PRAISE FOR *CRASH AND BURN*

"REALLY COMPELLING." —*CONAN O'BRIEN*

"It's great, it's honest, and it's **FUCKING BEAUTIFUL."**
—*MARC MARON*

"COULD BE A MOVIE." —*ALAN COLMS, FOX* News Radio

"Candid. **VERY CANDID."** —*ABC* News

"F-ING BEAUTIFUL." —MARC

ALSO BY ARTIE LANGE
WITH ANTHONY BOZZA

Too Fat to Fish

CRASH
AND
BURN

Artie Lange

with Anthony Bozza

A Touchstone Book
Published by Simon & Schuster
New York London Toronto Sydney New Delhi

Touchstone
A Division of Simon & Schuster, Inc.
1230 Avenue of the Americas
New York, NY 10020

First Touchstone trade paperback edition June 2014

TOUCHSTONE and colophon are registered trademarks of
Simon & Schuster, Inc.

For information about special discounts for bulk purchases,
please contact Simon & Schuster Special Sales at 1-866-506-1949
or business@simonandschuster.com.

The Simon & Schuster Speakers Bureau can bring authors to your
live event. For more information or to book an event, contact the
Simon & Schuster Speakers Bureau at 1-866-248-3049 or visit our
website at www.simonspeakers.com.

Interior design by Joy O'Meara
Jacket design by David Ter-Avaneysan

Front cover and step back photo by Paul Mobley
www.paulmobleystudio.com
Postproduction by Mike Campau
Back cover photo by Adrienne Ockrymiek

Manufactured in the United States of America

1   3   5   7   9   10   8   6   4   2

The Library of Congress has cataloged the hardcover edition as follows:
Lange, Artie, 1967–
Crash and burn / by Artie Lange with Anthony Bozza.—
First Touchstone hardcover edition.
pages   cm
ISBN 978-1-4767-6511-2 (hardcover)—ISBN 978-1-4767-6512-9 (ebook)—ISBN
978-1-4767-6559-4 (trade paper)   1. Lange, Artie, 1967–   2. Comedians—
United States—Biography.   3. Actors—United States—Biography.
I. Bozza, Anthony.   II. Title.
PN2287.L2833A3 2013
792.702'8092—dc23
[B]
2013035351

ISBN 978-1-4767-6511-2
ISBN 978-1-4767-6559-4 (pbk)
ISBN 978-1-4767-6512-9 (ebook)

To Mom & Stace

Without you there is nothing

———

Thanks Colin, Nils, & Amy

———

For Patience

For Love

For Adrienne

CONTENTS

FOREWORD

THE BUCK STOPS HERE

I must admit, for the first few days after Artie called to ask me to write this foreword I was confused. A few questions bounced around in my mind: How did he get my number? Is that on the Internet now too? Why me? Was I next on his list after Bin Laden (not available)? What can I possibly bring to these pages that someone more qualified (like Bigfoot) can't? After wrestling with the enormity of this task for a bit I decided to give it a shot because Artie and I have an interesting past. In case you didn't know, he was a guest on my first HBO show in the summer of 2009. With all due respect to the Mayan calendar and its prediction of doom in 2012, that day sure as hell felt for a while like the end of the world to me. I was told by Artie that his appearance on my show is covered in this book, so I won't go into too much detail about that night, however, it would be weird for me to not give my perspective.

First let me state that I, Joe Buck, was the one who had him at the top of the list for potential guests for the final segment of the show, which was to be a panel of comedians. I have been a fan of the *Stern Show* for a long time, and I knew Artie to be brilliantly funny, as well as a huge, smart sports fan. The "asks" went out, and Artie was one of the first to say yes. I was thrilled. Hell, I was happy to hear that *anyone* wanted to be on my show. Word came back that he was a fan of my father's work and that he really wanted to do it (considering how it turned out all I can say is that it's too bad my dad wasn't around to host). In the end, the panel consisted of Artie, Paul Rudd, and Jason Sudeikis, and to me, that was a solid lineup. Before the show, which was live, I went to the green room specifically to seek out Artie. I wanted to introduce myself and to let him know how big a fan of his I was. It isn't tailor-made hindsight to say that he was what anyone would call "jumpy" when I went to say hi and the look in his eyes was a bit unsettling. That said, I specifically told him that when he got out there he should "light me up, give me shit, and bust my balls" because I could handle it—at least that's what I thought. I wanted the show to have some edge and I wanted it to be different from any other sports talk show on cable, past or present. We didn't get there the way I hoped, but I think we accomplished that goal at least, huh? If you don't know what I'm talking about, a quick Internet search—which my daughters have been forbidden to do—will fill in the blanks. Artie did exactly what I asked and exactly what he was booked to do. And so began the LONGEST ten minutes of my life.

Artie lit me up. He had fun at my expense. And you know what? So what! It was a live show on HBO—AT NIGHT! He was raw, he was uncensored, and he was offensive. He was everything you can't be on a prime-time network but could be on cable. Yet somehow the network that airs highbrow classics like *Pornucopia*, *Cathouse*, *G String Divas*, *Taxicab Confessions*, *Real Sex*, and *Hookers on Ice* got mad. Like they would say on *Stern* when things are unfair—WAHHH! Don't get me wrong, it wasn't easy to take, but if Artie was messed up on horse tranquilizers, heroin, or just too much pudding, looking back, I really don't care. In his mind, as a comedian, he was booked to be funny on a cable channel that airs comedy specials from Chris Rock and Ricky Gervais and a long list of guys who say whatever the hell they want, however the hell they want, so why wouldn't he swing for the fences? Comedians on HBO are even allowed to say curse words—gasp! What else was Artie Lange supposed to do, tell knock-knock jokes fit for a Girl Scouts meeting? He had to go for it—and he did. Was he harsh and over the line? Absolutely. Was he so cruel that he made me cry or truly pissed me off? Absolutely not.

Two days after the show I asked HBO for whatever contact information they had for Artie and I called him. I wanted him to know that I bore him no ill will and that I appreciated him coming on the show, no matter how it had turned out. I needed to let him know that as far as I was concerned, it was water under the bridge and I was just happy to have met him after listening to him on *Stern* for so long. He said that he'd gotten that first laugh and got a bit carried away and that he was sorry if his appearance had hurt my chances for the show to continue. He followed with, "Anything I can do to help you going forward, I will; I owe you that." I took him up on that by asking if he would shoot the "cold open" for our next show. We'd do it in Times Square, he and I would appear together, and we'd poke fun at the incident and put it all to bed. The rest of the conversations, especially those with HBO, will be in my book someday, not this one. Artie agreed and a few days later, he and I stood in Times Square for an hour and a half shooting out in the open with hundreds of people filing past. He was great, and it was good to see him. The bit we shot killed in the room when it aired, and after the show a high-ranking executive admitted to me it was the right thing to do. It was over, well, except for the fact that every two weeks to this day somebody yells, "ARTIE LANGE!!!" at me as I enter a stadium somewhere. Once I got a Twitter account I also found out that, on average, every fourteenth tweet I receive would refer to Artie and HBO and probably always will. Fun . . . it's the moment that has no death.

I don't know Artie that well, but what I do know of him I like. No matter how many *Stern Shows* you've listened to or how many times you've seen *Beer League* or *Dirty Work* or seen him do stand-up, you don't know him well either. We don't know these larger-than-life celebrities as much as we think we do. Even though he revealed a lot about his life on the show every day, we don't know what shoots through his mind when he is onstage or ordering a hooker or contemplating a quick eight ball before bed. He is a complex dude who has a whirring mind that spins faster than most. As a listener I found his intelligence remarkable. He is a great mimic—think George Takei. He can remember lyrics from songs and lines from movies better than most—think *Godfather*. And he seems willing to lend money to people who need it, even when he knows he probably won't get it back—think interns. He comes off like someone who would be a good friend—the kind of guy who would give you (and a buddy) the shirt off his back. I like that type of guy, the world needs more of them. I read his first book and found out he was a momma's boy who worshipped his dad, the man who introduced him to baseball. That sounded a lot like how I grew up. After the family suffered the tragedy with his father and his paralysis, obviously Artie's life took a dark turn. But under all the hurt and the self-destructive behavior lies a good guy with a big heart who wants to do right. He is assisted in his career by his sister and still leans on his mom for help. Again, a lot like I do. I root for the guy, and I believe anyone who listened to his daily morning brilliance during his tenure on the *Stern Show* probably does as well. By the way, that show is like a test to me. For its critics it's easy to dismiss as trashy and vulgar. I maintain you have to listen through the bluster and outrageous conversation to hear the way they root for each other and get along. There is a lot of heart and honesty to that show and you don't have to listen long to really hear it.

There is no denying that Artie rocked my world when he appeared on my show. There is also no denying that I am there to help him if he ever needs it. We have a bond that is weird but since it gets brought up to me over and over again, I've come to understand it. That's a good thing because it probably won't go away, so why fight it? Artie has written two books now. That means he has asked for two forewords to precede his stories. Only Howard Stern and I have had that honor. That's cool to me.

This foreword represents my version of closure. No, not the part of Artie's go-to pants that have been reinforced more than once, but closure to the perceived feud between a guy who broadcasts a lot of Yankee games and a guy who bets on a lot of them. Enjoy this book, and if you haven't read it, go enjoy the first. And while we're at it, here's to Artie's next book, a hat trick that will be a combination of the first two: *Too Fat to Burn*. Oh, and Artie, FUCK YOU! Love, Joe.

—Joe Buck

CRASH
AND
BURN

INTRODUCTION

DALE WOULD NOT BE PROUD

All I can say is that you only realize how big your mountain is once you're laying motionless, helpless, and hopeless in the valley below. No one goes there on purpose, if you get what I'm saying, because the only way to find your personal low is to slip and roll down that mountain of yours, straight through to the bottom, no holds barred. Only when you're in that ditch, lying there in the muddy runoff you've made of your life, gazing up at the peak you fell from, do you truly know how small you are and understand how tall you used to be. Down there at the bottom you can finally see the invisible zigzag path you followed, reliving every lump you took along the way. You feel the pain of each one again, and some others for the first time, as behind you the avalanche you've made of your life crashes toward you in slow motion, engulfing the people you care about; stifling you with the debris of your existence. The view from that gully is a front-row seat to the mess you've made, but it's not the kind of show you want to see up close and personal. If you're lucky and if you want to, if you've got the strength and good people willing to pick up what remains of you in your life, you can make it out alive and climb back into the world. If any of you reading this feel like you're close to that pit, please read on: I've done your homework for you. At least I hope so, because I'd like to think the time I spent out of my mind will do someone some good. My life changed, so in the end it did me some good, but if I can keep just one person from suffering a fraction of what I had to, then it wasn't all for nothing. And that means something.

I crashed and burned. I rolled all the way down my fucking hill, man, and I did it in a very big way. It was a slow slide at first, easy enough to ignore, but in the end it was a race to the end and I lapped my best time. Only now can I see just how far back my slip and slide down to Gutter Town took me. I've gotta be honest, sometimes I'm impressed with myself, because I held out for a pretty long time going pretty damn hard before I fucked up good enough to wake up. Now that I've had enough time to think about it, now that I'm "alive" again for all practical purposes (sorry, ArtiesDeathWatch.com), I can pinpoint the moment that my descent began. Nobody slipped me that one pill that sent me over the edge; that's not the kind of thing I'm talking about. I mean the moment when I began to let duplicity rule my life, when lying to myself and to others, to whatever degree necessary, became completely acceptable to me. I didn't even shrug at it anymore. That's when I turned the corner into hell. I can tell you where it happened, and aside from my blackouts, what happened, but I don't know the why of this shit, only the how, so bear with me; I'm doing my best.

It was November 9, 2006. I was standing onstage at Carnegie Hall, one of the most prestigious concert venues in the world. It was built in 1891, and has hosted more talent than heaven. Back then I was still with my ex-girlfriend Dana, whom any fan of the *Stern Show* during my tenure there knows far too much about. At that time she and I had been together for five years, and we were starting to get very serious. I felt that she was probably the only girl who would marry me and so I thought pretty soon I'd do something about that. At least I knew I *should* do something about it.

Anyway, because of the *Stern Show*, my stand-up career had taken off and I was booked to play the most beautiful room that any dickhead comic like me could ever dream to play. It's almost wrong that they book comics there, because the place is far too beautiful for those walls to hear what I say to get laughs. But there I was, and it was a peak achievement for me. I hope to relive it someday and feel the warmth of those stage lights on me again. They didn't feel like any other lights that have ever shined on me, including the blue and red of law enforcement.

At the time Dana and I were fighting, mostly because of my habits, which were far from good. I was a decently functioning alcoholic and drug addict, with a concentration in heroin, coke, and whiskey. Really, I'd say I was cheating on Dana with heroin—that dirty opiate bitch will do that to you, ask any addict. I'd been fucking up regularly and obviously, so by then our relationship was dangling by a thread. We hadn't seen each other at all in the weeks leading up to the show, and things were so tense I wasn't even sure she'd show up. I didn't know if we were going to stay together, I didn't know if she'd even say yes if I asked her to marry me. All I knew was that I wanted her there to see me play Carnegie Hall. Even if we didn't stay together, it was such a special occasion and such a landmark for me that I needed her there, plain and simple, because she was so important in the grand scheme of my life. She was like another limb to me.

The gig also happened to fall on her birthday, so it was a coup to get her there considering the circumstances. My good friends the great comedians Joe Matarese, Jimmy Florentine, and Greg Fitzsimmons opened the show and killed. Howard Stern and a lot of people from the *Stern Show* were there, as were many members of my family. I pulled out all the stops for my set. I did over an hour, and I had my equivalent of pyrotechnics: I showed some sketches I'd done at MADtv on the big screen and worked them into my routine. I'm not lying at all: everything went over great and I totally killed. But that wasn't Dana's birthday surprise. I mean, I don't know, maybe she was surprised that I did so well, but she had another thing coming.

The last bit in my set was something I'd done the first time I did an open-mic stand-up, just a few blocks away from Carnegie Hall. I was nineteen at the time, and this occurred at the original Improv, which was thirteen blocks away on Ninth Avenue and Forty-Fourth Street. It was a song parody, which was appropriate for the acoustics, based on the theme song to the show *Cheers*, if it were a gay bar in Boston called Queers. And here's how it goes: "Going to bars where everyone's straight gets to be a rut / You want to go where you can get rammed in the butt / And Judy Garland's all they play / Sometimes you want to go where everybody knows you're gay / And they're not afraid to say, 'When I look at his ass, I lick my chops' and all the barstools have no tops / You wanna go where everybody knows . . ." And then I pointed the mic toward the audience and the sold-out crowd at Carnegie Hall shouted, "You're gay!"

"That's not the first time a large group of people has looked at me and shouted 'You're gay,' " I said. "It happened to me once at a family wedding in front of my Italian uncles when I was on the dance floor sucking a cock."

That was the perfect warm-up to bring up Dana for her birthday. "Hey, any *Stern Show* fans here?" Honestly that was the most unnecessary question anybody could have asked that room. The place roared. "So you guys know about my girlfriend, Dana, then," I said. More uproar.

"So it's Dana's birthday today. And she's here!"

Dana came onstage and I wasn't sure if she wanted to kill me or kiss me. But everyone was happy to see her in that way that fans of the *Stern Show* are always happy to see anyone that they've gotten to know over the air. Dana is not a ham in any way, so this degree of attention, right up there in her face, got her blushing redder than a whore in church. It got much worse when I instructed all three thousand in attendance to sing her "Happy Birthday." You can call me corny, you can call me Al; I don't give a fuck. I was trying to win some points with her, and it seemed like the best way to show her I cared. She was past her last straw with me, which demanded a giant gesture on my part, and as humble as she is, she loved it; I saw it in her eyes as we left the stage to a standing ovation. But that was the end of us; that very night was all she wrote.

Even if it had all worked out, it still would have been a sham, because I did the whole show with two bags of heroin in my pocket, despite the fact that I'd sworn to her I was clean at the time. I don't think the hall's patron, Andrew Carnegie, would have approved of me performing while "holding smack" as they used to say on *Starsky and Hutch*. I gotta say, it's pretty pathetic, because I didn't even need the heroin to get through the show. I wasn't even close to being that far gone (I still had all of that to look forward to); I just had those bags to celebrate, because at that point in my life I still enjoyed it and I still thought heroin was cool. Well, there was more to it than that; I fucking loved the escape and the long good night that it brought. I had disrespected Dana by lying about my use, and I disrespected the hall. I could have stashed it offstage in my bag or something. I didn't need to have the drugs in my pocket while I was performing, but I did, because at the time I thought doing that was cool too.

The heroin was a time bomb in my pocket, or an exotic animal I couldn't afford to feed forever. It was a fever I had to tend to but continued to ignore. At that point in my life, playing Carnegie Hall was the most significant thing I'd ever done, but as soon as the lights went down, all I could think about was the heroin. After the show I rushed through greeting my friends, family, and peers with the same enthusiasm I muster up ordering a Whopper at Burger King. They were all in my way, because all I wanted was to get to my hotel and sniff a few lines of heroin. It was great when I did—I hoovered up those lines at the speed of snort. I didn't have a problem; I was only extending the high of the show all night long. After that pit stop, I continued to the after-party, which was at the legendary Caroline's, about eight blocks away. They had a car reserved for me, but since it was a beautiful and unseasonably warm night, and because I was now high on heroin, I led a pack of my friends there on foot. It was a fun party, and it seemed like Dana was having fun. I hoped so, because I was intent on getting her back for good, which was why I had booked a room at the Ritz-Carlton overlooking Central Park that night but nothing was going to save us, because Dana knew I was high. She always knew when I was high, because she knew me better than anyone. But even strangers with a rudimentary knowledge of heroin behavior would have known I was high that night. I was all over the place. This next sentence would make no sense outside of the comedy world, but in context, it's further proof of just how high I was: Howie Mandel showed up and I shook his hand. Howie Mandel is a great guy, but anyone in the business, and most of his fans, know that he is the world's biggest germaphobe. He doesn't shake hands—ever—and that's the most normal, socially acceptable custom of his. So I did that, went in for the shake, and completely shat on his parade: the guy looked like he'd seen a ghost, and I've wondered just how long he boiled that limb to get my cooties off when he got home.

Dana and I left Caroline's at about two a.m. and took a cab to the Ritz-Carlton, and by the time we got there we were in a cage match–style fight. She was mad, and she had every right to be, and there was no talking us into making up. I kept at it anyway, half fighting, half apologizing, until finally, she couldn't take any more and wanted to go home. I had gotten us this incredible suite to celebrate and hopefully begin again, but at that point I didn't care.

"Fuck it," I said. "Fine. Let's go."

I drove her home, completely high on dope, which is something I did a lot, I'm ashamed to say. After I dropped her off in Jersey, I drove back to the Ritz and sat alone in my gorgeous twelve-hundred-dollar-a-night room, looking out on Central Park, sipping champagne, and snorting heroin all by myself until the sun came up. If that isn't a cover story worthy of *Loser* magazine, I don't know what is. Eventually I nodded off but awoke at nine a.m., depressed and still high. I couldn't look at those four walls anymore, so I hit the streets and wandered aimlessly around midtown Manhattan. I ate breakfast at the Astro Restaurant on Sixth Avenue: two eggs over easy, home fries, and a side of pancakes, plus a big fat glass of chocolate milk, because I love chocolate milk when it's served in a diner. I loved the food, and I hated myself. I walked out of there and bought the *New York Post* and the *Daily News*, then I went down to the subway and rode around on the C and A trains, like Charlie Parker used to, only without the genius talent. I spent about two hours hopping trains, just reading the papers. I didn't shower before leaving the hotel, and I'd been up all night so I probably looked broke and homeless, when in reality the night before I'd earned fifty grand playing Carnegie Hall.

When I couldn't ignore life anymore I went home, and when I got there and looked in the mirror I realized that my relationship with Dana was truly over. And I knew why. I knew exactly why: motherfucking drugs. Drugs are the cheapest kind of magic. They make life amazing for about three hours a day, and for that miracle, they make the other twenty-one a complete living hell. Drugs ain't worth it, because they may be a motorboat to some kind of paradise island, but their wake creates a tidal wave of shit. I was starting to smell that tide rolling in, but I was still dead set on surfing it. Who the fuck am I kidding? In November 2006, I was like Robert Duvall in *Apocalypse Now*, screaming at the top of my lungs to put the goddamned helicopter down so I could surf that shit tide myself.

CHAPTER 1

MY LIFE AS A PRIZEFIGHTER

By the end of my eleven-year career on the *Howard Stern Show*, by my count I had gotten into a fight with literally every single person that worked for the show. These weren't one-round back-and-forth sparring matches: these were heavyweight insult slugfests with low blows, no rules, and blood on the canvas by the end of them. They went way beyond the acceptable level of shit giving and taking that defines the *Stern* universe because I drove them there directly. I could get under the skin of the most good-natured member of the crew on their happiest day because that's just what I do. If I decided that they were out to get me somehow or just decided that I didn't like them (probably because they seemed happy and I was a miserable drug addict who got a perverse thrill from destroying everything good in his life) I would lock on to my victim like a pit bull, keep at it until I found their soft spot, and force them to lose their temper in a very uncharacteristic way. I could make people become someone they didn't like, which suited me fine because I didn't like myself either.

During my descent, I may not have been the best cohost, but I was one hell of a fighter: a slouching tiger, sleeping dragon, if you will. I might spend half a show sleeping, in other words nodding off on heroin, but I'd wake up with more energy than an angry terrorist, ready to rail away at my target until I reduced them to the level of anger, loathing, insecurity, and frustration that I felt every single non-high hour of my day. Like I said, anger was a sick thrill for me: it got me going, it blew off steam, and it made me feel alive. And obviously I didn't care about the consequences it had on the relationships in my life, so it became a bit of a hobby—the kind of hobby your friends have that you wish they didn't. Usually those friends aren't too receptive when you try to tell them that collecting paintings by serial killers isn't going to get them laid.

I got into a fight with Robin, I got into a fight with Gary, I got into a fight with Fred, I got into a fight with Sal, I got into a fight with Richard, I even got into a fight with Howard! How the fuck did I think that was okay? I got into so many fights on the air that they made a "Best of Artie's Fights" special after I was gone that they still replay all the time. I know this because every time it airs, if I go outside at all that day—even for just five minutes—someone in a passing car will roll their window down and shout at me about it. This sounds bad, but it isn't; usually they are informing me of this in a good way. The most famous of these fights was quite the spectacle, even in audio form, and if you're lucky or cursed enough to have seen the video of this event then you know exactly what I'm talking about. Aside from all that, this incident is significant because it marks a major downturn in my efficiency as a functioning drug addict. I am referring to a fight that stands alone: my battle royale with my old assistant Teddy.

In April of 2008, I completely lost it on Teddy one day on the air. I insulted him, I threatened him, I made fun of him in every way possible, and I topped it all off by throwing a cup of water at him. I'd been munching painkillers like they were Tic Tacs all night, so I was flying high that morning. I was also pretty exhausted. I'd been keeping up the schedule that drove me into the ground and had played a big LA gig that month after which I planned to relax and wean myself off of the drugs, which would have been the sensible thing to do. Instead I went to Amsterdam.

One of the *Stern Show* producers, Jason Kaplan, was having a four-day bachelor party there, and great people were going, including Howard TV cameraman Brian Phelan, who is one of my favorite people from the show to hang out with. The flight out was that night, just a few hours after our blowup. On the show that morning, Howard asked about the trip and if we were all packed and ready to go. I remembered that I'd asked Teddy to make a copy of my passport so he'd have all of my information handy for filling out customs forms and in case I lost it, which was a distinct possibility. Teddy was, after all, my assistant, and these are the kind of tasks assistants are told to do if they aren't on top of it enough to think of these things themselves, which was definitely the case with my flunky man-servant. The number of times Teddy didn't do things he should have done is almost as legendary as the number of times I fell asleep on the air during my last year on the show, but no matter what he did, I believed in Teddy because I liked the kid a lot and wanted him to be all that he could be. So that day, I expected that he'd done what I'd asked him to, regardless of his track record.

A couple of hours into the show, during a break, a kid who worked at Sirius—not even on our show—came up to me, handed me my passport, and told me he'd found it in the copier machine, where Teddy had apparently left it. This was a major fuckup, even for him, because if someone hadn't found that and returned it, we would have gone to the airport and I would have been completely fucked. We would have missed the plane, because there is no way in hell I'd let Teddy go and have fun if I couldn't, and by the time we got ourselves over there we would have probably lost two days.

At first I just thought it was funny. Shit happens; we all do dumb shit, and I've done shit that's dumber than most. Luckily my dumb shit has turned out okay . . . most of the time. So with all that in mind I did what any self-respecting wiseass would do if their friend—let alone their paid assistant—fucked up that big: I started busting Teddy's balls. During the next commerical break I went and found him and started laying into him in a pretty lighthearted way that was nowhere close to how rude I'd been to him in the past for lesser crimes. I considered it gentle teasing, which he deserved to say the least, but it didn't take long for this exchange to turn into something violent. It literally took one cross word from Teddy.

After the break, back on the air, I told Howard what he'd done and when Teddy heard me, he barged into the studio to defend himself. He was offended and defensive and took no blame, and this flipped my crazy switch, shifting my tone in the argument from civil to insane. I was outraged that Teddy wasn't at all apologetic; I really couldn't believe it. To me, there is no excuse for leaving your boss's passport in a copy machine that everyone in our office—which is huge—has access to. I wasn't going to let him make any kind of excuse, because there was none.

I went right at the punk, because that's what he was to me at that point, and brought up the fact that he owed me two thousand dollars. The exchange that ensued was crazy. I started calling him gay because one time he'd shortened the word "Bloomingdale's" to "Bloomie's."

"Who says that?" I asked. "He might be gay."

My reasoning was twofold: I'd dropped my mother and sister off at Bloomingdale's but I'd never been inside, I'm proud to say. The fact that Teddy had been in there multiple times and had adopted a nickname for the place was suspect. Referring to it as "Bloomie's"? I had a huge problem with that. Who says that? He's such a pussy. I took that train of thought to the wall and still wasn't done because by then pure anger and hatred were streaming out of me. Things escalated until I reached my breaking point, which was the moment Teddy said that I forced the money on him. Forced. It's still an insane notion, and in my state that was it, I was out-of-control pissed off. I'd loaned him the money, but the way he talked about it that morning sounded as if he felt entitled to it and didn't feel he had to pay it back. I fucking lost it and all hell broke loose. Before I go on I'd like to emphasize that I overreacted here and I do apologize once again to Teddy.

Anyway, I threw my water at him and dove across the desk hoping to get my hands around his neck. I missed pretty badly on both counts so I got up, sending my chair crashing into the wall and ran after him because by then he was out of there. It was the fastest I'd ever seen him do anything. Benjy, who is a comedy writer I love and adore who wrote jokes for Howard and sat right next to me for years, tried to stop me but he couldn't. As fat as I am, I'm strong as hell, especially when I'm angry. So as Teddy ran for his life, Ronnie, Gary, and a few interns worked together to hold me back. Hands down, this was my worst moment on the air, which is saying a lot considering my track record. Still, I know some of you *Stern* freaks out there probably think it's the best thing you've ever heard. As much as I think you're sick fucks, I hope you weirdos never change.

As I saw Teddy get away, I became more of a maniac by that point, enraged and inconsolable, and underneath it all embarrassed and ashamed. I saw Howard in the middle of it and stopped in my tracks, finally realizing what I'd done and what I was still doing. I wasn't close to cooling down, but I had a moment of clarity. Howard and the show meant so much to me, and in that flash I forgot whatever whirlwind of hate I was caught up in and got some perspective.

I stopped struggling, I stopped yelling, and I went and hugged him. "I don't deserve to be here after this, Howard," I said. I was struggling to hold back my tears. "I'm sorry I disrespected you and I'm sorry I disrespected the show. Good-bye. I don't deserve to be here."

There was about an hour remaining in the broadcast when I stormed out, and I had never done that before, even on my worst days. I got out of the elevator and onto the street thinking that I'd resigned because I'd meant what I said: I didn't deserve to be there. I spent the rest of the day walking up and down Sixth Avenue, completely out of it. After a few hours, with nowhere to go, I went to the movies and tried to doze off and forget about my life. I have no idea what I saw, I just remember people in the theater yelling at me because my cell phone kept ringing as calls and texts from concerned people came in. I know what you're thinking, but c'mon, you really think I know how to put that shit on mute? I just found out about this thing they call e-mail.

Everyone in my life called me that afternoon, all of them trying to stop me from going on the trip, but that wasn't gonna happen. I was so determined to carry on that I would have told the president of the United States or Greg Nettles himself that we'd have to have dinner another time because there was a bachelor party in Amsterdam that I had to get to. So that evening, with all this bullshit unresolved, without having talked to anyone since walking off the show, I boarded the plane with Teddy, Brian, Jason, and the rest of the guys and flew to Amsterdam, Holland, for four days of male bonding and good times.

I was at the very height of my heroin addiction, by the way, which, factoring travel, lies, and other people, made for a perfectly tossed salad of shit, dressed in piss vinaigrette. Our fight on the air was a giant danger sign to everyone around me, most of whom didn't think I'd come back alive from a city infamous for liberal drug laws and an ample supply of heroin, pills, and hookers. They saw a sugar-mad kid heading unattended into Candy Land.

Things started out all right because I slept through most of the flight, but what really helped was that I was booked into a different hotel than the other guys. I had the cash to burn, so I'd booked a suite in a five-star establishment a couple of miles away from them. The first night I crashed hard because I still had a lot to sleep off, but by four p.m. the next day I was rested and ready to begin my version of a well-earned vacation: isolation and getting high. I had no problem celebrating Jason's upcoming nuptials my way because in my mind that was still honoring him, so I got into a cab and told the driver to find me some fun. He took one look at me and made a beeline for the Red Light District, where I bought a bunch of pills from some guy on the street who was wearing a beret. I remember wondering if that was Amsterdam code for "dealer holding." As a rule, berets piss me off on sight and I refuse to talk to anybody wearing them, but this guy got a pass for life. He had every opiate I'd ever heard of, so I bought a sack of his pills, then went looking for a hooker, which is my chaser of choice for a double shot of opiates. I found myself a solid seven and negotiated a rate that would get her back to my hotel. This chick was a hooker through and through, which is really what you want when hiring a prostitute. Any guy who kids himself that a woman for hire is his girlfriend, even while it's happening, is a complete idiot. The fucking business is a fucking business, so act accordingly and everyone will go home happy.

This broad was amazing, just completely a prostitute. There was no way anyone at the hotel from the bellboy to the bartender to the desk clerk manning the graveyard shift was going to address her as "Mrs. Lange." And she was so accommodating: as high as I was at the time, I will never forget how understanding she was that I hadn't changed my American dollars into Euros. She and I spent the rest of the night talking, while crushing and snorting every flavor we could find in the bag of pills I'd scored. She spoke decent English, and we only had sex once, because like drugs addicts will do, the time we spent together was all about the drugs. I was enjoying myself, so the next day, I refused to get in touch with the other guys, even though they'd left me a few messages. I remembered back to shooting *Dirty Work* in Toronto in 1998, with Chris Farley, because Farley would pay whores to just sit around, smoke weed with him, and keep him company because he was lonely. That's where my head was at—after banging her once, I was fascinated by the idea of paying a pretty woman to be my friend for the day. I was as far gone as Farley had been: I just wanted to spend an afternoon with a friend who wouldn't judge any awful thing I did. When it comes to hookers the sex is secondary in my opinion. The love you rent from them isn't real, but it's unconditional, and when you're a using, struggling drug addict, love and a lack of judgment are exactly what you need.

I never got her real name, but I did make one up for this broad: in my mind I started calling her Whoreguide™ because the moment we got outside she'd start giving me the history of the city. She was incredible! I started enjoying her company so much that I dodged all the guys' calls and texts and took her on a cruise through the canals of the city. I was staying at The Dylan, which is a very posh hotel, and there were sightseeing boats parked outside in the canal waiting to take rich tourists sightseeing by water. It was downright wholesome: me, the guy driving the boat, and Whoreguide™ taking in Amsterdam's historical highlights together. We saw centuries-old town houses, government buildings, famous residences, the Anne Frank House—all of this and more lay on either side in all their splendor.

Once again I've gotta hand it to Whoreguide™: she was one informed whore. She knew more about the history of Amsterdam than the boat tour guide by a long shot. The only thing he taught me was where to get breakfast. That guy, whom for the sake of argument we're going to call Goebbels, had a crisp Dutch accent and high-strung voice. Basically he sounded like a friendly Nazi, the way a counselor at a Hitler Youth summer camp might be. His Aryan nature became especially clear to me when he started talking about the Anne Frank House, explaining in great detail how long her family had hidden in the attic with the kind of restrained glee that all Nazis have when discussing the suffering of Jews. Now that I think about it, he was more of a repentant Nazi while highlighting the finer points of the house and Anne Frank's story, as if he didn't want to reveal himself. It was all very rehearsed, and I felt like I was watching

Yul Brynner do his five thousandth performance of *The King and I*. Once he finished talking about the Franks, though, he became his sinister, joyful self again.

"Now," he said, his voice getting louder and his eyes getting wider, "if you look just past the Anne Frank House, you'll see a great place . . . for pancakes!" I kid you not, he shouted the word "pancakes" as if he were saying, "Heil Hitler!"

It really was a lovely afternoon and all three of us got to know each other so well, but as the boat returned to the dock I didn't kid myself: I knew it was time for Whoreguide™ and me to part ways. She wandered off down the street and I went back to my room to get high for a few more hours before crashing out. The next day I finally contacted Jason and the other guys and met up with them at a café near their hotel. This was no coffee joint—it was a Dutch café that sold weed, and we hung out all afternoon smoking a bunch of shit. All of us laughed like crazy, had fun, and somewhere in there Teddy and I made up. Afterward, I walked the two miles back to my hotel alone, enjoying a really nice marijuana high. As I walked through the streets of Amsterdam that afternoon everything was beautiful, and I felt at peace taking it all in, especially when I noticed the great place for pancakes that young Goebbels had pointed out up ahead of me. It couldn't have been better timing because nuclear-powered munchies had set in, and Nazi-recommended or not, I can honestly say that those were the best goddamn pancakes I've ever had in my entire life. I planned to fuel up there then take the Anne Frank tour, but unlike the Nazis, the pancakes won: I didn't have time for the tour after my feast, but I didn't care because the rest of my walk back to the hotel may have been the most relaxing stroll of my life.

That was the last I saw of Amsterdam, because for the rest of the trip, I barricaded myself in my room, getting high, sleeping, getting high some more, then sleeping it all off. I'm quite the traveler; I get the most out of my free time in a foreign city. I really should write a series of tour books. The guys tried to hang with me and kept calling, but they probably knew what was going on. We did all fly home together and all was well. I heard all about what they'd done every day and night and they heard all about how exhausted I was from doing stand-up and how happy I was to have caught up on my sleep (yeah, right). Teddy and I kept working together for another year or so, but after that fight he demanded that he not be my assistant—he wanted to be my "tour manager." I wish he had brought that up while we were still in Amsterdam; I would have turned right around and hired Whoreguide™ because she would have been a much better choice. As it turned out, I gave Teddy what he asked for, I made him "tour manager to Artie Lange," but fuck him: I still asked him to do assistant stuff, which he still did half-assed. Whatever, Teddy's a good guy, but by January 2009, he'd had enough of me regardless of his title and asked to be let go. I didn't want to, but I said yes. It was the end of an era.

CHAPTER 2

WHEN YOU GET TO THE BOTTOM THEN YOU'LL SEE ME AGAIN

Amsterdam was a nice little buffer between hell and me, one that included amazing pancakes, canals, a neo-Nazi, a lot of pills, and a little sex. I consider it one of my better ventures abroad, which I need to do more of, because I'm a creature of habit, but I'll tell you something—as soon as I discharged WhoreGuide™, the shit hit the fan. I know how wrong it sounds but it's true: saying good-bye to that well-informed whore was a turning-point moment for me. I wasn't in love, and no, we didn't part like Bogie and Bergman in *Casablanca*. I act dumb, but I'm not stupid, and I mean it when I say that this parting resonated with me in some way I can't explain. It wasn't conscious, but I think I knew that the end of this moment of dysfunctional domesticity with its historical tour and drug snorting meant letting go of the last bit of hope for normalcy in my life. I felt that good-bye down to the very depths of my soul because I was saying good-bye to trying or caring about keeping things in check. Looking back on all that came next, my soul knew better than the rest of me just how hard I was set to slide.

The great comedian Dave Attell warned me about a kind of greed that I was feeding way before it happened to me. I understood the urge he was talking about but of course I thought I'd always be too strong for it.

"Dude, you can get addicted to the money," Dave told me, late in 2006. "Fuck the drugs and booze, that's secondary. You can get rid of those. The worst thing you can get addicted to is the money." He was doing his show *Insomniac* at the time, so he was in the middle of it all, and had started to get sober. He had a really clear view of things.

The money was just like anything else according to Dave. I didn't agree because I always saw money as something necessary, not something fun like eating the occasional vegetable. I could only see getting addicted to things that are fun. It was necessary to have money to have fun, but money on its own wasn't something I cared to hoard the way I did, say, oh, I don't know, heroin, coke, and pills. Those are fun; those were something worth getting addicted to, but money in and of itself? Dave had to be high.

I don't remember if he was at the time, but I tell you, he was right. It happened to me, and how could it not? If you grow up without money the way I did, struggle doing stand-up, and then, in your thirties, start getting offers of seventy grand to fly to St. Louis or Detroit for the weekend, how could you not get high just knowing you'd become worth that much doing something nobody ever thought you'd succeed at? I didn't notice it warping my perception because like a foster kid who finally finds a home, I was so fucking happy just to be wanted. I didn't care about the schedule, the radio show, or what that plus the drugs were doing to me. After every big-ticket gig I did (before I got used to it—at which point I'd want even more) I'd think to myself: *Tonight I made more than my father ever made in a year.* That meant something to me, and soon it meant everything to me. Dave was right, all right: I got as high on that kind of thinking as I liked to get on Vicodin every morning. I remember Dave telling me that when chasing money started to change his thinking he felt like it chipped away at his sanity. He felt himself slipping into this craziness and stopped before he sold out and took whatever came his way. Losing his self-respect wasn't worth it to him. He's right about that too, but I had to learn about that little pearl of wisdom the hard way, through chronic trial and error—mostly error.

A lot of that hardheadedness comes from being a stubborn loser and an Italian-American male, but there's another factor that comes into play: being a comedian. It doesn't go for every single one of us, but four out of five dentists would agree that comedians are generally a dark fucking bunch. That bullshit cliché about tears of a clown is pretty true, and I've spent enough years in my disfigured psyche to know from experience. A lot of us funnymen and -women are like that, but don't ever feel sorry for us because trust me, we deserve it. Plus if we sense any degree of pity coming from you we'll treat you as nicely as we'd treat a WASP at Christmas Eve dinner.

Here's another reason why you should keep your pity to yourself: comedians like to see things go wrong. We really do, because that's what makes us laugh. W. C. Fields said it best when he was asked what makes a comedian laugh. His answer was one of the funniest and most truthful bits of brilliance ever spoken. "If you dress up a man as an old woman and throw him down a flight of stairs, that will make normal people laugh," he said. "If you want to make a co-median laugh, you'll need to throw an old woman down the stairs." I couldn't agree more; once you make funny your reason for being, nothing else but that which pushes the envelope to the extreme is funny to you anymore.

This is why I have a hard time with anyone being positive. Posi-tivity is not some spiritually superior state; it's a delusion that is so dull and obvious that I refuse to get behind it because it's just too damn easy. Being all about positivity is like being for world peace— I mean, who isn't for that? It's not like anyone is out there rooting for world war, so world peace is a joke of a cause. It's also a myth, because people like to fight and because they do, shit happens. Being for world peace is like lobbying for oxygen: it's the kind of thing best left to beauty pageant contestants from such as such places such as South Carolina.

Positivity really pisses me off, so as a comedian I feel it's my duty to do what I can to shoot it down where I find it, which is precisely what my Twitter feed, "Artie Lange's Quitter," is all about. The goal of Quitter is to discourage people from trying to do anything at all because most people aim too high and waste too much time. There's just no point in anyone making statements like: "If you work hard enough you can do anything," because it's just not true. I don't care who you are, sorry, kid, everyone can't become president of this country if they try hard enough. Aside from the occasional miracle, only white people from old-money families can be president. Are you one of them? If you're not, then give that dream up now.

If you ask me, everyone needs to take a moment to truly absorb the brilliance of the epitaph of the late, great writer Charles Bukowski. It's simple and it says it all. His gravestone says nothing more than his name, the years he lived, and two other words: "Don't try." Let this be your mantra, people, because it should be. Seriously, all of you, stop what you're doing, because you're just fucking it all up. Stop now, before you do more damage. Please, people, don't try. Because, really, you shouldn't. If you're honest with yourselves for a minute, you'll know I'm right.

The truly talented people in this world don't talk about the shit they do, they just do it. The average and completely useless, which accounts for most people, spend so much time talking about their lofty plans and goals that they never get further than that, and call me crazy, but there's nothing worse than hearing self-righteous, talentless people blabbing on about the positive, wonderful things they think they're going to do with their lives. They're pathetic. They need to just sit down and take a Xanax.

I prefer failures and self-hatred. Failing is honest because when shit goes wrong and you really fuck it all up, you can't lie about it. It's like robbing a bank and having the paint bomb in the bag of cash go off in your face. You can't hide a fuckup like that because your face is blue. I think there's some kind of truth in mistakes that big because at least they're honest. I'd rather fail at being anything than succeed at being "positive." I don't want to go to a Tony Robbins seminar and be accepted into his inner circle; I want to make fun of Tony Robbins, which, ironically, I'd find much more therapeutic, personally. I have a feeling Tony would almost respect that if he spent enough time with me to understand what I'm made of. Tony Robbins is such an icon of positivity that I experienced perverse joy telling people on the air on *The Nick and Artie Show* how I had become one of his followers and had been granted access to one of his most exclusive get-togethers: "The Running of the Deer." That special exercise reflects the very heart of Tony's personal philosophy, I'd tell them, and it's something he reserves only for select friends and celebrities. As my story would go, Tony had heard about the changes I'd strived to make in my life and decided to invite me to get up early in the morning at five a.m. and accompany him as he ran with the deer. He thought it might help me find the light at the end of my personal tunnel. After some trip I took to LA I told the audience that this dream had come true and that I'd run with Tony, Nicole Richie, Jason Alexander, and Chad Ochocinco, plus Tony's pack of deer. We'd defecated with them and all rediscovered our primal nature. I'm not sure what this says about me or my fans, but most of those listeners who called in that night had believed my story, so I couldn't find a reason why I shouldn't keep it up. I went on about it for four days, after which time I began to feel so positive because of this deception that I just couldn't take any more. I literally had sunshine coming out of my ass and was so happy that I had to do something about it. So I told them all that I was lying. And then I felt better about things again.

Getting people to believe whatever the hell I wanted them to became the backbone of what Howard and the *Stern Show* came to call "Artie's Wild Year," 2008. The year my book came out, the year the money and drugs took over, the year that everything started to go wrong. They even commemorated that special time with a special episode that captured what was going on in front of the curtain at least—which was a fraction of the chaos. I had, despite Dave Attell's warnings, gotten completely hooked on greed and took every gig, everywhere, no matter how tired I was. I'm not sure if I believed myself every time I looked at my schedule and blocked out the weeks when I planned to detox and calm down, all I know is that every time I set those dates, I broke them as soon as a paying gig came along. The thing is, I had learned to tell people what they wanted to hear years before that.

Now that I'm sober—aside from the odd fuckup (more on that later)—I've gotten the most satisfaction from tracing just how far back my dysfunction started. When the greed set in things definitely got worse, but they were already bad. Let me show you what I mean.

Back in '07 I played the Playboy Mansion for some charity event. I only made $10,000, but I didn't care, I had played Vegas the weekend before and made $100,000 at the Hard Rock. Plus, fuck it, I was playing the Playboy Mansion! This was a Rat Pack–level achievement in my mind, and I couldn't wait. They had all kinds of talent there that day: there was some band set up to play after me, and Sarah Silverman was on the bill too. The stage was in the grotto area, where I planned to have sex with some Bunny after my set.

As I took the stage, Teddy, who was my assistant at the time, went and got high with Sarah Silverman over by the world-famous monkey cages, whose inhabitants are known for masturbating openly and throwing their jizz at many a random passerby. Sarah is world-famous for having the most insane weed, which she does—her shit is just ridiculous, or maybe that's just how I see it. Here's why: back in the '90s—in 1993, I believe—she and I played a place called the Luna Lounge on the Lower East Side and that night someone got the both of us high. I don't even think it was Sarah, but we got so high that I don't remember much else. I have no idea how I did onstage;

I have no idea how she did. I don't remember anyone else or anything at all, aside from one thing. All that I remember clearly is that I ended up disrupting the lives of the ten people on the bus I shared with them back to Jersey from Port Authority sometime around three a.m. by standing on my head and yelling at them, letting them know that I had "evil in my mind" and that "I had to get it out." I guess I thought it would run right out of my skull if I did a headstand. Judging by how my life has gone since then, I was wrong.

Anyway, I went onstage at the Mansion while Sarah and Teddy went and smoked weed by the monkey cages. It's probably good that they weren't there to witness me bomb. I can't lie (anymore): I really sucked. It didn't help that Jerry Buss, the owner of the Lakers, was there with a huge entourage, plus the servers were a pack of hot chicks, which meant there were many reasons not to listen to me. I had to do twenty minutes to get the ten grand, but two minutes into it I started wondering how the fuck I would fill the next eighteen minutes, because what little self-esteem I had shown up with that day was somewhere below the stage. I started taking healthy swallows of scotch from a tall glass I kept behind me on the drum riser. After going back for what seemed like my fifteenth, I went to set the drink back down and stepped on something slippery. It was something the color and texture of French dressing, and since nothing has been confirmed or denied, I'm going with that. In any case, French dressing, or dressing of any kind had no business being on that stage, because, among other things it could have done, it caused my foot to slide out from under me, and like the world's fattest cheerleader, I dropped into an awkward split. I caught myself before I hit the ground, but in the process I completely blew out the seam of my pants. They were basically a tent without a door in a matter of seconds.

From taint to waist, the seat of my pants was fully separated, leaving my ass comfortably hanging in the breeze except that I wasn't alone in my backyard. The thing is, I was bombing so badly that I'm not sure anyone in the audience even noticed this. And my ass was facing them when it happened, but not one person reacted in any way. I know this because by then, just three minutes into this fiasco, I was already hyperattuned to every breath those ignoring-me motherfuckers took. All I heard was the unconcerned, self-involved chatter of their cocktail-party chitchat: I heard hot chicks laughing above the noise of plates of food being delivered. I could have broken my neck or had a heart attack and no one would have noticed.

There was a clock at the side of the stage that I could see too easily from wherever I stood. And that clock became my personal hell for the next seventeen minutes, as I watched it ticking away each minute I had to endure insult and injury to get my money. After my pants split in two, despite the fact that no one probably noticed, I shuffled up to the mic, keeping my ass to the back of the stage, where the band's instruments were, and when I got there I just started mumbling because I literally had nothing. I'd been doing stand-up for fifteen years by then; I'd seen all kinds of shitty rooms and taken on disinterested crowds, but all of the defenses I'd built up were nowhere to be found. I was reminded that day that no matter how great you think you are, shit like this can happen at any time, and when it does you probably won't be ready for it. I did what anyone completely unprepared would do: I kept mumbling. It was pathetic. Did I mention that I was at the Playboy Mansion?

Out in the crowd, the dudes at Jerry Buss's table were starting to make out with the girls, because all of them were probably on Ecstasy. They were all touching each other, and that's when I realized that I could not be more insignificant in this scheme of things. That reality check might have broken my spirit, but it wasn't so earth-shattering that I lost sight of what I had to do to get paid. The gig was below my usual fee, and it seemed like all I was going to get out of this was humiliation, so I was determined to get the cash. By then I had wandered my way through nine minutes, so I had eleven left to go. That might not seem like a lot in the real world, but in stand-up minutes that's a fucking lifetime. If you don't believe me, bring your best jokes to the next open-mic comedy night in your hometown and then tell me how you do. You can tell those jokes at home to your friends, you can time yourself and think you've got it all figured out, but you don't. When you're up there, minutes are hours, trust me. So I had the equivalent of one of the Police Academy movies left on the clock, and I had no idea what to do. Considering how well my other material was going over, I did the only thing that made sense to me and started singing "Dixie Land," as interpreted by my Elvis impression. I felt no need for an extravagant setup: "Everybody, sometimes I like to pretend I'm Elvis." That had to get people's attention.

No such luck.

Maybe the song would do it.

"Ohhhhh, baby! . . . I . . . .wish I was in the land of cotton / Old times there are not forgotten! Look awaay! Look awaaay! Look awaaay! Look awaay!"

No one looked, not even once, toward the stage. Anyone who's heard me knows I'm not a good singer, and most of my impressions are obnoxious, so you'd think that the racket of me on the microphone alone would have alarmed somebody—anybody. Nope, not that night, not a fucking soul. I should have announced that an ICBM was headed toward Los Angeles.

I looked at the clock again and saw that I had about six minutes left. I figured I'd started something with this Elvis thing, so I should stick with it. How could I go back to jokes after exposing them to my singing voice? I dipped into my bag of songs and pulled out the only thing that made sense.

"You know something, ladies and gentlemen," I said, still imitating Elvis. "I really like it when Elvis sings this here song. It really is one from the great American songbook." And then I launched into "My Way."

"And now . . . the end is . . . near." I started camping it up too. "Yes, it is, ladies and gentlemen, the end is near."

For the first time people started laughing, but I knew what was going on. They weren't laughing with me, but I soon realized they weren't even laughing at me. By that point I would have jumped for fucking joy to be laughed at or made fun of. No, the dudes busting up at table five were laughing at whatever stupid jokes the hot waitresses were telling them. I could not catch a fucking break. These girls, all of them nineteen, on Ecstasy, and asking where Jerry Bruckheimer's house was, were getting more laughs than I was.

I dragged my exposed ass through "My Way," and made that piece of shit last as long as I could. I drew in as much breath as I could, and I think I held the last "waaaay" for at least a minute and thirty-five seconds. I had one eye on the clock, hoping I could end on this high note, but that wasn't going to happen; I still had four minutes to go. Four minutes of hell ahead and no turning back, so I launched right into "Hey Jude." To make matters worse I forgot the words, which on any other night I know by heart. As anyone who has ever tried to sing "Hey Jude" can tell you, there's only one way out of it if you forget the words: head right into the "nah-nah-nahs" and pray for the best. Well, I did that way too early—I did it after like the third line of the first verse. It was a complete train wreck, but considering my set overall, I think it was the highlight. I was so painfully aware of just how bad I was that I wondered if the guy paying me was going to try to skip out on my check. I mean, technically he could claim that I didn't do a stand-up set, seeing how I'd opted to perform so many of my well-honed musical routines.

There are only so many "nah-nahs" a man can do, and when I'd exhausted them, the clock of doom informed me that I still had two minutes left.

Fuck me, I thought.

Then I started singing a truly earnest version of "Happy Birthday," somewhere between Marilyn Monroe's serenade of JFK and a crackhead trying to impress his dealer.

"I know it's somebody's birthday in the house tonight, and

I promised them I'd sing them a song, so join me, won't you, ladies and gentleman, in wishing that person, wherever they are, a happy one."

For the first time during those twenty minutes I actually started enjoying what I was doing, so much that I actually went over the scheduled twenty minutes by ninety seconds. I was really proud of that.

"Thank you, everyone, good night," I said after I wrapped up the song. "You've been really great."

It was a horrible night, but I knew there was some kind of prize awaiting me: I had heard that after the performances were done there would be whores galore and that they were all fair game. With paid-for sex dangling as the carrot that would numb my embarrassment, I shuffled offstage, keeping my air-cooled ass turned away from the audience's eye. "Great job, great fucking job, man," the MC for this fine event said to me, nodding his head like a nutcracker as he took the mic from my hand. Clearly he was high or maybe he'd been nowhere near the stage during my set for the last twenty minutes, because he was so enthusiastic that he clearly wasn't busting my balls.

"Give it up one more time for Artie Lange!" he shouted into the mic. No one clapped, no one cheered, no one did anything. I laughed out loud because that moment was funnier than anything I'd done up there—asking them to give it up one more time as if they'd even given it up one time. The band played a few songs as I stood there feeling like a loser, wanting another drink but not wanting to walk anywhere with my ripped-open pants. My mind was consumed with just one crystal clear thought: *Where the fuck is Teddy?* We've already covered how much I love the kid as well as how much he is capable of pissing me off, but I have to say, this night took the prize. Standing there with ripped pants, with no assistant in sight, I was pretty justified in my anger. I needed pants to cover my ass and I needed painkillers to cover my shame. And hopefully a whore to make me forget about all of it for the time it took her to blow me. This was the kind of party where pills were everywhere, that was obvious, but I wasn't in any condition to go asking around—I expected Teddy to do it.

As I stood there with my ass to a hedgerow, my blood began to boil because the kid was nowhere to be found. By that point the pain of my failure onstage had sobered me up, and just then one of the two guys in charge of the event came over to me.

"Great job, Artie, we really loved it," he said.

He had to be kidding.

"Thanks, man," I said. "I knew I had to try something special for this crowd, you know?" This guy had to be fucking with me.

"Well, you really did great, I mean it," he said with a big grin.

Then I noticed the camera behind him, taping us. If my pants were in one piece I would have shit them.

"That's cool, man, I'm so glad you enjoyed it. So, the camera—are you taping us?"

"Yes, we are."

"Did you tape my set too?"

"We did, but it's just for our purposes."

"Oh yeah?" I said. "What are your purposes?"

"Well, it's just a souvenir of the night," he said, smiling.

I kind of wanted to punch him. "A souvenir?" I asked. "What am I? A bobblehead?"

"That's funny, Artie!" he said, slapping my shoulder. "We're just going to show it in-house."

In my mind that was worse than having twelve-year-olds in Nebraska poring over it on YouTube. What kind of viewing party were they saving it for? If anyone ever watched it they'd see every bit of the crap sandwich I'd made that night.

"Oh, that's cool, man," I said. "It's not going to end up anywhere, though, right?"

"No, not at all."

After that exchange, he left for a minute and came back with my check for $10,000, which I immediately noticed wasn't made out to "Too Fat to Fish, Inc.," as it should have been. It was made out to "R. D. Lang," a famous Scottish psychiatrist who specialized in treating psychosis. He also died in 1989. *This is what I pay Teddy for, isn't it?* I thought. I didn't want to have a conversation with this guy about the check; I wanted to get into some new pants, I wanted pills and booze, and I wanted to be first in line when the hooker bus showed up. Where the fuck was Teddy?

"Uh, hey, man, thanks for the check, but it's made out to the wrong guy; I'm not R. D. Lang," I said. "From what I understand he was a great man, but he's dead. The check should be made out to 'Too Fat to Fish.' "

"What?"

Saying that name turned more heads than any joke I'd said all night.

"Too Fat to Fish, what's that?" he asked.

"It's the name of my corporation. It comes from something my mother said once."

There were a pair of girls talking to us and one of them thought this was literally the funniest thing she'd ever heard.

"Too fat to fish?" she squealed. "That's so funny! Where does that come from?"

The last thing I wanted to do with my ass hanging out, an empty drink, and no opiates in sight was tell some broad who didn't seem like a sure thing the too-fat-to-fish story. I told it half-assed and without the usual enthusiasm I bring to it, and it went over just about as well as my set had. When I finished it, the promoter guy and the chicks were staring at me blankly.

"That's it?" one of them asked.

"Yeah. That's it," I said.

"I thought there would be, like, more to it," the other chick said. The promoter guy started laughing.

"I'm sorry, J. D. Salinger," I said to her, "but that's as complex as the narrative arc is gonna get in this tale." Fuck her, that bitch was straight off the bus from Kansas City, destined to fuck Pauly Shore as her greatest achievement, and she was critiquing my storytelling?

"Hey, man, can you cut me a new check tonight?" At least I hoped to get out of there with my money. My dignity, what little I had, was a long-lost cause.

"No, R.D., I'm sorry, we'll have to mail it to you," the guy said.

Jesus, really? How much worse could this night get? The answer, my friends, is much, much worse. By the way, they did mail me the check, but it took eight months and a few phone calls to get it. Fucking R. D. Lang.

So I'm standing there at the Playboy Mansion, just a complete wallflower, with my ass to the bushes, having, in every way, the opposite experience that James Caan had his first time there (from '74–'76 he held the record for fucking consecutive Playmates, or so I've heard). His memory of his time there, however, has probably been lost in a jungle of enormous '70s bush. Anyway, I'd been dreaming of coming to this place since I was a teenager, and I'd finally made it, but there I was, unable to move, just bombing and repulsing people over and over. I mean literally, as I wandered around, everyone I met looked at me as if I'd just puked on them. It was terrible.

Just then I finally caught sight of Teddy, who was down by the monkey cages, laughing hysterically with Sarah Silverman, whom I'd had a crush on since 1992, and because of that I was beyond furious. They were having the time of their lives while I suffered through one of the worst sets of my career, and I was paying that kid to be there. I decided that if they started making out, if I had to watch him kiss her, I would gladly do the time in prison for the joy I'd have received choking him to death with my bare hands. Can you blame me? I was still standing there in ripped pants. What the FUCK?

"Teddy!" I shouted. "Ted-day!"

He didn't hear me (of course he didn't), so I shuffled along the hedge, keeping my bare ass to the bush, inching closer to them. My blood was boiling—literally boiling—with every inch I crept closer. I got within four feet and, fuck you, man, I was fuming by then.

"TEDDY!!!"

He turned, looked at me, then walked over. "Oh, hey!" he said, as if we were old friends running into each other at a high school reunion, just all full of good times and hugs. "What's going on? What are you doing?"

"What am I doing?" I asked, barely choking back my rage. "I don't know, Teddy. . . . What am I doing? Well, let's see . . . I just did stand-up comedy, which is the whole reason we are here. 'We' meaning 'you and me'; you're aware of that . . . right, Teddy? That's what I've been doing. Earning money. . . . So, how have you been? What have you been doing?"

"What have I been doing?" he said. Then he started giggling.

"Yeah, Ted, what have you been doing? What *are* you doing?"

Just then Sarah came up and was supernice in that condescending, patronizing bullshit way that she always is, and I love her for that character she plays, but wow, it couldn't have been worse timing. I still loved her then and now because she just walked up and gave me a hug.

"Do you want some pot?" she asked.

"Yeah, I do."

"Oh man, that's too bad, I don't have any more!" she said, grinning, all cute.

That's because she and Teddy had smoked all of it. Awww. Fuck me.

"And you don't have any more? Or anything better?"

"No, man," she said. "That's all I've got. Check you later, I've got to go onstage right now."

Off she went, and she went on and she killed. No, she destroyed. She got more laughs than George Carlin at Carnegie Hall . . . like, ever. I'm serious, and I hate to admit this kind of shit, Sarah that night at the Mansion made every dipshit within range completely crack up whether they wanted to or not, and I hated her for it. I couldn't even believe I'd been up in front of the same people. When she was finished she bopped off the stage and gave me another big hug (I mean, really?). "So, how was your set?" she asked. I wasn't even sure if she was being a bitch at that point, that's how subversive she was.

"Whatever," I said.

"Ohhh," she said, completely overdoing it. "Yeah? Not good? I get it."

"All right, I mean, it was fine. It was . . . whatever."

"It happens, man!" And off she bounced into the night, smug as a bug in a fucking rug.

She was right, I mean, it does. But this night, it was killing me. And I'd paid my assistant to make sure I didn't feel this pain!

"Ted, let me ask you something," I said, turning to him, hating his stoned Cheshire Cat grin. "Where the fuck were you while I was onstage?"

"We went to the monkey cages and got high, that's all," he said. "She had pot . . . and she's really nice."

"She's really nice? Why don't you go fucking be her assistant, then, Ted? I fucking needed you! I got offstage and ripped my pants, you even aware of that?"

Teddy was so high that the minute he heard me say, "I ripped my pants," he doubled over laughing. I know what that's like and I've been there, but the more he laughed, the madder I got. I wanted to kill him—like more than I usually wanted to kill him (because I wanted to kill that little cocksucker quite often). He could barely breathe, but when he could, he started calling Sarah over. She was a few feet away, surrounded by a circle of well-wishers fawning over her after her set.

"Hey!" I said. "Don't you dare call her over here, Teddy. NO! I am fucking serious."

He could tell I was mad, so he stopped, but he couldn't control his laughter or how red his face was at that point. If I'd told him that an asteroid was going to obliterate LA in five minutes he would have laughed. If I'd told him his parents had been killed in a car accident he would have laughed. He was a mechanical clown in a fun house, just laughing and laughing and laughing. I wanted to kill him.

"Dude, I know you're high, but you have to get me some fucking pants. Do you understand what I'm saying?"

More laughing.

"Teddy . . . Teddy! Hey, Fuckhead! Go be high, but do it now, get me pants—this isn't funny."

Looking back it amazes me that I kept him on for another six months. I know I was fucked up, but whose assistant is so inefficient that they can't find their boss a pair of sweatpants at the Playboy Mansion? Teddy was a waste of time, money, and space.

"Dude. Get yourself together," I said. "Get me some pants, a triple scotch on the rocks in a pint glass, and a handful of pills, right now."

"Why can't you go get your own drink? I've got to get the pants . . . that's a lot to do." He said that to me and he wasn't kidding. Now, listen . . . I'm not even sure if that kind of attitude happened due to me or if it was all that little snot-nosed bitch's fault. All I know is that I really never wanted to hear that kind of entitled attitude again.

"Teddy?" I said, inhaling slowly, trying to calm down (knowing I was way beyond calm). "I can't get the scotch, Teddy . . . but I'd like to. Want to know why I can't get the scotch, Teddy? Because my fucking pants are ripped!"

That of course sent him into hysterics. And made me homicidal.

"You're right, I forgot about that," he said, completely serious but laughing still, and headed off toward the bar.

He was that high.

The little prick.

The first thing he did right that whole day was come back imme-diately with my drink, at which point I told him he needed to score me pills, any kind of pills, as fast as possible.

"Why do you want pills?"

"Because I want to be high. High . . . high like you, Teddy, high off my fucking ass, laughing and having fun. Fucking fun, Teddy! Since you and Sarah smoked all the pot, I'm stranded. I need pills. Get me a Vicodin. Get me one right fucking now! This place is crawl-ing with shit like that."

"Scoring for you is against my morals, Art. I won't do it."

"Against your morals? Really? Your morals? How much do those cost to circumvent?"

"I've told you, I won't score for you."

"Your morals allow you to get high and talk to monkeys instead of doing your job taking care of me while I'm onstage, though, right?"

"That's different. You have a problem with drugs."

"Oh, right. I guess so. Yes, Teddy, I have a problem with drugs. No, I'd say *you* have a problem with drugs . . . because I don't have any! I need pants and drugs and you have neither of them for me! So as my assistant you need to handle my PVS: pants, Vicodin, scotch. Now get going and don't come back here empty-handed, you stupid little fuckwit!"

He didn't look happy, but then again he never looked happy whenever he had to actually do something for me. As usual, a threat-ening tone yielded results: first came another large scotch, which, much like the first, I treated the way a marathon runner would Gatorade, I sent him off again, demanding drugs and pants. Call me a skeptic but I wasn't willing to put my faith entirely in Teddy's hands, so I called over a scummy-looking staffer and proceeded to tell him about my knee injury. You know the one—the one that had started acting up, the one I "got operated on for" a few months back. That imaginary injury was just about killing me that night after my run-in with the French dressing, so I needed something to kill the pain.

"Man, I must have torn my injury wide open tonight. Can you get me something?"

In about fourteen seconds he came back with fifty Percocet, and being a true scumbag he wanted to charge me twelve dollars a pill for them—which, being a seasoned drug addict, I knew was a little high. Really, I was something to be proud of during my Playboy Mansion debut. I was the picture of class: ripped pants; a pint glass full of scotch; a useless, red-eyed, assistant in tow; haggling over the price of a pile of Percocet. At this point, does it matter that I did twenty minutes and bombed beyond belief? (Honestly, I'm not sure.)

I had $280 on me, so I couldn't afford all fifty pills, because this fucking guy wasn't budging on his price (really, dude?). If I weren't so desperate I would have lectured him about it, but I was so I did what I could and bought twenty of them, which came out to $240. Of course, seeing as this wasn't in any way my night, I didn't have exact change, so I gave the guy $250.

"I'll be right back with a ten for you, man," he said. "You'll be right here?"

"Yeah," I replied, knowing he wouldn't yet still hoping that he'd come back with my ten dollars.

I didn't get depressed about it for long; I had a bag of pills to swallow, and I got into it immediately. The only problem I had was that I was still a fucking slob wearing half a pair of pants. And my assistant was still nowhere to be found. The Mansion is decadent and there were people making out, half-dressed here and there, but it wasn't a scene out of *Caligula* by any means. Being sexy, touchy, and debauched is one thing; munching pills hand over fist out of a Ziploc bag out in the open is another—and that's what I was doing.

Teddy finally came back around then, and for whatever reason I asked him what he thought I should do about munching these pills at this party. I mean, why did I? But I did, and what did I expect this kid to say other than just one more retarded, idiotic piece of non-wisdom? I really don't know what the fuck is wrong with me when it comes to some of the people I keep around me, let alone pay for their "services." I very well may never have crashed and burned if I'd been smart and just made Whoreguide™ my assistant.

Teddy encouraged me to just walk to the bathrooms and not worry about my ripped up, open-assed pants or anything else and to go take my pills.

"It's the Playboy Mansion; no one is going to look," he said.

"Fuck it," I said. I was desperate. I had to turn this night around.

I walked to the Porta-Johns, pants ripped from balls to waist, French dressing on my sneakers, a warm, half-empty pint glass of scotch in hand, thinking that maybe, just maybe I'd be allowed to have fun at the Mansion.

When I was about fifty feet from the Porta-John, I heard hysterical laughter behind me—like crazy-person loud. It was fucking Teddy, still so high that he couldn't help himself! It wasn't just the sight of my ripped pants, it was me—that little piece of shit was laughing all out of control. He sounded insane, he was half-crying, he was doubled over like some gleeful maniac, making such a scene that everyone nearby was looking at him, wondering what the fuck was going on.

He couldn't contain himself, that little prick; he was pointing at me, crying, cackling at my fat, briefs-covered ass. There were people pointing in disgust, and all of them made me want to crawl inside my skin and never come out. I shuffled as fast as I could into the can, that Porta-John, spilling my scotch the whole way. I slammed that blue plastic door behind me and finally I was safe, and fuck them, I didn't care anymore. I had enough pills to get high. I had enough pills to get so high that nothing they could do or say would ever fucking affect me. I wouldn't give a shit what anybody thought the next time I opened that door. I reached into my pocket to get the pills . . . and I came up with nothing. I'd dropped my bag of Percocet. I'd dropped it somewhere between the bar and the bathroom door. Really, this night could not get any fucking better.

Just then I heard a knock at the door and thought more than twice about opening it. I mean . . . Anyway, I did so slowly, just a crack, and I met a young girl who introduced herself as one of the associate producers of the event (which is Hollywood code for bullshit artist who gets people coffee).

"You dropped something," she said, handing me my bag of pills. She was very nonplussed.

"What is this stuff?" she asked.

"Oh, that's just aspirin. Prescription aspirin. I get bad headaches. Thank you so much."

"C'mon, I'm not stupid," she said. That was debatable.

"Well, okay, it's not aspirin. It's something stronger. I've got a condition. Listen, you're not going to write about this, right? You are a publicist, aren't you? You realize that certain realities should be kept out of the press?"

"Yes. I'll make sure of that. We are here for charity . . . but you should get yourself together."

I excused myself, which was easy since I was already in the toilet, locked myself into the darkness of the Porta-John, and started eating my Percocet as if they were Flintstones chewables, taking down five in one swallow of scotch. The thing about painkillers and opiates of any kind is that they make you nauseous, even if you're an addict who loves them (like I do) and does them all the time. I felt queasy, but I didn't care. I kept going until the inevitable happened: I threw up.

Actually, that's an understatement. What I did was hose down the entire porta-potty with vomit as if I were a fire hose and there was a fire. It was violent, projectile-style puke and it coated the walls, the toilet, and the urinal in waves for about three minutes straight. Everyone outside heard it, believe me. I can still hear the echoes, and I'm sure they still can.

After the storm subsided, I heard a knock at the door.

"Boss?" Teddy asked quietly. "Boss? . . . Are you okay?"

"I'm fine. . . . I just threw up."

For a millisecond I thought that Teddy might actually care about me. Then that motherfucker started laughing again. Fuck him.

I wiped the puke off of myself as best I could with whatever still-dry, limp toilet paper I could find. I didn't have the means to get all of it off of me; I knew there was puke in my beard and I could smell it on me, above and beyond the smell of shit and plastic that had permeated the air beforehand. To me, I'd made it through the rain, so I ate a few more Percocet, because there was no fucking way I wasn't getting high tonight. I fucking deserved it. I'd crapped on-stage. I mean, please, what else was there besides getting fucked up by now?

I had eaten five pills and thrown them up, and since I still felt nothing, I ate four more. Don't judge me until you've had a night like this. If you do I suggest you take ALL of the pills you can find right away!

That was my plan. And here's how it went down. I'd bought twenty pills and I'd gone through nine, and I needed to save some for the plane. At that point, if I didn't have access to heroin, I was up to about fifteen painkillers a day. So I was cutting it close. I looked down and saw three full Percocets, completely untouched, sitting there in my puke. I'd sucked them down so quickly that I hadn't gotten a chance to chew them. Aside from the puke, they were virtually brand-new! I was such a fucked-up addict by then that I picked them up without hesitation and put them in the Zip-loc bag for later. I got puke all over the bag in the process, but that didn't matter because now it matched my shirt, my beard, and the rest of me.

By then my high was actually kicking in, so everything had sud-denly become beautiful in my mind. I didn't give a shit about the stares I received when I left the bathroom. Who were those fucking people anyway? I was high, I had no pants, and I had one mission: dealing with Teddy's insubordination. I started arguing with him immediately, telling him that if I were a corporation, and he were an employee, even if he were a high-ranking executive, he would be fired on the spot for his performance that night. It sucked; the kid was so stoned that nothing I could say got through to him, so he was, at best, halfheartedly apologetic for his lack of being the least bit on point. I fucking couldn't stand that shit, so I told him the only way to redeem himself was to find me pants, and if he didn't he'd be dead by the end of the week. At that point I didn't care about the pants anymore: I was so high that the wind on my ass was actually quite refreshing, and I was amused at all the idiots who kept pointing at me and giggling. Meanwhile Teddy had come down enough to realize that I was his boss and that he should probably take me seriously. And so things got even sillier.

I'd gotten two of my friends into the Mansion that night, the actor Jimmy Palumbo, who played Johnny Trinno in *Beer League,* and my friend Anthony, who produced it. Those two morons rolled up in Jimmy's 1982 Honda Civic. There were lines of limos, Bentleys, Maybachs, you name it, in that driveway, accompanied by one completely shitty Civic . . . with my friends in it. I was standing there with one of the promoter guys when my buddies pulled up, and the guy looked over at me like he was missing the joke. I mean, there was no joke, and that's the point he was missing. He then told me that my friends' car made me look bad and that I should never, ever have them back to the Mansion or any other place I wanted to make a good impression.

"Yeah?" I said. "I'll remember that. I told them not to take their nice car because this one would make me look more down-to-earth."

His frown said it all: my ripped pants, scruffy beard, and scotch-and-Percocet eyes were the epitome of class, so those losers, in that car, were definitely bringing me down.

Just after my boys showed up, I noticed that the "ladies of the night" had arrived, and it was a very dark night. These were the most hard-core—and I mean fucking hard-core—whores I've ever seen in my life. These were $20 crackhead cocksuckers from the mean streets of Compton and without a doubt I'd say a whopping two out of 150 of them were legitimately cute. It looked like for some this night at the Mansion was BYOB (Bring Your Own Bunny). It was never like that back in the day, which depressed me, but I was very high by then, so I didn't give a fuck for long.

My buddy Anthony asked one of the two cute ones how much a blow job would cost him.

"One thousand dollars," she said.

"Get the fuck away from me!" he said. "You're crazy." She was, because she wasn't that hot and I'm pretty sure that even if you tapped Tiger Woods's finest talent, you'd get more than a blow job for $1,000. Still, and this was the drugs talking to me, I sat there wondering what a thousand-dollar blow job felt like. What could she or any other chick possibly do to justify that price tag? I halfheartedly decided I'd try to find out.

"So it's a thousand dollars for a blow job, but what would you do for some Percocet?" I asked her.

"Nothing, I have my own," she said, looking at me suspiciously.

"Oh, you do? You like Percocet? Well, how much does it cost to buy your Percocet?" I asked. "A blow job is a thousand; how much is the Percocet?"

"They're not for sale, I don't do that," she said.

"Oh, you don't? So you're only a whore?" I asked. "You should think about diversifying your interests and pursuing drug sales. You really should cover a few other markets, honey."

She probably didn't even have Percocet. She probably didn't even know what it was, because she got so mad that she stormed off and told all the girls within earshot that I was a jerk-off. Thanks to me, none of the whores would talk to us, so none of us hooked up. Let me tell you, that was really adding insult to injury, because these girls had no business even being in the same zip code as the Playboy

Mansion. They were an insult to everything the place stands for, historically or otherwise.

There was no sex in the grotto for me, but that didn't stop everyone else at the party from getting their dicks wet. Before too long it might as well have been 1974. Actually I wish it had been 1974; I might have seen some hot chicks with feathered hair and great banana-boat tits. Instead I found myself watching a two-hundred-pound hooker with a tattoo of her murdered boyfriend's name across her chest blowing three goofy white record-executive types by the pool. I was the only one who saw this as horrifying. Her tits were flabby, her thighs were huge, and there was nothing sexy about any of it. Aside from my personal misfortunes, I'm pretty confident when I tell you that this was the worst night the grotto has ever seen . . . at least I hope so. If those rocks could talk they would pretend these events never happened.

The thing about drugs is that they can erase all of that kind of carnage, or at least make it all seem okay at the time, which is pretty much what happened to me that night. What I was seeing before me became a bad movie that I suddenly wasn't in anymore. Sure, I'd played my role onstage earlier, but I was high now, so that was yesterday as far as I was concerned. All the gross sex I saw was just ugly wallpaper, because everything was fucking fine, man. Wanna know why? Because finally I was fucking high!

When Teddy showed up with pants (I'd forgotten that I'd ever needed pants), he brought this pair of red silky pajama pants that could have been Hef's cast-offs. By then, that was so cool, I couldn't have been happier. Teddy . . . what a useless, cool guy I employed. I thanked him for those pants and then I ducked into the bushes, threw my ripped ones deep into the shrubs, and put my new ones on, and when I came back out, I felt like a beautiful mermaid. I strutted my stuff as if I were wearing a $4,000 tuxedo that fit me perfectly. I mean, these things were covering my ass and junk, but that was about it; they were nothing special. Actually they were tight, and I looked ridiculous. I was also wearing white Nikes that were smeared with orange French dressing, plus my jean jacket and some oversized fat-guy T-shirt, so alongside these red pajama pants I probably looked like Ignatius J. Reilly from one of my favorite books of all time, *A Confederacy of Dunces*. Or at least the way I picture him if he ever walked the Earth with you and me.

So I was definitely feeling fine, and in my mind I was looking really fine. And according to me, it was time to give Teddy some payback, because that fucker hadn't done his job. He had it coming, and nothing is better than fucking with some guy who has it coming, especially if your victim is completely stoned on marijuana. It's shooting fish in a barrel, it's clay in the kiln, it's just too easy. And that little prick deserved it. I even knew how I'd fuck with him: I'd make him chase down my incorrectly written check.

"Ted, listen to me. I need that check tonight. You have to find the guy and have him cut me a new one," I said.

"Dude, I can get that from him tomorrow."

"I'm paying you out of that check, Teddy," I said. "You don't get that, I've got nothing for you for this weekend of work." That got his attention.

Off he went, while my friends and I continued to drink and watch this sad pack of derelict Compton whores sucking and fucking goofballs. About ten minutes later Teddy returned and he told me that the guy had no more checks, which I already knew, and that they'd have to mail it, which I also already knew—because the guy who'd thought my name was R. D. Lang had already told me so and taken my address.

"Man, that sucks, Ted," I said. "I'm a little bit disappointed in you. I wanted to give you your money tomorrow. It's just gonna have to wait. Um . . . hey, did you tell him the address was wrong too?"

"No, wait . . . what?"

"Yeah, yeah, he's got the wrong address too. He's got it going to my mom's, which isn't right. That's gonna delay this even more. Can you go sort that out?"

This took Teddy at least forty-five minutes, long enough for my friends and me to totally forget about him altogether, until he came running up, all proud that he'd gotten it handled. I mean, Jesus, he didn't even suspect that I was fucking with him, which was great because the kid deserved all of it, but I still wasn't done, because there was just one last thing I could think of that could be wrong with the check.

"Listen Ted, you probably think I'm crazy, but I didn't give him the full nine-digit zip code for my address in Hoboken. I hate to do this to you, but I've lost checks—I've lost a lot of checks—and I really don't want that to happen anymore. Would you mind running that guy down and making sure he's got the full nine-digit zip on that address? I'm sure you don't feel like doing it, but it's better to handle it now."

That kept him occupied for another half hour, by which point, when he finally came back saying he couldn't find the guy (who was probably hiding from Teddy by then if he wasn't being blown by an overweight mother of eight), I decided it was time to go. It was one of the worst gigs I've ever done at one of the top places I've always wanted to play. That's life, though, isn't it? You can sit around thinking that some place is the Taj Mahal, but when you finally get there, you realize it's shit. Who knows, if I didn't care so much about drugs and money I might have managed to have a good time and maybe even do a good set. I was so in my head that when it started to go wrong up there, the paranoia, the false perception, and the lessened ability that comes with drug abuse defined what happened next. And the only thing that made it go away? Complete obliteration via puke-covered Percocet. Oh yeah, speaking of those, once I got back to my suite at the Park Hyatt in Century City that night I realized I'd left those at the scene of the crime: they were in my ripped-up pants, deep inside a hedgerow at the Playboy Mansion. Tell you the truth,

I hope they're still there. That would be the type of mark I'd be proud of leaving on the Mansion.

Without a fix of Percocet to get me through the day, my flight home was going to be more of a living hell than my set had been, times ten. I was in first class and Teddy wasn't, so the only joy I got was laughing at him as he shuffled his lazy ass back to coach. He was hungover and I knew it, and in reality that was all I had (aside from the obvious): ways to feel superior to him.

"See ya later, loser!" I shouted as he shuffled by. "Maybe I'll bring you something to eat, jerk-off. I'll let you know how the warm brownie and ice cream taste. Hey, do they give you champagne when you first enter coach? Ted, don't worry, I'll come see you after I watch my favorite episode of *Taxi*."

"Yeah, really funny."

I could make fun of him all I wanted, but it didn't matter; I was the one who was truly fucked. No amount of alcohol could soothe the raging, toxic headache brewing in my brain. Fifteen minutes into the flight I got the sweats because my withdrawals had set in. As soon as the seat belt light went off I was pacing up and down the aisles, asking for more scotch, praying that the anxiety and sweats and itch would go away, and knowing that they wouldn't. I'd planned it wrong, I'd not brought enough stuff to get me back to my home base in one piece. But all was not lost; I knew that I just had to get through the flight to be able to get myself shipshape again. Luckily I was met by a very, shall we say, "understanding" driver whom I had ridden with before. He picked me up at the airport that day, took one long look at me, and said: "Where we goin', man? I don't think you're goin' home just yet."

"No, man, I'm not," I said. "I'm in bad shape."

I borrowed a few hundred dollars off him (I told you he was amazingly understanding), and I won't tell you where we went to score, but I can tell you it rhymes with Shmarlem. That night we got me about two hundred Vicodin, and this guy was wise—I'd have to pay him that cash back with ten percent interest. That's how it was, and I considered it normal. Ah, fuck it, I don't even know if I thought it was normal. I didn't give a fuck what it was anymore. It was my life.

CHAPTER 3

SLIP SLIDIN' AWAY

If you're still with me by now, even if you weren't there the first go-round, you probably realize that 2008 was a banner year for me. My first book, *Too Fat to Fish*, debuted at number one on the *New York Times* bestseller list and remained a bestseller for nearly two months. When it went into paperback a year later, it hit the list again—the thing just didn't let up, because it somehow crossed over from interested people who knew me from stand-up or were just die-hard *Stern* fans to becoming its own entity, a collection of autobiographical stories that touched people. Making the *Times* list and the media that came along with it piqued the curiosity of people who didn't know who I was, but I guess they wanted to know what this weird book with the stupid title at number one was all about. I hope they found it to be entertaining, or at least purely disgusting—at the best I hope they found it enlightening. I'll also settle for educational, in the way that any video preceded by a don't-try-this-at-home disclaimer can be educational. That book is one of my proudest achievements, no matter what other heights I manage to scale, God willing.

Anyway, my stand-up schedule was as busy and lucrative as it had ever been and between the *Stern Show*, invites to Comedy Central roasts, and a few small acting roles, I'd tapped into everything I'd always wanted from show business besides banging Angie Dickinson and playing Jean Valjean in the Broadway production of *Les Misérables*. I also received the opportunity to give back to our country, which is something I'd always wanted to do. That year I went to Afghanistan with the USO to entertain our troops—a milestone for me—but I couldn't let myself enjoy it completely and had to fuck it up by scoring fifteen Valium at the airport in Kyrgyzstan while waiting for our Armed Forces transport flight out of that hellhole. I got so out of my mind that I had to be driven back to the US Army base to sleep it off for thirteen hours because I was deemed unfit to fly. This was the army, by the way, so they had the authority to strap me into a seat as if I were a box of emergency rations, but they chose not to—I was that bad. If I was what might be called "mildly ill behaved" at the airport, once they got me back on the base I really put on a show, because all fifteen of those black-market Valium, about 150 milligrams' worth because they were the biggest-sized generic pills—really kicked in. When they let me out of the car I proceeded to run around like a crazy man, until the top dog sergeant in charge caught up with me and told me in no uncertain terms that I was either going to bed or getting locked up in a cell by him personally. There's one thing I can say about me, which is that I rebel all I can to the furthest degree, always to my own detriment, but when true authority knocks and real trouble is at my door, I answer and at least try to fly right.

Sometimes it literally takes an army, though. I got the message and allowed them to escort me to my bunk, where I realized that I was more exhausted than I'd thought and had no more fight in me, because, despite my tolerance and stature, I'd snacked on enough Middle Eastern Valium to put down a horse. Still, I had enough wiseass in me to pop off and keep everyone within earshot awake for another hour, because I'd convinced myself that my misery was all their fault and so they deserved to be insulted. I've come to realize that I should just stay home.

After my USO tour I was reeling from drug use, living in a fantasy land, because like I've said, in Amsterdam I made this almost proud, conscious decision to let go and didn't give a shit about myself anymore. I didn't even try to pretend that I was attempting to slow down anymore, which, ironically, was the most honest I'd been with myself in years. I don't know if this will make sense to anybody else but me, but it was as if I'd gone to confession and I was the priest: I'd admitted my sin, and I forgave me. My self-appointed salvation was to keep heading on down that road without looking back. I was free; I really didn't care what happened to me anymore.

People started to slip out of my life, some quickly, some slowly: everyone from Dana to my best childhood friends, to family like my cousin Jeff, whom I'd never in a million years thought I'd ever lose touch with. I remember him telling me at that time that he hardly knew me anymore and that he only learned what I was doing by listening to the *Stern Show*. Jeff had always been an older brother to me, I'd always shared everything with him, ever since we were kids, and he'd been reduced to knowing as much about me as any given stranger with a Sirius subscription.

I saw all of this happening in slow motion, and I really didn't give a shit. I was too happily preoccupied with the money I was making and all the drugs it took to get me through the night. The affirmation I felt onstage some nights, when the people cheered, was a bonus. I refused to see that as anything real. The same went for friendships: whomever was or wasn't my friend was about as important to me as following women's college lacrosse.

Just getting through my professional engagements took all of my energy, so what most people concern themselves with, all of those things that make up what anyone considers an average, functional life, were annoying to me. I was like a hair metal band in the '80s demanding a straight line from the limo to the backstage door: my line went from the *Stern Show* to my weekend moneymakers to my drugs to my bed, wherever that bed may be. Anything else was a problem, anything else got in the way, and I hated anything else. If I ever got lonely or horny I called a whore, but between my six-a.m.-

to-eleven-a.m. on air schedule during the week and my nocturnal stand-up and opiate weekend netherworld, I barely had the time or taste for them anymore.

I was in the worst health I'd ever been, just a drug addict limping through life, yet somehow I got more done in 2008 than in any other year I've spent in show business. All of my achievements came with a price, though. I was nodding off on the air, which is fine if your radio show is being heard by twenty-five people in Ossining, New York, at three a.m., but I was one of the main players on the *Howard Stern Show*, where six million people listened to me snore every time I "dozed" off (which was a hell of a lot). That wasn't enough for me either, so I stayed on the comedy circuit, playing Vegas, Atlantic City, and all points that paid well in between, raking in the cash and snorting up the drugs in places far enough away that I could evade the eyes of those watching me back at home. I had it all worked out, and even when I saw it was a sham, I kept pushing until it all fell apart.

It was perfect timing too, because I'd finally gotten my close-up, thank you, Mr. DeMille. The success of the book earned me repeated spots on *Letterman*, *Conan*, *Kimmel*, too many live radio shows to name, and just about every local TV entertainment show in America that I cared to do. I'd have the publisher organize book signings and press wherever I did stand-up, meaning that every single hour of my weekends away from *Stern* was occupied. I'd do press in person or on the phone when I got to wherever I was playing and after I got offstage I'd sign books at a bookstore or at the comedy club until every single person who showed up had bought one, gotten their photo op, and had me sign their copy. Some nights I'd be at a table in some bookstore after a gig until four a.m., and so long as I was kept well lubricated and was allowed to smoke, I would have stayed there signing and greeting my fans until I passed out.

Take a look at any picture taken of me during my book tour— I look near death. My skin was gray, I was heavier than usual, I was smoking and drinking like there was no tomorrow, and I wore the same clothes every day. If I had to describe myself I'd say I looked like a guy whose skin was uncomfortable with having him in it. And I wouldn't be wrong, because my body was starting to give out. You know you're not healthy when your face matches the yellowish-gray stack of newspapers in the corner of your apartment.

As I wrote in the paperback edition of my first book, I completely short-circuited the day I was scheduled to participate in Comedy Central's roast of Bob Saget because I'd been playing Russian roulette with my opiate addiction and I'd finally chambered the bullet. I was sick, going through serious heroin withdrawal because I'd been abusing a drug called Subutex to get me from my weekend benders into my somewhat "sober" workweeks. The drug isn't meant to be used that way, and if you use it incorrectly you'll end up very, very ill, as I did.

I tried to plead the flu, but they wanted me to be a part of this thing so badly that Comedy Central was ready to hire a private jet to fly me to LA, complete with a doctor on board to get me well enough to perform. My cover was blown and for once there was no way I was getting away with it, so I had no choice but to admit that I was drug sick. I told my lawyer, Jared Levine, the truth, and he did his best to handle it. You know it's bad when you can't even get yourself onto a private jet with a doctor waiting to fix you up. It's pretty sad but the truth is, nothing could get me out of bed that day, physically or mentally—and I didn't care. I'd hit the wall head-on at full speed, like a fly slamming into the radiator grille of an eighteen-wheeler doing seventy-five on I-95. It was the end of the road, and like that fly, my asshole slammed through my brain, turning me into an unrecognizable stain.

The roast was taped in August, and my missing it was a big red flag for my friend Colin Quinn, who had been talking to me regularly for months about getting help. He saw this slipup as the tipping point—it was going to be life or death for me from here. This is when he and my sister, Stacey, began talking regularly, trying to come up with a plan to save my life.

They were right, of course, but I managed to keep them at bay for a while, until my next major public slipup in November, when I appeared on *Late Night with Conan O'Brien*. I love Conan dearly and he and his show have always been incredibly gracious and kind to me. This marked something like my twenty-fifth appearance on the show, which is a milestone. Unfortunately I have no recollection of it whatsoever—it's another trophy in my hall of blackout. I'm not kidding; I've watched the footage many times, each time hoping that something I see triggers even the slightest degree of recall. Let me try again right now. . . . Yeah, sorry, I've got nothing. I did a major television appearance in a complete blackout. I know there is some stoner out there who thinks this is really cool, who is probably the kind of guy who shouts "play 'Free Bird'!" at the end of every concert no matter what band is on stage. I'm glad I'm your hero, tough guy, but it's for all the wrong reasons.

The *Conan* people have been more than kind to me over the years when I've been less than sober, but this was the last straw for them because being buzzed or on drugs is one thing, but disrespecting Conan and the show is something else and it's not forgivable. And I couldn't have been more obvious: every single joke I told was drug related. I was clearly so tired of my own shit or just so bold, feeling so untouchable—or not caring—that I was like a serial killer trying to get caught. When I wasn't making blatant drug references I kept cutting Conan off midsentence with lines that made no sense at all. Go YouTube it; you'll see what I mean. I really couldn't have been more obvious about being fucked up and I couldn't have been more insulting to Conan.

I knew I'd blown it, but I still didn't think I'd been that bad, because I tried to book another appearance a few months later to continue promoting the paperback version of *Too Fat to Fish*. Honestly, I was shocked when they refused to book me, for the first time in ten years. They'd had me on when I had nothing going on, but now I had a book that had hit the bestseller list twice and they wouldn't have me. The producers were very honest with me: they told my manager that they knew I was high the last time I was on the show and that they weren't willing to risk that kind of train wreck again.

Despite these repeated fuckups, which continued to grow in scale, I wasn't willing to admit that professionally I was slipping. I saw these events as setbacks and pains in the ass, something as inconvenient as my new habit of forgetting to shave for three weeks. I just kept on, and to be honest, the holiday season was fucking great for me that year. Each week *Too Fat to Fish* sold more copies and I was asked to do bigger gigs for more money, so overall my life was good. I had money to burn and no shortage of offers to make more. I'd gone through a bunch of assistants, but it felt like I'd found one in my friend Michelle, whom I flew up from Florida to help me out with all of the things I had to do on my book tour. I sent her back home for the holidays with plans to resume our working relationship after New Year's.

As Christmas came around I spent as little time with my family as possible so that I could spend the most time possible doing drugs alone in my apartment. The holidays made me sappy, so I also made an attempt to salvage my relationship with Dana—something I'd realized was a lost and useless cause long before that last stretch of the year between Christmas and New Year's. The damage had been done, and I was the last to admit it, but understanding that finally made me feel free of Dana. At the same time letting go of the idea that she and I might get back together someday made me feel more alone than I'd ever thought possible. You'd think that I'd want to be with my family when I felt that way, but I didn't. I didn't feel like I deserved their love and attention; I deserved to be as alone as possible, so I wallowed in it.

My mother and sister were understandably distraught over me at this point. I felt like I had an excuse this particular year, but due to drugs or withdrawals I'd missed four Christmases and four Thanksgivings in a row, and in an Italian family, that is equal to treason. I'd just not show up, and I never had a good reason. Some years I didn't even call to say, "Merry Christmas." I'd promised them this year would be different, but it wasn't, and when I didn't materialize, my mother called me and said something I'll never forget.

"Art, do you have any self-respect?" she asked. She was crying too. "Do you really hate yourself this much? This is craziness. Art, you are killing me."

She was right, so I did the only thing I could: I got defensive and changed the subject. "Ma, you know if it wasn't for me you'd be living in a closet somewhere, don't you?" I said. "Dad left us nothing! I bought you a car, a town house, and I've helped you with everything."

My mother then said something so poignant and from the heart that it cut through my haze of bullshit, straight to my core. "You don't realize that I'd rather live in a closet and have you be happy and drug-free, spending the holidays with me, than be in a mansion and have you in the condition you're in and not even here with us? You matter to me, not this goddamned house!"

The fact that I was making about $3 million a year and giving my mom the life she'd never had got me off the hook for missing holidays in my mind, but that day she set me straight. When my dad told me to take care of my mother and sister I thought he meant financially, so I thought I was doing the right thing—and then some. Dad was on his deathbed at the time, so I took this request very seriously, and honestly I believe that is what he meant, but there's more to life than that. When somebody truly loves you, they want you, and they want you around more than they want any material belongings you can provide. The time spent with a loved one is more valuable than any amount of money in the world. The problem was, I'd forgotten all about that.

I was so far up the ass of my own career and my own chemical needs that I couldn't see daylight anymore. But, hey, I've always thought daylight was overrated—the thing I hate about it most is that it makes it easier for people to see you. Keeping up with this theme, I'd transformed my apartment into something out of a nightmare edition of *Hoarders*, which suited me fine. If it kept people away, great. This wasn't entirely my fault, by the way, because hoarding can creep up on you just like an opiate addiction, especially if you're in the position to get fan mail. I can't speak for The Beatles or some tweenybopper like Justin Beeker or whatever his name is, but I can tell you that anyone associated with Stern gets an ungodly amount of fan mail. Put it this way, when members of the Wack Pack, like High-Pitched Mike, get bags of mail at the studio, you can imagine how much I'd get as one of the primary cohosts. My fans are important to me, so I'd have our office manager, Tracy, put all of my mail in large white bags that I'd leave in my corner of the studio or in my office until the piles became to large to handle. Then I'd insist on taking them home with me, believing that I'd actually find the time to read and respond to every letter. I'd throw these bags—kitchen-sized garbage bags—into the trunk of the car driving me home and have my driver carry them upstairs and dump them in my home office, where they'd sit, untouched until my Mexican housekeeper Salma reached the end of her rope and threw them out. After a while she stopped asking me if that was okay because I always said no but never noticed when any of them disappeared.

The hoarding didn't end there: I also stacked up copies of the *Post* and the *New York Times* into piles that grew as high as the Chrysler Building. My very patient maid also asked me nicely if she could throw those monstrosities out, and I didn't fight her there, I always said yes, but by the time she decided to ask, probably because

I was so difficult about the fan mail, there were so many unstable piles that she needed a forklift to move them (this came in the form of my doorman). Over time, the stack developed a color scheme, which ran from gray at the top to yellow at the bottom, and I remember the day Salma removed the oldest stack, because I recall catching a glimpse of the first Gulf War headline getting turned over into the garbage bag. She did her best to keep the place neat, but Salma was fighting an uphill battle, because besides my newspaper compulsion, I kept papers everywhere, most of them handwritten notes filled with half-baked jokes and ideas for new stand-up bits. These were inspirational and somewhat important items, but the negative degree of organization I had going on made it pure luck that I ever saw any of them again once I set them down. It was like dropping something into quicksand. To this day I still don't use a computer, so napkins and bits of legal pads trail behind me and probably always will, but I've learned to keep them somewhere they won't get lost if they're actually important. I've gotten used to using my phone, but I still hate typing anything, so the most you'll get out of me is 140 characters or less. And I still don't do e-mail. That's way too much for me, so don't even suggest it.

My diet in those days consisted of nothing but pizza and chicken parmesan bought exclusively from one place: Uptown Pizza, the place closest to my apartment. I was loyal to them and still am for several reasons. First of all, I don't need new and challenging cuisine; I like what I like and when I find it done well, I'm happy to eat it every day. Second, these guys took exactly eleven minutes to deliver my order—believe me, I timed them, because that is the kind of thing that I amused myself with in those days. Uptown makes great food, and since I used to mention them on the air every once in a while, Richie, the owner, never let me pay for anything ever again. I loved that, but honestly it got to be ridiculous. I liked their cooking so much I would have ordered just as often—and trust me, I actually wanted to give these people my money! But every time I'd try to pay the delivery guys for the food (let alone a tip) they'd refuse and run away from me like scared bookies fleeing John Gotti, saying that Richie would fire them if they took so much as a dime from me. I started getting a complex; I mean, maybe Richie thought I was connected or something, so I asked one of the delivery guys I saw regularly what Richie had said about me.

"'Artie Lange never pays for anything,'" he said. "That's what Richie tells us. If he hears that any of us take your money, that guy loses his job."

I know I'm not the only "celebrity" who gets this treatment, but there's one thing about this story that sets it apart: this guy Richie we're talking about had died of cancer the year before. He'd been dead for over twelve months, and his staff was honoring his wish as if he'd come back from the dead to fire them if they took my cash! Before he passed, he said I was not to pay for anything—ever. After I heard about this I became even more determined to pay them, so I started dropping twenties and fifties in their pockets if they didn't agree to take them. I will always be beyond touched and flattered that Richie thought so highly of me that he put that unwavering law into place, but after he'd been gone for a few years, I had to ask them to stop.

I also ordered from them so much that I had all the delivery guys in my pocket and so I began to use them (and pay them) to do whatever errands I needed done. As my world narrowed to a pinpoint, these tasks got more and more complex to the degree that I feel confident saying that if I asked, they'd help me move a dead body, right now, so long as it was within their delivery radius. I didn't need them to bring me drugs, because I had that covered, but they brought over just about everything else, allowing me to stay in my apartment for days on end.

"Hey, man, it's Artie," I'd say when I called Uptown. "Bring me a Sicilian pie and two one-liter bottles of Pepsi."

"Okay, you got it, Mr. Lange."

"Also, stop by Rite-Aid and get me some Advil and a carton of Marlboro Lights. Then stop by King's Grocery and pick me up four value-sized packs of Peanut M&M's, some Kit Kats, and a box of Tastykakes," I'd say.

"Anything else?"

"Yeah, then go to Starbucks and get me a caramel macchiato, large. I'll see you here in twenty minutes?"

"Twenty minutes."

I got so out of control sometimes that they'd need to send two guys to carry it all. That didn't matter; they did it always, they were never late, and they never fucked up my order. I couldn't have been happier, knowing that once I was home, I'd never have to leave. I had no girlfriend at the time—if I'd had one that liked to live the way I did then you'd probably not be reading these words, because we'd be dead. The only things that got me out of my cave was work at the *Stern Show* and my stand-up gigs, which took up a lot of my time, thank God.

By the way, I wasn't really fooling the people who were closest to me. I was a visible mess that no one could contain or ignore. I'd stopped caring, and somehow I thought that meant no one else cared either. If they did they had no right to as far as I was concerned. That's why I was truly surprised one night in late December '08. During one of my more enjoyable evenings of solitude and drug abuse, sitting on my couch watching *SportsCenter*, I heard a knock at my door and looked through the peephole to see my sister Stacey red-eyed, nearly in tears. Next to her I saw a dark sleeve, definitely a guy, and to be honest, I was so constantly paranoid by then that I figured that must be a cop. This was either an arrest or intervention and I decided real quick that whichever it was, I wasn't having either.

"Stacey?" I said. "Um, what are you doing here? And who are you with?"

"I'm with Colin Quinn, Art; he wants to talk to you."

This wasn't expected at all. Of the two options, this was an intervention and she wasn't kidding around.

"C'mon, Artie, open the door," Colin said. "I just want to talk to you, that's all."

I hid my drugs, tried to arrange myself, and let them in, because Colin is one of the smartest, funniest, greatest comics on the planet and I respect him immensely. Even though I wanted to, I wasn't going to leave him hanging or refuse to see him, because he's a true friend and a great person. What I hadn't realized was that he and my sister had become very close because she needed help dealing with me, so she'd turned to Colin, begging him to help get me into rehab. This wasn't a typical intervention, though they had packed a bag for me, had chosen a place in upstate New York where I could detox, and were ready to drive me there immediately.

I refused to go, of course, no matter how many different ways my sister asked me. Colin did his best to lighten the mood with spot-on imitations from *Goodfellas* and *The Godfather*, which got me going. He and I went back and forth trading lines like that for half an hour, which isn't exactly what you see during your average episode of *Intervention*.

"Listen, guys," I said after the imitations had run their course. "I know I have to go to rehab, but I can't go to rehab now. And right now I refuse to go. Let me try to make it to Christmas this year. I'd like to spend Christmas with my family. Then I'll do what we all know I have to do."

"Artie," my sister said, looking me dead in the eye, "you know you're not going to make it to Christmas. You haven't made it in four years. Enough of the bullshit, enough of the lies. You need to go to rehab and you need to go now."

"Stace, it's not just that. I want to go to Christmas and I will go, but I also have work and I can't miss that."

"We already talked to them, Artie," she said, not missing a beat. "Gary and Howard are fine with you taking all the time you need."

"You talked to Howard?" I asked. I was shocked and not happy at all.

"Yes, I did. And he's fine with it."

I couldn't shoo that fact away; that meant this was real and things were bad. As much as outsiders think the entire *Stern Show* is a group of misfits being cruel to each other and making fun of the world around them, Howard and the staff, down to the last man and woman, truly care about one another. Sure, it's a comedy show, so it's crazy and the mood is always irreverent, but we are all sensitive people and all I can say is that Howard cares—really cares—about everyone. He was genuinely concerned about me and had been for a long time and had tried to get through to me many ways, but I wasn't having any of it. I know that Howard still cares about me and wants to see me defeat my demons. That knowledge is one of the things that keeps me going because I respect him more than I do myself most of the time.

Howard wasn't kidding when he asked Chris Rock on the air, in the spring of '09, "Chris, you're a smart guy; please tell me, how do I help Artie?"

"Howard, I hate to say this, man, but you're going to have to fire him," Chris said without missing a beat. "If you fire him, that might wake him up."

I was sitting right there, by the way. "That's a great idea," I said. "Thanks, Chris."

"Artie, I'm trying to help you out, man," Chris said. He yelled it actually, because that's how Chris says anything. "If Howard fires you, it might wake you up! You'd be fired, you'd be out of a job, and it'd be your fault. It would be a consequence of your actions that you could not ignore."

Chris was right, and I think deep down Howard knew it, but Howard is such a kind guy that he couldn't do it, because he's the type that just can't fire people no matter how much they drive him crazy. The list of *Stern Show* employees past and present that prove this point is very long. Howard would rather be inconvenienced by putting up with people he hates no matter how bad a job they do than take away that person's living. That is how he thinks and it's coming from a place of kindness, so firing is just not in his vocabulary. I'd like to think that even at my worst I was still contributing to the show in some small way, at least enough that no matter how bad it got, Howard was able to keep rooting for me to get it together, hoping that it would all work out in the end. His attitude rallied everyone else behind me and all the staff did everything they could to help me, day in and day out.

Howard really tried; he took the time to set me up with a shrink, and said that if I needed a week, a month, six months or a year to get better, he'd support me and I'd have a job waiting. "Artie, I want you to do what you've got to do," he kept telling me, and he meant it. Howard also set up a meeting with his agent, Don Buchwald, who is a brilliant guy and a class-A problem solver. Don came up with a plan to dig me out after I'd called in sick two Mondays in a row after spending the weekend on the road doing stand-up. Howard said this couldn't keep happening, so he sent me to Don to have him figure it out, and it was very awkward because this was the first time Howard had had to address this issue. I met with Don and my agent, Tony Burton.

"Here's what I think, Artie," Don said. "You should work stand-up according to a schedule that I'll write up for you. You're doing too much right now and you need to get it together. We don't want you to make less, we just want you to work less, so you'll do fewer gigs, but for bigger money. You'll only do venues of four to six thousand seats and you won't do as many, so what will happen is that your shows will become events, not some regular thing any schmuck can see every month. We'll get you traveling less, which takes a lot out of you. If you let me book things for you, we'll have you on the road once a month at most, only playing for big money."

That made total sense to me. It was amazing advice actually, but I didn't follow it. Like everything else I intended to—I just didn't do it no matter how hard I said yes, even when I meant it.

"I like that plan, Don," I said. "That sounds perfect, man. Let me just get through this year and finish out all my preexisting commitments and then I'll start doing that." Yeah, right.

Anyway, that day in December, Colin and Stacey weren't letting me off easy. Stacey had taken the lead, so I figured I'd shot this whole rehab idea down once she folded her arms and gave up arguing with me. I was in the clear; Santa had come early to Artie's house. I hadn't counted on Colin picking up where she left off.

"Art, if you don't like the sound of that place upstate, don't worry about it; it's not the only solution, you know," he said. "Believe me, I know plenty of places, and they come in every flavor."

He told me about a rehab in South Florida called Hippocrates, which isn't your average detox and rehab—it's much more holistic. They teach "lifestyle change," which involves teaching people to adjust their diet for one thing, and if you want to go the whole hog, they'll teach you the benefits of juicing and eating vegan once you get the drugs out of the way. If you let them have their way you go in a junk food–eating junkie and you come out a yoga-loving swami. They look at diet and lifestyle as something that must change alongside addiction if someone is really going to be free of it. This sounded like a cult to me. I tried to put on a poker face.

"What if you go there?" Colin asked. "It's not even like a rehab, Art; it's more like a South Florida resort where you'll get through withdrawals and then learn about healthy living. You can go between Christmas and New Year's and stay a month. It's pricey, but you've got the cash. You'll lose weight and you'll come back with a tan. It will be a vacation."

Maybe it *was* a cult, but that part sounded great, because I was fucking exhausted. I really was, and I couldn't remember the last time I had taken a vacation. The drugs weren't fun anymore; they were an anchor dragging in the sand, just as much of a nag as my loved ones were when they were trying to help me. I was too tired to help myself or do much of anything else but try to stay on the hamster wheel I'd built for myself. This Hippocrates place sounded like Club Med compared to keeping up with my bullshit, and I don't know if Colin and Stacey had just worn me down or if for the first time I felt like I'd actually been presented with an option I could live with. Whatever it was I agreed to go, which was a small victory for Stacey and Colin. It had taken them two hours of talk to get through to me, but they did it. We called the place and made me a reservation: I'd arrive the day after Christmas, because I swore up and down I'd be there. The place cost something like ten grand for two weeks, and I booked myself in there for a month. We then called Gary to inform the Stern camp that I wouldn't be back until January 17, and they wished me the best.

It goes without saying that my sister was right—I didn't make Christmas; I was neck-deep in withdrawals, sweating and itchy and not giving half a shit about the holiday season. I called my family but they'd all heard it too many times by then. So I did what any self-disrespecting drug addict would do to honor the season of giving and the legacy of Jesus Christ: I drove to downtown Newark and bought Oxycontin off the first street dealer I saw, then sped back to my apartment and spent the day high and alone. I was reading *Exile on Main Street: A Season in Hell with the Rolling Stones* by Robert Greenfield and was so into it that I made notes in the margin of every page that dealt with Keith Richards's desperation during the deepest depths of his drug abuse. I also watched *Dog Day Afternoon* a lot. Over that Christmas I think I watched it three or four times. And as I had for years, when I'd get high on anything and lay around my apartment alone, I'd listen to the Allman Brothers' *Eat a Peach* over and over again. That was the scene. It so seasonally cheery, I can't believe I didn't have anyone over for a holiday meal. Anyway, the next morning I made my flight to Florida and brought a healthy supply of Subutex, the opiate blocker drug that I used to avoid withdrawals. I figured I'd need it at Hippocrates and that it would help me reach the first stepping-stone on my path to healthy living.

That might have worked if I hadn't been abusing it for the previous three years, using it as some kind of safety net instead of its intended purpose as a detox drug. When I knew I couldn't get heroin or strong enough opiates for twelve to twenty-four hours, I'd start popping Subutex like Certs to get me through until I could score again. That's not what it is intended for, but that's how Dr. Artie used it. The thing about Subutex is that it contains enough of an opiate to keep your body from going into the shock of withdrawal, so you get high to a very mild degree, but after you take it, if you ingest real opiates of any kind for the next twelve hours you become violently sick, which is how and why I missed Bob Saget's Comedy Central roast. My chemistry schedule, especially when I got bad, was to do as many opiates as I could find for four days—Thursday through Sunday usually—before turning to Subutex to skip through the withdrawals and slip back into the workweek at the *Stern Show*. I also used it when I had a stand-up gig and couldn't score drugs before I got there. There were weeks when I was doing Subutex, weeks when I was abusing opiates, and weeks when I was doing both, which was a dangerous proposition. So my body had all kinds of dependency going on.

At Hippocrates I had my own room, and as nutty as that place is, their program works. Their philosophy was beyond anything I'd ever been exposed to, because to me you were either on drugs or you weren't, you were either functional or you weren't, but they didn't see things that way at all: they took your whole body into account. The drugs were just one piece of the puzzle to them, and I was shocked to find out that the drugs were the least intimate thing they cared about. They aim to get your entire body clean, then teach you to eat right and then to live right. I'm not what you'd call an armchair nutritionist, but I feel fine saying that they have a very unusual view of eating right, which is tied more directly than the food chain itself to shitting right. And like I've said, they are the kind of people who aim to be involved every step of the way.

They had group meetings about this, which involved getting everyone in a banquet room to listen to a staff member explain their program in the kind of very positive up-with-people speak that I loathe. I'm serious, that kind of shit makes my skin crawl worse than day three of heroin withdrawal. This introductory seminar made me want to throw up, which I'm not sure they would consider beneficial because it didn't involve pulling anything out of my ass.

You see, they were obsessed with shitting, which they got to immediately after the happy talk died down. They told us that when you shit, you should keep your legs up, which unbeknownst to most of humanity is the "proper" way to shit. To assist us in assuming this position and unlearning years of improper shitting, they gave each of us a little step to put under our feet on when we sat on the bowl. It's amazing that we've put a man on the moon but most of us still don't shit right, because as I now know, only with your legs elevated can any of us—detoxing addicts, health nuts, normal people—properly get their shit on. I was so glad that someone told me how badly I'd been misusing toilet bowls since my first day out of Pampers.

They worked their way backward with us, telling us that to get our digestive tracts back in shape we would need to consume plenty of green drinks, yogurt, and more vegetables than I'd ever seen or eaten in my entire life. There was no fruit on the menu, however, because fruit is high in sugar, which is forbidden, as is caffeine and anything else that gets you buzzed in any way. To enjoy an apple a day at Hippocrates you'd need a note from someone in charge— I'm completely serious. Our diet consisted of nothing but flavorless organic things like celery, none of them fun, all of them aimed at cleaning you out.

It didn't stop there; actually it didn't even begin there. Every morning of that first week, a Jamaican woman of about sixty years of age woke me up at seven a.m. with a gentle knock at the door followed by a not-so-gentle green colonic to my ass. She was as chipper as Jiminy Cricket, making small talk while she slipped a tube up there and sent this healthy, organic green cleanser that you could probably also use to fertilize your lawn into my poop chute. She'd smile the whole time, chatting away, asking me questions about my life in her thick, upbeat accent. We'd talk about my favorite bands, my hometown, sports, and whatever else, while this algae shake went into my ass, swished around a bit, then flowed out into a bag, carrying Chinese rocks and God knows what else with it. The whole process took about twenty-five minutes, and since it happened every day, she and I got real chummy, because let me tell you, if someone probes your ass every morning for a week you'll either become best friends with them or end up killing them with your bare hands. Seeing as I was there to "make some changes" I "stayed positive," though I hope to never, ever have that much traffic going the wrong way up my body's one-way street again.

At the end of the first week my sister came to visit me, and she wasn't happy to learn that I was still taking Subutex. I hadn't told her I'd brought it and I wasn't sure if they'd allow it in, but I explained to the admitting physician that I'd been using it for years and that I'd have a seizure without it. I don't know if that's true—it probably isn't—but they bought it. Anyway, Stacey felt like I was still high all the time because of it. She felt like I wasn't taking any of this seriously and that I was just wasting everyone's time once again, and we had it out in my room.

"Artie, I can't do this anymore," she said, enraged. "I'm going to have to give up on you. I've reached the end of my rope."

To me, this whole thing—the "intervention," her criticism of my life, all of it—came down to money. At least that was the only subject that might give me an edge up on her. Really it was all I had, so I went for it.

"Why can't you let me live the way I want to live, Stacey?" I shouted. "Let me do it my way and I'll buy you a fucking car! Whatever you want, just leave me the fuck alone."

That made her want to punch me in the face.

I kept saying stupid shit like that during my first week at Hippocrates and I believed all of it, but things had started to change. I'd lost some weight, I'd gotten some color back in my face, and I felt better. I saw it, I felt it, and I liked it, but that didn't mean I was buying the lifestyle they were selling. My sister sensed that, so she stayed on in West Palm Beach for as long as she could, until eventually she had to get back to her job in New York City. I said good-bye and told her I'd see her back at home after my time there was done—and she gave me a look that said she wasn't betting on it.

She was right again, of course. I was scheduled to stay at Hippocrates for another two and a half weeks, but it took me precisely twenty-four hours after Stacey's departure to decide that I was all fixed up. I checked out, I rented a car, I drove to Miami, to South Beach, and checked into a $2,000-a-night suite at the Setai Hotel. Then I started drinking the minibar, one small bottle at a time, no chaser, mixing everything from Sambuca to tequila. I ordered room service, I got smashed at the beach bar, and I started living it up like the world was going to end tomorrow. The party was back on.

The *Stern Show* was also back on, so each morning, since I'd be up, I'd start listening to them talking about how I'd gone AWOL from rehab. They'd wonder what I was doing, where I might be, and when I couldn't take the speculation anymore I checked in by phone. I was completely fucked up, sitting there waiting for room service to bring my breakfast at six a.m., having drunk all through the night. They patched me in to Gary right away, then to Howard, live on the air.

"Artie, where are you?" Howard asked.

"I'm at a hotel in South Beach, Howard!" I said, somehow proud of myself. "The rehab I was in was great, and I did so well there I got to leave early. I'm in Miami, and boy, am I going nuts!"

Just then the food arrived and I made the Asian guy who delivered it tell everyone exactly what I'd ordered. It was funny because he had a very thick accent, which made the word "pancakes" sound hilarious. I really couldn't get enough of it, so I asked him to say it about five or six times.

"Artie, get back here as soon as possible," Howard said, dead serious. "We're all worried about you."

"All right, all right, I'll come back tomorrow."

I didn't do that, of course: I partied for two more days, spending an insane amount of money before I got on a plane home. It was completely retarded: aside from my bar tabs, drinks at the pool, and room service bills, I bought a $7,000 watch that I wore exactly twice. I ended up giving it to a drug dealer when I had no cash and owed him money. He took it for $3,000, which is about as great of a value depreciation as you get driving a sports car off the lot. I also met some girl in the lobby who saw me buying the watch in the gift shop and we got to talking. She kind of recognized me, which means she recognized that I had money, and after we had a bunch of drinks at the bar we went to my room and out on my terrace, in broad daylight, overlooking the beach, she gave me a blow job. I remember drinking a Jack Daniel's and water, admiring both the view of the coastline and the top of her head blowing me and thinking to myself, *Nobody gets it. Why would I ever want to stop partying? This is great! Fucking rock and roll!* What a perfect prick I was. I had become that asshole who'd forgotten every single value my Italian-American family had instilled in me.

It couldn't last forever, because no high can, so my last night there I had dinner at Nobu with my former assistant Michelle and I remember listening to myself, knowing I was lying, telling her how I'd get clean the minute I got home.

"Oh yeah?" she asked. She has these insanely expressive, beautiful eyes, which she squinted up at me and sarcastically said, "How?"

That was all she needed to say. Both of us knew I had no answer, so we simultaneously started giggling. "Yeah," I said, kind of mock frowning. "I don't know how I'm gonna do that."

I flew home the next day and went back to the show and made light of all of it. I told all my crazy stories and at once I felt like the status quo had returned. I'd gotten through the holidays and 2009 had arrived and everything was fine—right? It was a new year, and a week later I found out that another one of my dreams was about to come true.

The success of *Too Fat to Fish* drew the attention of the kind of mainstream media that had ignored me until then, one of which being *Rolling Stone* magazine. I'd always wanted to be in those pages because what warm-blooded American rock-and-roll fan wouldn't? I was overjoyed to hear they wanted to do a feature on me and had assigned a reporter to follow me around during the first two weeks of January. They didn't want a manufactured photo, they wanted me in my element, at home, with no pretense, so they asked to have the shoot take place at my apartment. That sounded perfect.

This was really important to me, so I hired my former assistant Michelle to come in to town to make sure everything went smoothly. That didn't keep me from oversleeping the day of the photo shoot because I'd done drugs all night the night before. I had no awareness of the wreckage I was leaving in my wake. I saw my abuse as harmless to anyone else but me just as much as I saw it as necessary to my existence. I'd do drugs, sitting there watching the clock tick away the hours, knowing I should get some rest but continually procrastinating, telling myself I could handle it. When something important was scheduled for the next day I'd tell myself I'd get the rest I needed after I snorted just one more line. There'd be time to sleep after that high. And then it would wear off and I'd convince myself that I'd be good to go after just one more. And then one more. I was always running out of time because time flies when you're getting high. The thing was, I pretty much always showed up to my engagements, maybe unprepared, but I was always there, so what was the problem?

That was my train of thought in the hours leading up to what in theory was one of the proudest moments and greatest tokens of success in my life. I guess I was truly laying myself bare before one of the most legendary magazines in the world by getting numb and hungover, but it was so far from being premeditated. As usual when I was on a bender of any kind, I slept in my clothes and didn't shower, using all those minutes to chase the high or hover in between sleep and euphoria.

I had to fly Michelle in from Miami to be my stand-in assistant, because as I've mentioned, I'd burned through four assistants in the New York tri-state area, none of whom could deal with my drug abuse and insanity. No one wanted to work for me, even on a short-term basis, even for one day—it was that bad. She'd tried to rouse me and yelled at me to get cleaned up, but I don't even remember that happening. She got so frustrated that she took pictures of me sprawled out in bed and eventually showed them to me when I woke up.

"This is you getting ready for your *Rolling Stone* photo shoot," she said, deadpan. She has a great sense of humor as well as immense patience, that girl. The pictures are hilarious: I look like Oscar Madison rolled up in bed after a bender.

She stalled them for about twenty minutes, but after a while there was nothing else for her to do but to admit I was still asleep.

"Artie, the photographer is here," she said loudly, standing in the doorway to my bedroom, banging on the wall as hard as she could.

"Oh yeah?" I said. "Hi, photographer. Give me just a minute."

I rolled out of bed with the grace of an obese otter with a hangover, still high on opiates and booze, my eyes crusted shut from sleep. I looked like a piece of furniture left out on the lawn after a weeklong orgy at Versailles. I was overweight and gray-skinned, my eyes still pinned from smack and my hair standing up like I'd been electrocuted. I was just forty-one, but I looked seventy-five. My beard was entirely gray and all I could think to put on for this shoot was a green corduroy jacket, a pair of gray sweatpants, and white gym socks. Somehow I thought a shirt wasn't necessary. *Mister DeMille,* I thought, *I am ready for my close-up.*

The photographer was an effeminate Asian fellow. "It's nice to meet you, Artie," he said, looking at me strangely. "Why don't you go and get ready."

"What do you mean?" I said. "I am ready. Were you expecting me to be wearing Yves Saint Laurent?"

"Oh," he replied. "Fine, then." He looked like he'd smelled fresh dog shit.

And the thickest silence you can imagine fell over the room.

I started chain-smoking as they set up their lights, moved my books around, and tried to make an artful backdrop out of my belongings. I kept going to the bathroom every fifteen minutes to crush and snort more pills. I didn't care how obvious it was, and it was obvious, because every time I returned all eyes were on me.

As the photographer prepared to shoot, the hair and makeup girl approached me, looking truly terrified. There wasn't a foundation, eye shadow, brush, or spackling tool on Earth that could have made me look healthy, sober, or normal, but God bless her, the girl fought the good fight. She put powder on me, trimmed my beard and the rest of it as best she could. It didn't help matters that I wouldn't stay still, because the more high I got the more abusive I became toward the photographer. I chose to torment him by quoting movie lines he clearly didn't know.

"How about a Fresca?" I'd say to all of them. That's a line from *Caddyshack* from the scene where Ted Knight says it to the guy who plays Noonan. No one had any idea what I was talking about. They were probably too young to even know what a Fresca was.

The assistants kept joking around, trying to make light of it, but my comments were pointed and just so off that the mood got awkward and dark real quick. I remember the two guys taking test shots and doing what they could to distract me from what had become my main objective: pissing the Asian guy off, which I was doing in the time-honored spirit of self-destructive rebellion. In the end I'm pretty sure they used one of those test shots, because the image was the most grotesque, embarrassing, and unfinished one you can imagine. Basically I looked like Vic Tayback, who played Mel on *Alice*, on a crack binge.

Norm MacDonald had this sweet little piece of advice for me—too late, of course—after he saw this murder scene they called a photo. "First of all, you never let anybody with a camera into your home—ever," he said. "That's the first thing you should know."

I wish that the photo was the worst thing about the whole debacle, but it wasn't: the article was much, much worse. It was what two-bit gossip columnists call a "takedown," just an insult wrapped in a veil of fake authority and so-called journalism. Who knows, maybe it was due to my behavior at the photo shoot that they chose to send a woman writer who'd gone to Wesleyan or Vassar or one of those other broad colleges, who basically hated me on sight. She was a typically forgettable Upper-West-Side-Central-Park-jogger type who couldn't be more different from—or more judgmental of—someone like me. I've become pretty skilled at knowing when someone doesn't like me, particularly women, so I knew it wasn't going to be a "fluff" piece, but I had no idea it would be such a hatchet job.

Everything in my life was going so well professionally, and it's not like a biased article by some no-name broad in *Rolling Stone* could change any of that, but still, I'd hoped that my moment in such a historic magazine would at least reflect who I was. She just couldn't get past her own bias enough to do her job. The day the magazine came out I bought one at the newsstand and realized immediately that this was another bittersweet victory in my life—this one more bitter than sweet.

On the cover, you see, was my hero, Bruce Springsteen, and there was my name just above his picture. After I'd read the first five words of the article on me, I literally prayed to God that Bruce flipped by those pages on me on his way to his article and never, ever read it. Let me tell you why, the photo was terrible, but the tagline was worse, it quoted me calling myself a loser. How can you ever really come back from that?

I remember Norm MacDonald being on the *Stern Show* the week the article came out and defending me when Howard suggested that I appease *Rolling Stone* by not bitching out the writer on the air as enthusiastically as I'd started to do. Norm cut Howard off actually, which is not something anyone does and gets away with.

"Howard, that fucking broad really railroaded Artie," he said. "He shouldn't be nice about it at all."

I'm pretty sure I was still drunk that morning, and I was definitely high on painkillers, so Norm's comments really got me going, so much so that when I went on *The Wrap-Up Show* with Gary I really let it go. The best way to combat a blatant attack like a shitty article is to avoid giving it any attention, which I didn't do, of course. I started insulting everything about the reporter and the shitty job she'd done. In the process I called her a "cunt" about eighteen times, give or take a few cunts. Someone told her about it, of course, which is generally what happens when you say anything insulting about someone on a radio show with six million listeners. The broad responded—of course she did—on some blog somewhere, calling me low-class and obnoxious. Now, if she'd done her homework for the article, she would have known this about me already, just like she would have known that I've made those two traits work wonders for me professionally. Stating the obvious is no way to get back at someone who advertises what they are to the degree that I do, so her comment stung about as much as a bee would a rhino's ass. Anyway, that's the last I heard from her, which depresses me because I thought we'd really connected and that these differences were just growing pains. I was looking forward to summering together on Cape Cod each August.

When you're a comedian with any visible degree of success

and you meet comedians on their way up or those just struggling to make it to the middle, most of them ask you for advice. I'm sure it's like this in every industry, but comics are so full of overanalytical self-loathing that I'd bet my bank account that these little pep talks take longer to get through or get out of than they would, say, a CEO of Boeing Aviation chatting with a recent business school graduate. Comics think too much, they feel too much, and most of them really hate themselves, so you can imagine what happens if you open up that can of worms. You'd better want to, is all I can tell you, and if you don't, you'd better have an escape plan.

Norm MacDonald has perfected the art of this conversation because he's had years of practice. It started in the mid-nineties when he was on *Saturday Night Live*, and it only got worse in 1999, when he starred in his own network sitcom, *Norm*. I've seen comics latch on to him hoping to get pieces of wisdom long before I ever had to deal with anything like that, and I envy what he came up with, because it's both true and the best way to keep the conversation brief. Here's Norm's line when a comic asks him how to break into the "major leagues" of the business: "Well, I don't have all the answers, so I can't tell you how to get in, but I sure can tell you how to get out." A quick review of his television career will confirm that he's an expert at achieving and then abandoning success, so you should take his word for it. The rip cord out of a mainstream career for any comic according to Norm is a well-placed racist or homophobic joke. He's not wrong—just ask Michael Richards: that guy got out of the business in literally two minutes.

After that stint in rehab, I kept going to work, no matter how fucked up I was. I'd show up with my ass crack hanging out, in three-day-old clothes, stinking and high to heaven, but I still showed up. There's this theory out there among *Stern* fans that I missed work a lot of the time, but that's just not true; I didn't miss work. I was there all the time and when I wasn't sleeping live on the radio, I was funny all the time, every time. I was able to seem normal somehow . . . crazy, sure, but normal and functional. Only in my last few months on the show did I ever miss a day, because by then things were really falling apart. That's because I knew what I was doing: if my dealers couldn't get me what I needed I knew how to score on the street in downtown Newark or Jersey City. I could keep myself supplied well enough so that I would seem normal for those four hours a day that I had to be on the show.

When I got on the road I had to sleep all the time because that's where my ruse was up. From Teddy to my road manager Tim, and J.D., who did video for me on the road, they began to see what I couldn't hide. I never wanted to travel with drugs, so the road became a test; I'd get as much shit as possible into me before I got on that plane, trying to plan it all so that I'd not go into withdrawals until I was back home, safe, in range of where I could get enough drugs to get me on track to show up for my job at *Stern*. When I left town for a weekend of stand-up I'd time it out so I'd get to my room and pass out and still be high when I woke up to go onstage a few hours later. If I could get on a plane home just as my withdrawals were starting, I knew I'd be fine because I knew I had something stashed in my apartment and if I didn't I knew exactly whom to call or where to drive to make those cramps stop. Coming home was literally going to heaven for me for all those months I was doing all those lucrative stand-up gigs every single weekend. If we landed and I was hurting, I knew as soon as I was in my car I could make it. I had it planned out that far. I mean, any flight delay was like death to me, so you can imagine just how often this fragile ecosystem I lived in got completely imbalanced.

This was far from exact science, let me tell you. We are talking about a guy who was trying to do all the drugs he'd need in a weekend by the time the five-o'clock bell rang on Friday. The road became going from the plane to the car to the hotel room where I'd blacken out my hotel room. I mean, blacken. Literally I'd duct tape the curtains down. Around that time, a friend of mine had told me that a buddy of his who was a heroin addict would get so light sensitive that even the little green light on the smoke detector was too much light for him. What this guy would do is chew a piece of gum and stick it over that little green light. I'm not sure I'd ever even noticed those lights before I'd heard the story, but all I know is that I couldn't sleep an hour in any hotel room bed if I could see that light from where I was lying. I'm not even a gum guy, but I started to buy gum at the airport just so I'd be able to stick a piece over the little green light. I obsessed over it, and there were terrible times when I found myself with no gum to chew, and before then I'd found gum to be a completely useless item. But once it became my method of blacking out the light in a hotel room, gum became very important to me. There were, however, times when the hotel I was staying in would need to send a maintenance guy with a ladder to place my piece of gum over the smoke detector light. I'm not a diva; I was happy to do it myself, but sometimes the ceilings were too high for me to reach. It got to the point that I couldn't sleep properly without gum on that light. Chewing gum, strictly to place over the smoke detector light, became part of my ritual, and ask any drug addict—the ritual is what it's all about.

I was starting to lose it. And thank God that at this point stand-up was all instinct for me, because I'd stay in my hotel room until the last possible minute and take the stage without mentally preparing in any way. If I had to go on at eight p.m., I'd be in the room, in bed, until 7:55 p.m. The promoter, my road manager, everyone, would be ringing incessantly; they'd knock on my door nonstop, but it didn't matter. There were many times when they all thought I was dead, and to be honest, I don't blame them. All I'd ever say was that I was real tired, which I suppose I was. I was never lying; then again, was I ever really telling the truth?

It was this crazy: I'd get up when I absolutely had to, and if I couldn't deal with my hair situation I'd put a hat on. Usually I'd be wearing the same clothes, so I didn't have to worry about getting dressed, and I'd go straight to the stage, literally from bed, and I'd do an hour of comedy. I guess that is some kind of miracle. And if I was anywhere within range of my home in New Jersey, I'd drive there myself or demand that I be brought right home afterward because home is where the heart is, and in my case, it was also where all of my drugs were.

I was scared to travel with drugs, which is why my life on the road got so nuts. I'd read all those stories about Keith Richards and the Stones smuggling shit and getting busted, so there was no way I was going to do that as one dude on my own. So I did what I could: I top-loaded my consumption so that I'd be high enough to get through the weekend until I could get home and get more. I didn't have much of a choice, really. It wasn't logical at all and it was a risk every single time, but I did think it was fun in a very sick way, and I know why—because I love gambling. Gambling is my biggest vice and this was a huge bet I was placing every week, wasn't it? Taking all the opiates I'd need to get through the weekend and home again before the withdrawals kicked in and stabilized me enough to make it to work in some kind of decent shape the next morning? That's one exciting fucking wager! It sure beat betting on college basketball.

There were more than a few times when I think I OD'd before I even left the house on Friday. I gave myself these seizures a few times that I can't accurately describe because all I know is that I blacked out and then came to a few minutes later. I was a doctor without a degree: I'd tally up all the hours I had to be gone from my stash and then dose myself as I saw fit. At the time I was doing one-nighters in theaters instead of two-nighters in a club. And thank God I was, because I'd be dead right now otherwise. I'm not kidding; if I'd been doing clubs at that point in my life I would have either been arrested or I would have died. Most likely I'd have been arrested for trying to take drugs on a plane. And then I'd probably have died.

The *Stern Show* was my priority, and I kept it that way until the very end, when I was so far gone that I did miss work and it was glaringly obvious that something was very wrong with me. Up until then, I was fine. But I'm still not sure how. There were weekends where I had those ministrokes before I even left my house and was still so banged up by the time I got to the gig that my body would hit some sort of wall. Can you blame it? I was hardly in the best shape to begin with. I'd get off work at, say, eleven and have to fly at four, and would spend those three hours before my flight to St. Louis doing as many lines of heroin and popping as many pills as I could manage. I'd arrive, go right to bed, and then wake up the next day and fulfill my obligations. There were times when I'd sleep a full day, do what I had to do, and go right back to my dark hotel room to sleep until the flight home. There were times where I didn't shower for three or four days while on the road, slept in my clothes, got home, and slept in my clothes again for a few hours, then went right into work at the *Stern Show*. I wasn't capable of showering until I was high enough to function.

Listen, I didn't *look* good because I was heavy, but if you listen to those shows I was always funny, and I always showed up. The times I didn't show up on *Stern* became very famous because they blow everything out of proportion on that show. If it happened as much as it seemed like it did, I'd have never kept that job as long as I did, and that's the truth.

I was tired and my road schedule was crazy and that's what I told them, and they had no real reason to believe otherwise. I would say the *Stern Show* knew I had a real problem only in the last few months I was there—the fall of '09. And that's when Howard came to me aggressively with his agent and suggested that I stop the stand-up schedule. Their plan didn't work out, mostly because I was making 100 grand a weekend, and why would I even think of stopping that? I had money coming in hand over fist, I was juggling people getting me off drugs and bringing me drugs—what else could I want? It was the kind of action that I found exciting.

I was successfully able to keep what I was doing in my private life away from the *Stern Show* because I showed up there and was proficient at my job. The rest of my life, however, was chaos on a level I can't even describe. I had to keep all of that as far away from the *Stern* universe as I could. And I did, successfully—until the fall of '09, that is.

CHAPTER 4

PARTIE LANGE AIRWAYS

In late 2007, I remet someone whom *Stern* fans will remember from my final days on the show, a guy known to me and mine and them as well as Helicopter Mike. I don't know how much any of you believe in fate, but there have been too many coincidences in my life for me to ignore the possibility that fate is fake, and this guy is one of the biggest reasons for that. I have no recollection of meeting Mike the first time, but when I heard the facts, enough of them lined up to make a believer out of me. I've got a strange type of memory, by which I mean if you mention a date to me, whether it's last month or twelve years ago, there's a ninety-percent chance that I'll immediately remember exactly where I was that day without needing to check a calendar or date book. If I played a gig on the day in question, most likely I'll remember the venue, as well as the promoter and who opened for me if anyone did. If any major-league play-off events took place on that day (excluding basketball), I'll probably also be able to tell whether I placed bets that day and whether my team won. My recall is basically prejudiced because those facts and a few others are consistently the only things I've retained. It's a window into my soul that very close friends, bookies, drug dealers, hookers, and ex-girlfriends are the characters that most densely populate my memory lane, and that's only because they are the ones who were there when my favorite activities occurred. I can't help it, and it often offends me on behalf of those who should occupy more space in my mental scrapbook, but what can I say? My lopsided mind chooses to retain most clearly memories of the activities that involve the action my nature loves best. I hope everyone else understands and hopefully realizes I do care . . . I've just got my priorities.

I meet a lot of people in my line of work, and back when I was all Partie Lange (which, by the way, will be my on-air name if I'm ever forced at gunpoint to become a "morning zookeeper" on Z100) I spent a lot of time whiling the night away with strangers. I loved every minute of it; I just don't remember much about it. So right now, once and for all, I'd like to apologize to all those people I've hung out with after a gig or at wherever the party has taken me over the years because I probably don't remember shit about you. All of you strangers who became fast friends, please don't be hurt; I know we may have figured out the cure for cancer and the meaning of life that night all before the sun came up. I mean you no offense, but don't be surprised if I look at you in terror when we meet again, as if you're my own personal Mark David Chapman.

Since getting sober, the limitations of my biased recall have become crystal clear to me, and I've got no choice but to embrace them and acknowledge their existence. I have to work with them or else they'll be a huge problem. I did this begrudgingly at first, like a government admitting a budget deficit or a KKK Grand Dragon admitting that we have a black president. But eventually I did admit the truth to myself in the only way I know how—by finding the humor in it. Here's an example from a few months ago that says it all. I was in Midtown Manhattan, walking to work from the parking garage at about seven p.m., going to the studio where my radio show on DirecTV/Sirius is recorded. I was almost there when a kid stopped me to say hi, like my fans usually do. He started telling me about how we'd met at a rest stop just outside of Portland a few years back, where I was heading to do a show.

"Man, that sounds great, but it couldn't have been me," I said, laughing, thinking the kid should have done a little homework before coming up with this ruse to get a photo and my autograph. "Must have been a different fat, homeless-looking guy, buddy; I've never been to Portland."

"Yeah, you have, Artie, I swear to God," he said. "It was totally you. We shot the shit for about twenty minutes. Here, I'll show you."

He pulled out his phone and proceeded to show me a picture of the two of us standing under a sign, at a rest stop, that said WELCOME TO PORTLAND.

"You don't say," I said.

That moment was more sobering than half the AA meetings I've attended. Not only did I not remember the kid—like at all—but I didn't even recall one thing about being in the city. Nothing about playing it, nothing about the hotel, the motel, or the Holiday Inn— I'm talking, I drew a complete blank! I had to have spent at least a full day there plus the day I did the gig, so it was crazy to me that it was all a black hole. It made me think and wonder just how many more moments of my life I've lived through in complete blackouts, and I've come to accept the fact that the number is quite high. Now that I've pledged to do my best each day to keep myself on the other side of that void, I see every reminder like this one—as uncomfortable as they are—as a welcome reminder. Which is good, because in my case they're going to be plentiful. In fact, those of you who see me again, do me a favor and tell me where we may have met, because I could use a clue. Just watch my expression when you do, so that we'll both know it if my memory dice are coming up snake eyes again.

Anyway, the first time I met Helicopter Mike is an event occupying space in one of my blackouts—from the sound of it, one of my better ones. The following will be my version of a *Law & Order* re-creation, because the facts were all gathered from the eyewitnesses there, me not being one of them, though I was playing myself.

The season: winter. The location: the Patchogue Theatre, Patchogue, Long Island, which is a great, intimate performance space that holds about fifteen hundred people. I'd headlined there a few times before and I've always found the great people of Long Island to be nothing but a welcoming and wonderful audience, so I was pretty excited for this show. I was even more excited because it is striking distance from my apartment in Hoboken, aka the Arthur Lange Resort and Spa, where I would be able to adhere to my proper health regime, take my constitutional, and get large doses of that all-important cure-all, "rest," that I was so fond of at the time.

Teddy was still my assistant and road manager then, and I believe J.D. was still attempting to make a documentary about my life on the road. Completing the *Stern* revue that night we had Long Island native Sal the Stockbroker opening up as well as Reverend Bob Levy. Long Island is definitely *Stern* country, so we had Brian Phelan, all the Howard TV people, Sal's parents, you name it, plus every die-hard *Stern* fan who could be there in the house that night. The backstage area was packed to say the least because Sal and Levy alone invited their entire extended families, each with plus-threes.

We were pushing the limits, but the theater and promoter really took care of us: all the dressing rooms were stocked with booze and sandwiches. There were people smoking weed nonstop in every greenroom. I was partaking heavily at the time, so I helped myself to everything, and I loved everybody I saw (though I remember none of you) because with all the weed and whiskey flowing it was a fucking good party. I was pretty buzzed as showtime approached, though, so I knew I had to take it down a little and find someplace to relax.

It was a freezing cold night in January so there was no way I could slip outside to escape the circus. I was going to have to figure something else out. On my way into the artist's entrance I remembered seeing a bus parked out back. It was a huge, real comfortable-looking, well-worn but upscale tour bus: just the kind of ride where a '70s rock fan would love to spark a doober. When Teddy saw me getting shifty he knew I needed some privacy. I sent him off to ask around about the bus.

"Art, that bus belongs to Lynyrd Skynyrd, and it's here because they're playing the theater later this week," he said when he returned a few minutes later. "Their tour manager is here tonight, though, and he said that if you want to chill out there, it's cool with him."

Usually I turn down shit like that because I don't like owing anyone anything; for better or for worse I'm more comfortable with people owing me things, but that night Skynyrd's bus was just what I needed. Plus I was dying to see the inside of it. I didn't even care what incarnation the band was currently in and how few of the original members were in it, Skynyrd is an institution and I had to know how they rolled. In 1977, hanging out on their bus would have been cooler than doing blow with Ryan O'Neal at Studio 54, and I knew it. At this time, in 2007, it was more morbid curiosity, but fuck it, I needed someone to give me three steps toward the door leading away from the chaos backstage, and who better to do that than Lynyrd Skynyrd?

Me, Teddy, and J.D. went onto the bus, where we met Mike, who wasn't familiar to me at all, beyond seeming like the kind of really nice Long Island guy I had met a million times. We got comfortable on the bus and I was grateful for that; I lit up a cigarette and Mike told us a bit about himself. He said he'd been in the army and had spent five years serving in the Gulf War under the first George Bush, then came back and served fifteen years as a cop for the NYPD. He'd since retired and now did security for bands, currently Skynyrd. I was so thankful for that little bit of peace before having to perform that I asked Mike if it was okay for me to pass out in the back lounge for a half hour or so, and he said yes, so that's what I did.

When Teddy came and woke me up he was beyond chipper, just oddly excited. Usually he was pretty drab and openly resentful about having to wake me up or do anything at all for me, so there had to be something going on, I just didn't know what it was.

"Art, you're not gonna believe this," he said, grinning.

"Probably not, Teddy. And I'm not sure I even want to hear about it."

"Just come out here."

I got up, rubbed my eyes, and walked down the hallway into the main lounge of the bus.

"What is it, Teddy? You're acting like a horny dude on prom night."

"Look at this guy," Teddy said, pointing at Mike. "Look at him. Does he look familiar to you at all?"

"I'm looking, Ted," I said. "I just met him when we got on the bus, so yeah, he's familiar."

"You've never met him before?"

What the fuck is this? I thought to myself. "I'm looking at him, Ted, and no, I haven't seen him before," I said. "Mike, I'm a little fried, so if we've met before I'm sorry, but your face isn't ringing a bell."

"You've definitely met him before," Teddy said.

"That's great, Ted, and thanks for letting me know. Let me ask you something—are you my assistant or do I pay you to make me look like a dick?"

"You've met him, I'm not lying, and this is the craziest story I've ever heard, so it has to be true."

"No offense, Mike, but Jesus Christ, Teddy, are we really doing this? All right, let's hear it." To his credit, Teddy wasn't lying, this story is one for the books, even for this one.

In 1992, when Helicopter Mike was still an NYPD beat cop, he got a call on a night that he happened to have a rookie along for the ride. There was a kid on the corner of Second Avenue and East Seventeenth Street in Manhattan claiming that a guy whom he'd seen doing stand-up comedy at Comic Strip Live had kidnapped him. Supposedly the comic and the kid had been drinking at a bar after the show when the comic asked the guy to get him cocaine.

When the kid said he didn't know where to get any, the comic got mad and strong-armed the kid into driving him to get cocaine. The comic was in the kid's car and refused to get out until he was driven to get drugs. That was the long and short of what dispatch told them.

Mike and his partner took the call, rolled up, and found the kid in his car with me in the front seat. The kid confirmed everything they'd been told. He said I was the comedian he'd just seen in the club (probably right) and that we'd gotten to drinking (of course) and that I was doing coke (whatever) and when I ran out, I insisted that we take his car to get more (who doesn't like cocaine?). Then I got into the passenger seat and wouldn't leave. Since I didn't have any more coke I fell asleep (that's what happens) and he couldn't wake me up (right again, and good luck with that).

"I'm afraid of this guy," the kid told the two cops. "You've got to get him out of my car."

There was no way in the world for me to refute these facts, so when Mike told me the story I didn't even try. I was a regular at Comic Strip Live from '92 through '93, and I was doing all the coke I could get, drinking whiskey like water, and having blackouts the way yuppies take "staycations." I remember doing a lot of strange things at night, but the few clear memories I have don't come close to the number of stories I've heard about me, almost all of which involve me forcing people to get me drugs or threatening them if they didn't give me the rest of theirs.

When I heard this story in 2007, it was embarrassing but it wasn't a surprise. Believe me, I was dying to be offended, wishing I could get in this guy's face and yell: *This is an outrage, you bastard. How dare you! I was a junior at Dartmouth at that time!* I wish I were more like Travolta, able to point to films I was doing, insisting I was out of town, on set, or off helping the needy for every time I was accused of soliciting a male masseur. Spoiler alert: I'm not Travolta, so I didn't flinch when the guy told me I'd taken a kid hostage because I'd run out of coke.

"Yeah, man, now that you mention it that could have been me," I said, "so let's assume it was, and I hope this is the beginning of a great story. But what happened? I don't have a record, so you couldn't have arrested me."

Mike laughed. "No, man, you weren't arrested that night. The ending is much better than that."

Mike confirmed what most of us have probably guessed at one point or another: cops don't like doing paperwork and who can blame them? So rather than arrest me, which would have involved waking me up and taking me in, he decided that both the kid and I were such idiots that we deserved to spend the night together. The kid, by the way, was also visibly drunk, so cleaning up the mess would have meant a lot of paperwork and waiting for a tow truck to impound this knucklehead's car. Instead of dealing with any of that, Mike and his partner told the kid they'd take his keys, lock them in the trunk, and then take the trunk key with them. The plan was to leave him there in the car with me for a few hours until their shift was over. By then the two of us would be sober enough to go home.

"That okay with you, kid?" Mike said.

"Well, I . . ."

"It's either that or we're arresting you and taking your car, and I just don't really feel like arresting anybody tonight. And in this situation, you're both going downtown. If I were you I'd shut up and sleep it off."

The kid had enough of a functioning brain left to make the right choice, but I think it took all three of them to talk me into the backseat, where the kid joined me. That sucked for him, but if another squad car found him sleeping in the front seat, legally he could still be busted for DUI—take note of that, you drunks. The cops found a shitty blanket in his trunk, gave it to him, and apparently left the two of us back there to spoon.

Mike isn't a cop anymore and since we're now friends he's admitted to me what I've always suspected: cops do that kind of shit all the time just to fuck with people. I mean, wouldn't you if you were a cop? Pretty much if they don't want to do paperwork and you're on the margin of illegality and not hurting anybody, there's a good chance they'll clown you before they arrest you if they're feeling lazy. Making a fool of you kills two birds with one stone, because it teaches you a lesson and makes the cops' shift funny for them.

It was winter, it was cold, and they'd taken the keys to the car, so there was no heat. Two hours later, the backseat of that sedan was a meat locker, or so I'm guessing. Mike and his partner arrived to find the kid shivering, awake, terrified, sad, and blanket-less because I'd pulled it off him, wrapped myself in it, and was snoring, happy as a pig in shit. I'd also wrestled the kid's jacket off of him and had that around me too. I wish some camera had caught that when it happened. The cops could barely contain themselves.

"You've got to wake this guy up," the kid begged them. "I have to go home. I'm freezing to death and he's a fucking asshole!"

I'm not sure how long it took or what they had to do, but Mike remembers that they finally woke me up around 5:30 a.m. and that I was still a very drunk and very belligerent asshole. I refused to get out of the car because apparently I'd come to believe that the car was mine, and so I had no idea why all of these people were bothering me. I kept telling them—all of them—to get the fuck off of me and get the fuck out of my car because I had to sleep. I'm telling you, sleep has always been very, very important to me. I don't think the entirety of the situation ever really dawned on me, but eventually Mike and his partner managed to load me into a cab and send it off to Penn Station. Throughout that process, I've been told that I kept telling them that "this city sucks," that Mike and his partner were fags, and that they could "fucking keep Manhattan," because I had to "get back to Jersey where the cops aren't fags." As Mike told me this, all I kept thinking was that this was definitely me, because those are all things I would say, and said often, while wasted.

A couple of years later Mike was watching late-night television, minding his own business when he saw my mug on MADtv. He'd been telling the story of that night at parties and around the station since the day it happened because it is so outstandingly ridiculous. He'd never forgotten my proper name, Arthur Lange, because how could he? So when the credits rolled, he saw "Artie Lange" and did the math, and he couldn't wait until the morning to tell his partner, so he called him and woke him up.

"I'm telling you, it's the guy," he said. "I can't believe he ever made anything of himself."

"You really sure? It's like hearing the Easter Bunny lays eggs."

"I'm telling you, it's him."

They were right to doubt my future prospects—even my own grandmother did, and we Italians are proud people not prone to admitting these kinds of things. This was my mom's mom, Grandma Caprio, who prayed to various Catholic saints asking them to guide each of her sons, grandkids, nephews, and everybody else through life. One day I walked in on her praying to Saint Joseph and asked her what she was asking him for.

"All of my sons are carpenters, so I pray to Saint Joseph because he is the patron saint of carpenters," she said. "I ask him to keep my sons safe in their work and to make sure that they always prosper." She went back to praying.

"Grandma Caprio, can I ask you a question?" I said.

"Of course, Arthur, what is it?"

"Do you pray to a saint for me?"

"Yes, I do."

"Really? Which one?"

"For you I pray to Saint Jude."

I thought that was great! I loved the Beatles, and I loved the song "Hey Jude." I didn't even think to ask anything more, I felt like Saint Jude had to be rock-and-roll and Grandma Cap knew that. How cool was it to have your patron saint be Saint Jude? That mirage lasted about a week until I made the mistake of proudly telling my uncle Bruce how great it was that Grandma Cap prayed to Saint Jude for me.

"She prays to Saint Jude for you?" he said and doubled over laughing. "Saint Jude?"

"Yeah, Saint Jude," I said. "I thought that was really cool. You know, like 'Hey Jude.'"

"Do you know what Saint Jude is the patron saint of, Artie?" My uncle was nearly pissing himself.

"Um . . . no. I mean . . ."

"Saint Jude is the patron saint—" He was really cracking up; he had to pause to catch a breath. "He's . . . the . . . patron saint . . . of hopeless causes!"

Fuck me. Well if there's one thing that can be said about her, it's that Grandma Caprio called them as she saw them.

Back to the story, once Mike and his partner realized that the guy on MADtv was the same Arthur Lange they'd sent back to Jersey all those years ago, they became fans. I'm not sure why; I guess it had something to do with the age-old tradition of rooting for the under-dog, without which teams like the Mets would have no fans. Or maybe they just respected me for beating the odds.

"When I saw you were playing here tonight, Artie, I could have just locked the bus and gone home, but I stayed because I wanted to meet up with you again," Mike said.

"Really?" I said. "Why? I mean, I was an asshole. That's the dumbest story I've ever heard. It's only funny to me now because I don't remember any of it. It's like you're telling me about some idiot I'll never meet."

"I have my reasons, Art," he said. "First of all I think you're a funny motherfucker, but I also think I can help you stay out of trouble. I'd like to get to know you, if you're okay with that, and if you get to a point where you'd like to make some changes in your life I can help you with that. I've done this successfully for a few other people in your situation. That's really why I stayed tonight, to be completely honest."

So that's how Mike became a regular in my life, just another character populating my path to the crash, and like most of them, he jetted out before I burned. I'm not mad about that at all, because Mike really did his best to help until he had to do what he had to do. At this point, who's to say? There's no stopping someone who doesn't want to stop, so what can anyone's best intentions even accomplish? Once I agreed to take him into my world in that capacity, though, Mike did try to keep me away from drugs and keep me away from everyone who might give drugs to me, but he had no idea just how many options I had available in that department.

But that was really phase two of our friendship. Right away he became essential to me because of his connections to private jets, helicopters, and small planes—basically whatever gangsters, drug dealers, or Elvis would use to get around. I hate airports and I hate flying, so flying private was great, plus as I became less and less on top of my game, Mike became more and more irreplaceable because nothing can salvage dysfunctional lateness quicker than a private charter. Within a few weeks of knowing Mike, every gig I'd booked along the Eastern Seaboard from Niagara Falls to Baltimore and points farther south became much more fun. I wasn't going to be terribly screened by the authorities, so I could even sneak pills and heroin on board with me, which was a great help in avoiding withdrawals and getting to work on time Monday.

We took helicopters to every casino within range and in typical rock-and-roll fashion, one night (in the wilds of Connecticut, which isn't at all rock-and-roll) we nearly lost our lives. When it all went bleak for a moment, I distinctly remember being aware of the fact that Connecticut is one of the places, if not *the* place, that I'd least like to die. There is nothing at all remarkable, cool, or legendary about

Connecticut. If Jim Morrison were buried there, no one would visit his grave.

I was scheduled to play Foxwoods Resort Casino in scenic Mashantucket, for four thousand people. It was a totally sold-out show for which I made ninety grand plus an extra twenty grand as a bonus for selling it out. I brought my regular road guys at the time: J.D., Timmy, and Mike to fly us up. Since Mike wasn't officially hired to keep me off drugs yet, I was flying high on heroin and had some more in my pocket. At that time snorting lines of dope was all I really cared about. I'm not saying I'd turn down a handful of pills if someone gave them to me, but I remember really loving heroin like nothing else at that time.

I'd done quite a few lines before we left and was looking forward to putting on the huge headphones and zoning out in the back of the helicopter, maybe catching a few winks of sleep, and then landing and going right to the stage. We planned to arrive between six and seven o'clock, which left me plenty of time to relax before the curtain came up at eight, and I was actually impressed that we'd left early enough to arrive in a timely fashion. Considering how inefficiently I did everything else in my life by then, this was remarkable. It gave me an irrational feeling of well-being, and a delusion that I really did have it all under control, when it came to my career at least. And maybe I did that night, but what we didn't count on, and what I wasn't prepared for, was that no one at Foxwoods was as on the ball as we were.

I've got nothing but great things to say about Foxwoods; it's a paradise up there in the middle of nothing at all, and that's no exaggeration. There's literally no civilization of any kind for miles around. It's on an Indian reservation, so when you arrive, however you get there, you go through a limbo of backwoods emptiness until the place appears ahead of you out of nowhere like the Emerald City in *The Wizard of Oz*. Foxwoods has the only bright lights you see in a county otherwise composed of shit. I find it fascinating because there it is, this gorgeous, top-notch entertainment facility smack in the middle of white trash–ville. The people who live there follow the Yellow Brick Road of Foreclosure to the Great Oz's Fun House. They gamble away the deeds to their trailers, and no one's wearing ruby slippers.

The place shines so brightly that you can probably see it from space, but as we approached it that night in February of 2009, the helipad and landing tower were black as night. I had no idea at first because I was sleeping (I mean nodding out), but apparently no one had gotten the memo that we were arriving by air. We circled for about twenty minutes while Mike tried to get someone on the radio and Teddy called people on his cell phone. If you've never been in a helicopter, let me tell you why everyone wears headsets as big and soundproof as the earmuffs they hand out at shooting ranges: helicopters are fucking loud! They're basically an engine with seats below it, so I imagine that those phone calls Teddy made sounded like a guy calling from the inside of a vacuum cleaner. At least he tried; he's not a bad kid, Teddy.

We kept circling, which started making me nauseous, and woke me up from my "nap." I go in circles enough in my mind that I don't enjoy doing it in real life, so I turned up the sound on my headset and used the microphone to ask Mike what was going on. I was actually really excited for this gig, enough that I'd brought a decent set of clothes to wear, which is something I never did at that point. I was proud of myself for taking that extra time, to think about my appearance, and to think ahead, so as a gesture, this outfit meant a lot to me. I sure as hell wanted to be sure I had enough time to change into it.

"What the fuck!" I shouted into the microphone attached to my headset. "Why aren't we on the ground yet?"

"No one's in the tower, Art; I have nowhere to land," Mike said. "We're waiting for them to turn the lights on or else we're going down in complete darkness."

"Really? I've got serious money on the line, Mike. I have to start on time."

As we kept circling I got progressively more pissed off; they kept calling and radioing and nothing happened. It seemed like an eternity passed before we were finally told that it would take half an hour to get the lights on—which would put me onstage over twenty-five minutes late.

"Oh, fuck that!" I yelled. "Mike, if we don't get our asses on the ground and get me to that fucking stage, I am losing money, which means none of you are getting paid. You've got to land us right now!"

Mike looked over his shoulder at me with a funny look in his eye. "Okay, man, I can do that. Just don't expect it to be smooth."

"Well, don't kill us either, dude," I said, "I have to be onstage on time, alive. Is this going to be some *Apocalypse Now* shit?"

"Yeah," he said, grinning maniacally. "Look at them breaks, soldier!"

He flew about a half mile from Foxwoods to a space where he thought he could put the whirlybird down. It was ballsy because he had no idea for sure what was down there, but he didn't hesitate. He brought us down slowly, looking out for power lines, until it was clear that we were above an empty field. There was a cabin nearby and nothing else, so there was plenty of room to land, so he went for it successfully. We got out of the copter in the dark, trying to figure out where to find the nearest road. Out of nowhere a huge flashlight went on and blinded us.

Then we heard the sound of two shotguns being chambered.

"Now, tell me something, boys," this grizzly voice said. "Who the fuck are you? You a bunch of terrorist motherfuckers?"

Beyond the light I could see three redneck biker types straight out of Central Casting: shaggy beards, cutoff jean jackets, overweight. They were a father and two sons, two of them holding shotguns, one holding the flashlight, all of them with open cans of Bud in their free hands. Clearly they thought the race war started by Barack Obama had arrived in their backyard, just as their dear old pappy had predicted.

"Guys, it's okay," I said, with my hands up. "Relax . . . I'm a comedian."

I was hoping they'd recognize me. None of them did.

Even now I don't think any amount of heroin I could have done earlier that night can justify a statement as retarded as *It's okay, I'm a comedian*. They should have shot me on sight, and if we ever cross paths again I will understand if they decide to. But as these things often do in a way no one can plan, my idiotic off-the-cuff statement broke the ice.

It took me a few minutes to convince them that I wasn't lying, that I really was a comedian and that I had to be onstage at Foxwoods in fifteen minutes. After a round of pointed cross-examination ("You ever been on TV?" "Why we ain't never heard of you?" "You ever met Dane Cook?") they eventually believed me. When I told them that if they drove me to the casino they'd be my guests at the show, which included all the Bud they could drink, we became fast friends. I've got to admit, I'm not the best negotiator—I probably could have gotten myself a ride for two cases of Bud and nothing more if I pushed it. Then again, if I were Jeff Foxworthy, no bargaining would have been necessary at all. If I were Jeff Foxworthy I could have walked out of the helicopter and just said, *Hey, guys, you might just be a redneck if you land a copter in someone's backyard in the dark!* and they would have taken me right to the venue and named their next out-of-wedlock firstborn after me. Looking back I can say one thing without a doubt: I was high enough that I assumed entertainers on their way to Foxwoods landed in their backyard all the time, so I didn't understand how they weren't used to this. And that is the most liberal, douche bag, Hollywood assumption I've ever made about anything in my entire life.

"So this probably happens a lot, right? You guys should start charging for helicopter parking."

There was a long pause. "This ain't never happened before," one of them said. "You're the first set of numb-nut dumb-fucks to ever set a copter down here. You're lucky we like you. If we didn't, we'd have filled you full of buckshot for trespassing already."

They loaded all of us into a pickup truck and drove us down a dark dirt road to Foxwoods, where I got onstage with about two minutes to spare. I saw the promoter afterward, who was having such a great time by that point that I'm not even sure he knew how close a call the entire night was. He thought it was hilarious that we'd circled the tower and had to land in a field, as if it were an orchestrated entrance, or some bonus joke I'd worked out for the night. That guy had to be stoned out of his mind.

I would have made more of a stink about the helipad being out of commission, but how could I be mad after he handed me a check for $90K plus another for $20K as a bonus? Money makes all things okay because it's the great equalizer; that shade of green is everyone's favorite color. So after I got paid, everything that went wrong up to that point transformed into a joke. And the night wasn't over: I had heroin left to do, which was a good thing since I had a book signing that took three hours, during which I drank all the Jack Daniel's I could handle. Finally, at three a.m. I was done and we got a ride back to the *Deliverance* brothers' backyard, where Mike was waiting to fly us home.

Before we took off I gave those hicks five hundred bucks for driving us to the gig and letting us use their yard, and for the first time in my life I had someone refuse to take a tip. I'm not kidding; these guys were living in a log cabin but somehow they were insulted by me offering them that kind of money. They probably thought the cash was fake. I'm serious, they looked at it and at me like I was an alien holding space coins in my three-fingered hand. It was awkward; they just stared at it for a minute then huddled up and talked about it before saying no. I'm not sure they'd ever seen that much cash in one place before. They didn't trust it, like I was offering them exploding gum. I guess they figured that all comedians aside from Dane Cook and Jeff Foxworthy are clowns, so our money must be as useless and fake as balloon animals.

— — — —

That's how it began, and soon after that, Mike started doing security for me too.

What Mike could provide symbolized freedom to me, but Mike the guy was someone else. He knew what was going on with me and was disgusted by it, and since he's a smart dude who has seen a lot, he didn't come at me right away about this. He silently observed me for a while and he kept his opinions to himself and minded his own business. But after we'd been on the road together a good few months, one night in Niagara Falls, after we'd flown up to the gig in one of his planes, he took me aside.

"Artie, why don't we have dinner together tonight?" he said.

I did my usual thing: "Nah, man, that sounds great, but I'm gonna crash; it's been a long week. I gotta rest up for Monday."

Mike didn't flinch, and he didn't let it go. "Do me a favor, Art, just eat with me. We can do it in your room. Just real quick, then you can go to sleep."

We went up to this big suite that the promoter had given me and we ordered a couple of cheeseburgers, and after a while Mike said what he wanted to say.

"Look, Art, I know what's going on with you," he said. "I know you're doing drugs and I know the type of drugs you're doing. And I know you're battling them. I know this not because I've done it but because I have friends who have. I also have friends I've helped get off it."

Mike mentioned a well-known rock-and-roll guy whom I am a very big fan of (whose name I can't mention, sorry), and he told me that he was able to successfully get that guy clean.

"That's great, man," I said.

"Yeah," he said. "But you have to be ready."

"Yeah."

"And I don't think you are right now," he said. "But if you are ever ready—I mean really ready—let me know. I'm not pressuring you, I'm not judging you, just if you're ever ready, let me know, because I can do it. I can get you better."

"I appreciate that, man," I said. And I meant it.

I liked Mike for being straightforward about it, and I liked him for being both all-business and very understanding about what I was dealing with. I could tell he hated it and I could tell he wanted to shake me out of it. I could also tell that should I call on him, he'd be there for me. I knew he'd give it his all and he'd be compassionate and that he'd never be a pushover. That was something that I knew was nonnegotiable when it came to me; whoever got me clean had to be firm and incapable of being swayed by me. I appreciated Mike for telling me very clearly that I had to be ready and for insinuating just how "ready" that meant. He understood that I wasn't, because he probably knew better than I did at the time that I had a lot more fucking up to do.

Even though I didn't let Mike take control of getting me clean for quite a while, that didn't stop me from telling friends and family who knew I was starting to lose it that he was helping me out with the drugs. The guy has the kind of aura about him that people just trust, so he served this purpose perfectly. I also began to hide my drug use from him, choosing to play this cat-and-mouse game, pretty much hoping that I'd fool him along with everyone else in my life. I wasn't fooling him at all, of course, because Mike knew something that everyone should commit to memory: there is no way in hell that anything or anyone can keep an addict from what they want. The relationship between addict and addiction is impossible to penetrate, whether their poison is booze, gambling, crack, sex, opiates, chewing gum, or collecting fucking teddy bears. A true addict will be faithful to their addiction above all; it's the only thing they'll never cheat on or lie to. And nothing will ever change that relationship unless the addict, and only the addict, decides to change things and break up with their main squeeze—addiction. There is no magic pill and there is no easy solution, and that's just the way it is. This unassailable truth is based on a premise that is so simple that you'll thank me for sharing it with you if you don't already live your life by it: you can't change anyone, so don't bother trying. I don't care if you don't believe me on this point, because I know for a fact that someday you'll have to admit I'm right. If I were you I'd do it now. Humans are all the same and people are going to do what they want—addicts especially—until they, and only they, decide that they don't want to do what they're doing every day anymore. Whether you're an addict or just someone who knows one, trust me, you'll all be a lot happier once you stop trying to believe anything but what I just told you.

By this point in my life, the cycle that ended up dragging me under in the spring of 2009 had begun, fueled by my addiction to opiates and aided by my inability to say no to any professional opportunity. I literally said yes to every meeting, gig, or business-related introduction that came my way. Which was ridiculous because I could barely get through the week. It just goes to show how much drugs can make you think you're doing great when you're really limping along looking like week-old trash. Most of the business obligations I signed up for weren't even necessary! Some were a complete waste of time and only a handful were golden opportunities, and all of those, for the most part, I fucked up. The following is the story of the one I fucked up most royally. And boy, did I.

The guy at the center of this story must remain unnamed; he's the head of a very high-end, multibillion-dollar hedge fund. My friend's wife was his executive assistant, and when she heard that I was looking for investors to put some capital into developing my website, she arranged a meeting for me with her boss. The moneyman was a fan of mine, both of my stand-up and my presence on the *Stern Show*, so potentially, our partnership was a natural fit. We met in his office, which had the most beautiful view of Central Park I'd ever seen, and we talked about what I wanted to accomplish with the website and with my career beyond Stern, and we got along well enough that we made tentative plans to do some business together. We also agreed that this guy and his wife, plus my friend and his wife, would come see me do stand-up in Detroit in two weeks, and we'd all fly out together on the company jet. We were all chummy, agreeing to stay a few extra days in order to hit the town properly, which would include a run through Windsor, Ontario. For those who don't know, just across the water from Detroit, in Canada, sits Windsor, a paradise of strip clubs and brothels full of beautiful women. I couldn't wait.

It wasn't meant to be, because this business love affair lasted as long as it took me to do the one thing no one should ever do on a tour bus or a private jet—take a horribly toxic shit. Trust me, let your intestines fall into your underwear, stick a softball up your ass, do anything, but find a way to hold it in if you ever find yourself on a rich guy's private jet. Because there's no way to hide it—even the smell of a miniscule rabbit pellet will be detected.

I'd had the Detroit gig booked for a while and I was excited for it, because Detroit is an honest town that likes to laugh, likes to party, and will not be fucked with. Going there with Detroit natives, arriving in high style, was just so cool to me—it was like being flown in by helicopter to see the Stones back in '78, which is something I think about often and wish those thoughts could take me there.

So for the sake of telling this story anonymously, let's call the main guy "Hedge Fund Guy" and his wife "Mrs. Impossibly Beautiful Hedge Fund Spoils" because the woman was completely stunning, a half-Asian ten, dressed to the nines. Keep in mind we were taking a jet to a comedy club in Detroit; not exactly an occasion to don your Oscars-worthy finery. But she was all decked out just to see me, of all people, do stand-up. This woman possessed the kind of beauty that demanded respect, because not only was she blessed with genes that few people have, but she was putting in the work and doing the upkeep. It's not easy being hot (just ask me); those women have to do a lot of work to maintain it.

The other people on this jet were equally well dressed, well educated, and sophisticated. It looked like they were all going to dinner at Dorsia with Patrick Bateman, not into Detroit with Artie Lange. I was pretty self-conscious in my sweatpants, green corduroy jacket, disheveled hair, and gruff demeanor (can you blame me?), so I did the only thing that made sense to a derelict like me who found himself in company like that: I snorted a lot of heroin.

For those of you who haven't done heroin and don't know much about opiate addiction or abusing other drugs, first of all don't do it. Don't do opiates at all. Stay away.

There is no worse curse I could wish upon my enemy than opiate addiction. It's an albatross that you can never truly remove from around your neck. At best you make it invisible and keep it at bay before it drags you into the depths. Now that I've gotten that off my chest (ha ha! get it?), let me tell you what happens when you're a true opiate/heroin addict and you get a generous amount of that stuff in your system: you need to take a shit immediately. I'm not talking about some workaday crap that you can pull off on the side of the highway rest stop. A full toilet and some privacy are required.

That's the brand of shit I laid down on that plane, in the very nicely decorated cubbyhole of a toilet at the front of the cabin. It was a completely horrible, inhuman crap—literally the most disgusting, foul, odorous shit a human being has ever dealt. How do I know this? I dealt it, I smelt it, and everyone else on the plane did too.

I should have seen it coming; since we were flying private I'd brought a large bag of heroin with me, which I hadn't planned to dip into until after the show, but these people were all so perfect that I needed to be numb just to be in their presence. I started hitting it hard the second we got on board, and of course I couldn't stop, so I kept returning to the bathroom every few minutes after the seat belt sign went off.

"Artie, are you okay?" one of their beautiful wives asked me after my third trip to the head

"Oh, yeah, yeah. I'm great, couldn't be better."

I didn't want to shit on the plane, believe me, and since it wasn't that long of a flight I figured I could hold it, but I was wrong again. After a while, my ass was going to let go wherever I was sitting, so I figured I should at least do the right thing and put it in a toilet. As a longtime abuser I've had the misfortune of polluting many toilets with toxic human waste, but I have to say that this particular instance took the cake. It really was that bad, just one of the worst heroin shits I've ever shat. For all the things I don't remember doing in blackouts, this is something I wish I could forget. If I think about it too long the stench will come back to me and I'll gag.

It takes a little over two hours to fly to Detroit and my bowels gave out about forty-five minutes into the flight. We had been making small talk the whole time, all while I kept getting up to do more drugs, then returning, trying my best to keep everyone laughing. I wanted to be as charming as I could be to make up for the obvious fact that I was trash and they were treasure. I wanted to show these lovely people that I am smarter and more well read than a Google search of my name might suggest. I didn't go to college (because college is for losers) and I barely graduated high school, but let me tell you something, for most careers, none of that shit matters in the real world. If you read a lot, stay up on current events, have a curious mind, and aren't lazy when it comes to learning about what's important to you, you don't need a degree. I've met plenty of Ivy League morons I'd run circles around if life were the Olympics.

I have no idea what they thought of me before then, I just know what they'll remember me for: the hurricane of shit that came from my ass. After too many lines I knew I had no choice, so I went into that little closet and let loose the mythical Kraken from my crack. The plane was so small and sleek and efficient that everyone else heard all about it because the can was no more than five feet away from them. They were enjoying a quiet night and civilized cocktail-party chatter, which made it all worse, because this shit was not going quietly into the night: once my pants were down, I let it go, and my ass sounded like it was killing Sonny on the Long Island Causeway in *The Godfather*.

There is a very specific type of heroin- or cocaine-induced shit fueled by the copious ingestion of those drugs which causes your body to empty itself so suddenly that you feel like you're sitting above a thunderstorm. You're not really even part of it, it's that much bigger than you are. The worst part about it is that, like lightning, it can't be controlled, plus the thunder is really loud. It also leaves evidence of its destruction behind, and when you're a heavy guy, that becomes an issue because it's not exactly easy to wipe your ass properly. Imagine how much harder that is when you're high and in a Barbie-sized bathroom. And, just beyond the folding door a plane full of beautiful, rich people are listening to you.

I was fucked: I'd put on a show I had no intention of starring in and I couldn't even clean myself up because I could barely move. On top of that I had to go back out there and make small talk with people who couldn't be nicer or more intimidating to me. Did I mention that everyone was hungry when we took off? All they could talk about as we taxied down the runway was how great the catering was on the jet and how they couldn't wait to dig into the sushi and seafood they'd arranged for. I felt bad that they were about to sample that sushi with a coating of my shit stench on it.

Since I'm coming clean here (ha ha!—get it?) I'd like to admit that I also completely shit my pants on that plane, which I'm even less happy to admit is something I'm no stranger to doing. I don't remember the first time it happened, but I know for a fact that during that phase of my life it became a regular thing. It began to happen so much that I made a game of it by stashing my shitty underwear in the corner of the balcony of whatever hotel I happened to sleep in that night. This was a one-sided game, because the maids who were my opponents had no idea that we were playing, and by the time they did, I'd already won. It was an Easter Egg hunt where the eggs were all brown and only one kid was looking. Here's how I would play it out: if I shit my pants completely, I'd find the most tucked-away corner of the room and stuff them in there in such a way that the horror of what they held wasn't visible from a distance—only picking them up would reveal the "goods." To balance this cruel joke that I completely enjoyed, I'd leave a $20 bill on the dresser. That was my sarcastic thank-you. In my mind here's how it played out: the maid would come into the room and think I was a great guy for leaving such a huge tip. Then they'd find my pile of shit in those underpants on the balcony and realize that $20 wasn't even close to covering what they deserved.

Believe it or not, if there's one thing I would change about that flight to Detroit it wouldn't be the shitting, my unclean ass, my stinking underpants, or my inability to go fifteen minutes in their presence without doing heroin. The only thing I'd do differently would be somehow keeping the jet's caterer from serving an amazing meal. That was the coup de ass if you will, because the moment I came out of the bathroom and met everyone's disgusted stare, exactly then the staff began to roll out these gorgeous plates of sushi. Can you think of anything less appetizing to eat with the scent of fresh shit hanging in the air? So let me remind you once more of the cardinal rule in show business: never shit on a private jet (or a tour bus). If you do, everyone will know, because the smell flows right through the ventilation system and there's no getting away from it.

As I mentioned, another thing you can't get away from when you're fat is the inability to wipe your ass well, especially in cramped quarters (such as airplane bathrooms). That's the kind of hygiene situation I was working with when I returned to my seat next to Hedge Fund Guy, which made matters infinitely worse. The smell never dissipated because it was right there around me like the worst kind of halo. I can't explain how awkwardly silent the remainder of that flight was. The food remained untouched, mocking me as my fellow passengers tried not to talk because that meant they'd need to breathe. I was responsible and everyone knew it. There was nothing I could do to redeem this. I was also high as hell, so at the same time I didn't care because all I wanted to do was nod off. In the moments where I realized just how disgusting a human I was I toyed with the idea of breaking the ice and saving the situation by just coming out with a joke that addressed the deathly stink and made fun of my crap. This horrid, rank odor was literally a four-hundred-pound gorilla in the plane.

I ended up nodding off, and to make matters worse, about twenty minutes before we landed I woke up hungry and forgot all about what I'd done long enough to eat one or two of the shrimp cocktails, some cold cuts, and a lot of sushi as they looked on, truly horrified. I pretty much used my hands too. I didn't know what their problem was: I saw food in front of me and I ate it.

It goes without saying that Hedge Fund Guy was a fan of Artie Lange, but he, his wife, and their friends/my friends really weren't into Partie Lange. That guy sucked as far as they were concerned. Partie Lange lost Artie Lange his potential investor: they all came to the gig, but we didn't hang out afterward and I never heard from Hedge Fund Guy again. All those plans to go to Windsor were forgotten quicker than Brendan Fraser's last movie.

After the gig they came backstage, however, to say their hellos (which were really good-byes), and that is when I knew it was over. To this day it's a sore subject with my friends, so we've all nonverbally agreed to never discuss it again and we've adhered to that every time we see each other. For the record here's how that last conversation with Hedge Fund Guy went backstage.

"Great show, Artie; we really enjoyed it," he said.

"Oh, good, I'm glad," I said. "Your seats were okay?"

"They were fine," he said. "Listen, we're not going to Windsor, Artie."

"Oh, cool, okay," I said.

"We are going to dinner, though, if you'd like to join us, but I don't think you'd like the restaurant," he said, his message crystal clear.

The guy was a major player, and he was a huge fan. He ran a multibillion-dollar fund and he really wanted to invest in my career; he saw profit in my website at a time when every comedian was looking to evolve in that area. The purpose of the trip was for us to talk about it and get our plans beyond the ideas phase. I knew this and I wanted this; in fact I went out there with the goal of landing his support, because he had the means to make it happen. But I was so fucked up and so screwed up and it went so bad that all I did was make sure he'd never talk to me again. I've got the benefit of hindsight going for me now, and what I see in the rearview when I think about this story is a symbol of just how fucked up I was. This was a major opportunity for me—and a rare one—and I let it go right through my fingers. I was so embarrassed about it that I just didn't care to even try to rescue it. I let the pieces fall where they might and just looked down at them as if I had no choice and played no part in the matter.

That flight was the end of the relationship. I did my set and didn't even try to go with them to eat after the gig. They invited me—I still can't believe they were that polite—and that's clearly where we were going to talk business. But I didn't care anymore, so I didn't go. I was too fucked up to do anything but make an excuse and let something else of value drift away.

"Thanks for the invite, but I'm gonna go crash in my room."

That was about all I was capable of. That trip was a microcosm of my life because my life had become a series of excuses that allowed me to "crash in my room." What I didn't realize is that everything I was trying so hard to keep under wraps in those rooms was on the verge of escaping, ready to blow the doors off and come out into the light for all the world to see.

CHAPTER 5

EYE OF THE STORM

I continued to zigzag from gig to gig with Helicopter Mike in the spring of 2009, and he continued to remind me that if I was man enough, he would be able to get me off the shit that was becoming less fun and heavier than an anvil on my back every single fucking day. I never doubted Mike's intentions either, not because I thought he was charming, but because I knew from other people who knew him that I wouldn't be the guy's first rodeo: he'd helped a number of notable rock musicians get off heroin. That was all great, except that I was just too much trouble. I told him I wanted to rid myself of the drugs but I didn't want to have to take time off from my career to do it. He actually agreed to work with that and said we could accomplish it together as long as I was serious about tackling my problems when the time was right. When I was ready, he said, he was up to it—but I'd better mean it and not fuck around.

When I was finally ready, I told him so and he told me that he'd need a partner to have his back: Joe the Cop. I hired them both and they planned out exactly when, how, and where they would see me through detox. Joe is a really good guy, just a typical Irish cop from Queens, a real salt-of-the-earth type guy who reminded me of every friend I grew up with. Of course, that meant nothing to me when

I was retching and reeling from opiate withdrawal. At that point he was just a stick figure that wouldn't get me drugs.

The first thing those guys did was bring two drug-sniffing dogs over to my house in Hoboken and down the shore in Red Bank and those mutts literally found anything that had ever had drugs even next to it. I was actually in awe of them, which numbed me to the fact that every single stash I had was being discovered and trashed before my eyes. I mean, seriously, these two dogs were finding rolled-up bills in bathrobes that I hadn't worn in months, sniffing out the stench of crusted heroin that at that moment I wanted to snatch out of their mouths just for being so fucking good at their jobs. These fucking canines found my old stash spot in my Hoboken apartment, and even though it was empty and had been for a few weeks, they freaked out as if it were Scarface's desk. That was the moment I truly realized that I'd been found out and that this latest round of bullshit was over. That was when I knew that I had to try; I had to put myself in the hands of these guys at least. I had to sweat this shit out and see if there was anything left of me.

This had been a long time coming.

— — — —

I'd spent the previous half year hiding all of this the best I could, by hiring people, firing people, just padding my life from any kind of true vision. I rehired my old assistant Melissa (who is a very sweet, very hot former Dallas Cowboys cheerleader) because she was the only assistant who could deal with me without losing her mind. By early spring, she was my seventh PA in twelve months—lucky number seven. Here is how randomly I determined who should be working for and with me. Tim Sullivan, whom I'd met backstage at a Springsteen concert because he was connected to that camp, became my new road manager, starting with a fund-raiser I did at Caroline's, just because I wanted him to. I paid Tim ten grand for taking care of those gigs, not because it was actually very much work at all, but just because I wanted him to be on board "Team Artie." I even made Teddy get Tim up to speed at a gig in Boca Raton before I officially fired Teddy. I really didn't care much about etiquette, and my business management was beyond remedial.

I hadn't forgotten the plan that Howard's manager Don had laid out for me—less road time and fewer gigs for more money—that I'd agreed to start in the new year (meaning the year we were in, that was now nearly half gone). I did want to do that, but like everything else that was good for me I kept putting it off because I was overtaken with greed and drug lust. I decided I needed to put that plan on hold until the start of 2010, because I convinced myself that before I could change anything in my professional life and risk a potential decrease in my income I had to bank as much money as possible. I had two mortgages, I had spent a lot on my shore house, and I was spending even more on drugs and gambling. The deeper I got into my booze and drug problem the more I enjoyed gambling—on football, basketball, baseball, boxing, you name it. I also started playing blackjack a little too enthusiastically at every single casino that booked me—and there were a lot of them. The more I partied the more I lost and the less I cared.

Let me give you an example. During Super Bowl weekend in 2008, I played the Mandalay Bay in Vegas and was paid $110,000. I went on a real nice tear and had a great time. Between the booze, the drugs, the strippers/hookers, and all of the gambling I did, I netted $10,000. Actually, after paying my booker his commission on the $110,000, I lost money. Keep in mind my room was paid for, so in two days I spent $100,000 on "fun" and bad decisions.

I kept on like this, thinking everything was peachy, even when Dr. Drew called into the *Stern Show* and asked to have me on the next season of *Celebrity Rehab*. The producers of the show offered me $200,000 to do three weeks on the show and Howard said he'd be happy to give me the time off because he thought it was a great idea.

"Fuck that," I said on the air. "I'm not going to some fucking tele-vised bullshit rehab run by a quack."

Dr. Drew was very civil about it and pointed out the obvious: "If a person wants drugs they're going to get drugs. I don't think my program will work for Artie right now because I can tell from his at-titude that he doesn't want it. If we try to push him it won't work, but I can tell you this, Artie, if you don't get into a rehab program soon and make some changes, things are going to end badly for you."

That pissed me off so much that I went on a tirade about Dr. Drew, with him right there on the phone.

"How can you even call yourself a doctor?" I said. "You're a show biz whore. I mean nothing to you; I'm an opportunity. You're all about show business not about helping people. You are only talking to me because you're a *show biz whore.*"

I was completely wrong of course. As I found out later, Dr. Drew is the furthest thing from that; he genuinely cares and he is a real counselor whose motives are true. He's not in it for fame, he's in it to help—fame has come his way because he's really good at his job. I'd never learn this firsthand because I eliminated that possibility with my behavior on the air that day. Drew finished off the interview with Howard, but it was obvious that he'd put my file in his trash bin, if you catch my drift. Not too long afterward I learned that my suspi-cions were correct when Lisa G from Howard 100 News brought us a quote about me that Dr. Drew had given in an interview not too long afterward. Basically he said that he'd wanted to help me because it was clear that I desperately needed it, but that my feelings toward him were too strong and too aggressive for anything in his program to work for me. He said my attitude toward him was too vicious for us to ever make progress whether we were under the microscope of *Celebrity Rehab* or not. This of course sent me into an even more heated round of badmouthing, first Lisa G then Dr. Drew, until How-ard just cut me off outright.

And that's when I told Mike I was ready—as usual a little too late, but ready nonetheless. Better ready late than never ready, right? The plan was to lock me in down at my shore house during our next hiatus from the *Stern Show*, which was in April of that year. These two weren't kidding: Mike wanted to get me off all opiates, and wasn't hearing me when he realized that Subutex—the opiate inhibitor/replacement I'd been abusing—was as much a part of my diet as any of the obvious other drugs. I realized how serious he and Joe were about this when they handcuffed me to my bed in my bedroom down the shore.

"Yeah, I get it, dude, you don't need to remind me that you were once both cops," I said, my attitude still intact.

"Oh, we know you know that, Art," Mike said. "I'm doing this because you lied to me about the Subutex. We are not allowing that to be some kind of bridge for you. We're doing it all; we are getting you off everything. It's time."

"Hey, Mike," I said.

"Yeah?"

"Fuck you."

The next four days were the ninth circle of hell. It rained nonstop, or at least it was raining every time I was conscious enough to focus my eyes beyond the window past my bed. It was raining like hell, gray everywhere, and I wanted to fucking die. No, I wanted to kill Mike and Joe, because they were to blame for this in my mind's limited focus. Wave after wave of nausea, sweats, and crawling itch washed over me as whatever I cried out for went unanswered. After four days, my body had been so wracked with cramps and spasms that they took me out to get a massage, just to ease my sore muscles. I've never felt such relief at any other point in my life.

They brought me right back and threw me into my room again.

I got through the physical addiction just as my vacation from *Stern* ended—literally. It was hell, but Mike and Joe saw me through. They told me later that at the worst of my pains I promised them money, whores, whatever they wanted if they'd just get me some dope. The amount of dollars I was talking about was insane, but they knew I had it, so I need to thank them again for taking the high road. Or, as it were, the nonhigh road.

Each time I begged them to get me or let me get drugs I threw a bigger number at them, but they didn't bite. The best image I can give you of what I felt like is Linda Blair tied to that bed in *The Exorcist*. If you're bad enough into opiates the physical addiction becomes so deep that your muscles don't function right without the drugs in your bloodstream. That's where I was: in withdrawal I started spasming uncontrollably, my body jerking itself in so many opposite directions that I pulled muscles in my neck, my legs, and my back. I could not get comfortable in any way. I was hot and cold at the same time: I'd sweat in the shower and be freezing to death under a down comforter. I'm not kidding at all when I tell you that I would have punched my best friend in the face as hard as I could to get drugs and make it stop.

By day three I could see the light at the end of the tunnel and by day four I felt somewhat human. It took a full seven days, because of the extra opiates I'd been sneaking, for the predicted four-day Subutex withdrawal to be over, but once it was I was clean of everything for the first time in four years. That was really something to be proud of for me and it definitely had an effect on my mood. The color returned to my face and the confidence I got from beating my demons inspired me to start exercising a bit. I promised myself, honestly this time, that I'd stick with a nonopiate lifestyle as long as I could—and I did.

I went back to the *Stern Show* clean, and I kept that up for quite a while.

Before I knew it I'd dropped forty pounds in just over a month and a half, because I'd gotten so heavy that it came right off. I started a no-carb diet, I started walking and jogging every day, just moving around for once, and I took long intense steam saunas to help clean out my system and drop more weight. Seeing those results made me incredibly happy. I felt in my heart that I'd turned a corner, and every time someone I knew told me that I "looked more alive," I felt great. Believe me, that's far from a compliment because the implication is that the last time they'd seen me I'd looked like the walking dead.

Around that time I was approached by some reality show producers who wanted to do a show on me, so I let them follow me around for a while. I ultimately turned it down on the advice of my manager, Dave Becky, because it was clear that these guys wanted a train wreck: the show's working title was *Saving Artie*, and if that isn't a recipe for relapse I don't know what is. It was hard for me to say no because it's hard for me to say no to anything because deep down I still think that all that I've achieved could disappear at any moment. I fought that instinct and said no to this and I'm glad I did, but it just goes to show you that show business is all about timing. If these guys had shown up six months earlier we'd have had a show in the can in three weeks without even trying.

Before I knew it I'd been clean a month, which was so unfamiliar to me after so many years of abuse that I felt like I'd climbed a mountain without even breaking a sweat. For once I didn't feel like a loser, a pussy, or worse, a quitter, for being sober. I actually liked it and thought it was cool. I joined a gym in Hoboken and I started going every day to do what I could. I'm not going to kid you into thinking I jumped right into Tae Bo or the Insanity workout, because I was in such bad shape that moving around regularly at all was a lot for me. But it was progress, which was a new and very welcome concept in my life. For once I didn't start making fun of something positive in my life.

My gym was right next to a tanning salon and one day as I was walking by I saw, literally, the most stunningly beautiful girl I'd ever seen working at the counter. She was so gorgeous that I stopped in my tracks and did a completely obvious double take. I didn't care if she saw it, I had to stare at her to make sure she was real, so for a few minutes I stood there silently outside the window, creepier than a pedophile at a school-yard fence during recess. I wanted to talk to her but I didn't know how I could pull it off. This may come as a surprise, but I didn't really know my way around a tanning salon, so I had to think of something because this girl was beautiful enough to make a guy like me enter one of those places blind.

I realized as I went through the door that I had no idea what kind of bullshit things anyone could even ask about tanning, just to start some kind of conversation. She was alone at the counter, so I had that going for me, and just before she noticed me coming, I saw, off to the side, an old-fashioned shaving chair.

"Hey, do you do shaves here?" I asked her. "I'm going to my buddy's wedding next week and I'd like to get cleaned up." Thank God I didn't have to ask for a tan.

"I'm not sure," she said. "Can I get back to you? I'm just filling in for someone, and the manager isn't here right now."

"Okay," I said. I wasn't even listening because I was too busy staring at her the way a starving man would look at a filet mignon through a restaurant window. "Yeah, that's fine. If I give you my number, will you give me a call when you find out?" This was already a step in the right direction.

"Sure."

I then made the lamest joke ever. I asked her what nationality she was.

"I'm Russian," she said.

"You're rushin'?" I said. "What's your hurry?"

And she laughed. *Oh boy*, I thought, *I can't believe this*. I was in great shape with this girl, because if she'd laugh at a joke like that it was a really good sign that the rest of my material was gonna kill.

I hung around a little while longer making small talk and cracked her up a few more times until I felt confident enough about how we were relating to ask her if she'd like to go to a Yankee game some time. It turned out she was from Cherry Hill, which is in South Jersey down by Philly, but thankfully she wasn't a Phillies fan. That would have been a deal breaker, but instead it earned her points because it was clear to me that this girl had good taste, since she was from down there but knew enough to be a Yankees fan. I was becoming more smitten by the minute. "Let's go to a game, but how about we do something before that one night?" I asked.

"Yeah, that would be great," she said, smiling.

I couldn't believe my luck, this was amazing! She was twenty-five, her name was Adrienne, and that is officially how she entered my life. She met me in the best shape mentally and physically that I'd been in a long time, and after I got to know her I warned her about how I usually was and what I'd just come through. I'd referred to myself as Hurricane Artie for a while by then because there's no better metaphor: when I was in full-tilt dysfunction I was a storm that destroyed everything in its path with an "eye" that made people think everything was okay just before the most destructive wind and rain hit them.

"Things are calm now," I told her, "but hanging out with me you're entering a hurricane, which could be bad, but I swear, I hope things will be only good now. For the first time I really want to try."

She took it in stride; she was sweet and young and beautiful and a breath of fresh air in my life. And lucky for me she was willing to take a chance on me. After the first time we met I saw her the very next day when I realized that Norm MacDonald was doing a guest spot on the season finale of *Saturday Night Live*. What better way to impress a girl than to take her to the *SNL* finale after-party?

SNL flew Norm in to do his impression of Burt Reynolds for a celebrity *Jeopardy!* sketch that included Will Ferrell as host Alex Trebek and Darrell Hammond as Sean Connery—an impression that seemed to get better every time he did it. Will Ferrell was hosting the show that night, and he and I had been friends for years—we'd been in *Old School* and *Elf* together. We enjoyed each other's company and always cracked each other up, so this was going to be a great night, not to mention a great season finale. The same night my good friend Colin Quinn was doing the last performance of his brilliant one-man Broadway show *Long Story Short*, in which he discussed the economy, the fall of our society, and the history of the world, all in just over an hour. Colin's show was as genius as his shows always are, and I was so envious of him being able to bring such intelligence, current events, and informed opinions to what was at its core a great piece of stand-up comedy that I had to see his swan song. I also wanted to see him personally and let him know that I was doing all right because he'd always been such a steadfast source of support for me when it came to beating drugs. Backstage at his show I ran into Mandy Stadtmiller from the *New York Post* and we chatted awhile, which resulted in her running an item in Page Six the next day saying that I was fifty pounds lighter, had a tan, and looked like a human being for the first time in a while. I have to say, that made me feel pretty good! I made sure to show Adrienne that piece of news because I needed all the proof I could get to make her believe I was worth her time.

After Colin's show, which was in a Midtown theater, I walked over to *SNL* at 30 Rock and hung out with Norm in his dressing room. While we were there I met Bobby Moynihan, the heavy kid who joined the show in 2008 and looks eerily like a younger me. I also saw the great comedy writer Jim Downey, who is a friend I hadn't seen in years, and Norm and his assistant Lori Jo, and I just had a blast. It felt great to be out there on the town, sober and enjoying myself, because I'd had no idea I was even capable of that, but I was. I couldn't remember the last time I'd been out among my peers just having fun, totally sober. It had probably never happened. I have to say it was a great help that the whole time Norm was wearing the crazy Burt Reynolds wig and mustache because I was so transfixed by it that I didn't think about anything else. First off if you haven't seen it, YouTube Norm playing Burt Reynolds on *SNL*—his impression is uncanny and hilarious. He's naturally got that same twinkle in his eye that Burt has, so when he puts on that getup he looks so much like Burt, down to the fake hair, that it gets surreal after a while.

I called Adrienne from the dressing room, again, trying to impress her. "Hey, I'm up at *Saturday Night Live* and my friend is on the show tonight—a couple of them actually—and it's the season finale, so there's an after-party downstairs in Rockefeller Center. Do you think you'd like to come?"

"Yeah, that'll be great!" she said.

So that was our first official date—the *SNL* finale after-party, which was in a bar/restaurant on the first floor of Rock Center. It was half-inside, half-outside, and since it was lightly raining, the whole scene was very romantic, with people kind of huddling under the canopies, and all the lights of the buildings twinkling through the mist. I sent a town car to pick her up and bring her there, but I had one small problem: I didn't have a cell phone, so she couldn't call me when she arrived.

"You don't . . . have a cell phone?" she asked, confused and a little concerned. For a twenty-five-year-old, someone who didn't have a cell phone was like someone who didn't have a head. Instantly I was a weirdo.

"Yeah, I'll explain it to you later," I said. The truth was that now that I'd gotten clean and sober, Helicopter Mike, Joe the Cop, and my family insisted that I not have a phone for a while for obvious reasons. I'd hoped to avoid laying all my cards on the table with this girl right away, but it looked like I'd have to. At least not before I impressed her with *SNL*.

I needed to give her a number, so I borrowed my fellow comedian Craig Gass's cell phone to call her, and when I asked him for it, he looked at me with the disdain of a twenty-five-year-old. I told Adrienne I'd wait outside of Radio City until she got there, and that's what I did. Half an hour later I was standing there in that light rain when the town car pulled up and she got out, looking even more beautiful than I imagined she would. I think about that moment every single time I pass by Radio City, which was every weekday for the most of the first year of my radio show, since our first studio was just a block south of there.

Adrienne got to meet Will Ferrell and a few other people she thought were funny on that night and we did the rounds and had a great time. She drank, but I didn't because that was going to tempt me back to the dark side, and she was totally cool with that. We found Craig Gass and I returned his phone, and he took one look at Adrienne and understood why I'd been so intent about borrowing it. I had a weird interaction with actor Paul Rudd, which foreshadowed a much weirder one that would happen a month later on *Joe Buck Live*. During the *SNL* broadcast I'd told Craig Gass that I thought Rudd sucked and wasn't funny, so as he and I and Adrienne walked by Rudd, Gass said loud enough for everyone within ten feet to hear: "Hey, Artie, there's the guy you said sucked!" That's Gass for ya, but Paul is such a classy guy that he shook my hand, smiled, said hello, and took it in stride.

It was a great first date and we had so much fun that afterward we went back to my apartment and stayed up until seven a.m. just talking, barely even kissing, just getting to know each other. It was very sweet and once the sun came up I drove her home. When I got back to my place and got in bed all I could think about was when I would see Adrienne again. I felt like something really cool was starting, and for once I felt like I might be capable of having something that cool and that real in my life. At that moment, everything seemed possible.

━━ ━━ ━━

I'm not sure I ever got used to having the details of my life made public as instantly as they are when you're a cohost on the *Stern Show*. It is weird and unnatural and for the brief periods when I was sober

I felt just how strange that reality is with every cell in my being. Everyone is on the spot on the show, which is half the appeal to the audience, but during my last days there, when I was really going down the drain, I felt that spotlight on me more than ever and it was hot. When I started dating Adrienne, for the first time since joining the show I realized that the attention I always saw as an advantage could be a problem because for once I had something in my life I wanted to keep private. Maybe I'd learned a lesson after having my entire relationship with Dana broadcast over the air, or maybe I was just sober—who knows. All I can say is that this new relationship was special, so I didn't want to fuck it up and I didn't want anyone butting into it. I wanted it to grow on its own, but that was impossible, of course, because there was no way Howard and Robin were going to let it be. That's just not how it works on *Stern*, so I got hit with a million questions, and I had to honor the show, so I answered most of them. I ended up giving up more details on the air than I wanted to; put it this way, from the start Howard and Robin heard more about Adrienne and me than my closest friends had. I couldn't help it: it was Howard and it was Robin and if I didn't satisfy them they'd make fun of me for four hours every morning until I did. The whole thing made me very self-conscious, and it also made me realize that I really wanted something serious with this girl.

The microscope of the *Stern Show* has other consequences too: when Howard turns his insightful interview eye on you, he's got a way of luring anybody in the world into revealing more than they ever thought they would. The problem is that in his presence, even though you know you're on the radio, most people (even his co-hosts!) forget just how many people are listening. This phenomenon caused problems with every single woman I dated during my time on the *Stern Show*, whether it was just one night or a few years, and Adrienne was no different.

I got myself into even more trouble when it came to sharing my opinions of famous people. I'd be talking as if Howard and I were just on the phone shooting the shit and I'd say off-the-cuff things like "I saw that Chelsea Handler's show and I don't think she's that funny, do you?" A simple above-the-belt comment like that became, in the hands of some reporter interviewing Chelsea a few days later, me saying she wasn't talented and didn't deserve a talk show. This actually happened. I can't blame Chelsea, because that version was an insult, so she responded and my simple opinion started a mean-spirited conversation between us via the media—because we never talked to each other directly about any of this. While we're on the subject, Chelsea's response to me was actually funnier than most of her shows: "Artie Lange? He's grotesque. If I could find one who would, I'd pay any woman five hundred dollars to sleep with him. Honestly, any woman willing to sleep with Artie Lange, I'll pay you five hundred dollars right now to do it." I'd just like to say, Chelsea, that your assertion is complete bullshit. I have many friends who will testify, under oath, to the cold hard truth that I've gotten plenty of women to sleep with me for as little as $250.

Anyway, things were going all right. I was seeing a shrink that I liked very much, and I was enjoying my life and the world in a way I hadn't in years. I kept up my sobriety for four solid months, even as it came time to record my second live DVD, *Jack and Coke*. I'd been working on my stand-up act for about a year and a half, and by Saint Patrick's Day that year I felt I'd perfected it and was ready to capture it, so I put the wheels in motion. We shot the thing on May 28, 2009, at the Gotham Comedy Club, which is owned by my friend Chris Mazzilli. I had an hour and a half of material that I'd do for two different audiences, and we'd compile the DVD from there.

I couldn't think of a better title: *Jack and Coke*, two great tastes that taste great together, even though I was clean and sober (and happy) and enjoying neither at the time. That is when I felt that I was at my peak, and sometime just before that I told Mike and Joe that I didn't need them on the road with me anymore. I felt that I had my sobriety under control and could handle it all on my own. I even invited the two of them onstage and talked about how they'd gotten me sober. It was a very emotional moment, but it was completely delusional on my part because it came just five short months before I tried to kill myself. I wish I'd listened to Mike when he told me that I needed a year of nonstop, twenty-four-seven supervision. I really do.

The sobriety I was so proud of onstage that night wasn't going to last. A week later I slipped up, but going into the taping I was on top of the world when it came to my addictions. I had the Howard TV guys on board to produce the thing for me and it eventually became a Comedy Central special, which I'm very proud of. It didn't air until the following January, and there was no way I'd miss the premiere, even if I had to listen to it from under the covers in my bed on a psych ward. That happened, by the way.

Like I said, *Jack and Coke* was shot on May 28, 2009, and it was craziness backstage because I'd invited everybody I knew. Adrienne was there because we were going out regularly by then, and I was just so happy when she was around because I still couldn't believe she wanted to be with a guy like me. But she did, and we were becoming really close, really fast. Both of my sets killed that night, so the product is really great if you ask me. If you ask any critic on the planet I'm sure they'll disagree because generally the "art" I make, most "tastemakers" hate.

Overall that month of May was hectic as hell for me. When you're a cohost on a four-hour-a-day radio show that starts at six a.m., you're basically fucked because if you have any kind of life or engage in any activities that are somewhat nocturnal you're setting yourself up for extra stress. There's a reason why I slipped back into drinking, then into drugs not long after this: I did every single thing that they tell you not to do when you're freshly sober. They tell you not to jump into a relationship—did that. They tell you to avoid adding extra burdens to your work life—did that with my stand-up schedule, the DVD taping, and every other commitment I piled on. They tell you to avoid situations that are full of temptation where you've indulged your addictions in the past—did that by going right back on the road, into comedy clubs and casinos where I could get anything I wanted whenever I wanted it.

It should be obvious by now, as if it weren't already obvious in *Too Fat to Fish*, that I'm an addict, so the kinds of temptations available to a comedian on the road are dangerous for me. It was stressful enough for me to avoid them just living my professional life during this period of sobriety, and it really didn't help that I'd managed to break every rule they give newly sober people. Looking back, the worst mistake I made by far was piling on the live gigs and other professional responsibilities—in particular the ones I really didn't need to do. The stress of it all is what got me in the end, and some of it just so wasn't worth it. It's pretty easy for me to pinpoint exactly where and when this started. Yeah, without a doubt it was the benefit for Captain Janks. That gig cost me a small fortune, kicked off my decline, and left me with a case of post-traumatic stress disorder that still kicks in when I think about that moment in time.

For those readers who aren't maniacal die-hard *Stern* fans, first I'd like to welcome you, and second I'd like to say a few words about Captain Janks because I'm pretty sure you have no idea who the hell he is. Janks is a *Stern Show* Wack Packer, meaning he's one of the oddball flunkies that Howard has collected over the years who call into the show regularly and are on the TV specials and possess some special (as in "special ed") skill that Howard finds amusing. Janks, whose real name is Thomas Cipriano, is a gas station attendant by day last I heard, but the guy also happens to be a master prank phone caller who has been at it for *Stern* fans for fifteen years. I've got to hand it to him, Janks fools everybody, from CNN to the lady down the street, and what he usually does, once it's obvious that the victim believes him, is randomly drop Howard Stern's name into the conversation. He'll keep doing that until the person on the other end of the phone realizes they've been pranked, which is usually the best part of the call.

So, the day after the *Jack and Coke* taping, on May 29, 2009, I was scheduled to do a benefit for Janks, who had gotten arrested for multiple counts of taking payment for appearances and not showing up. The guy barely had the money to hire a lawyer, let alone pay for his court fees or post bail, so he was stuck in jail and had been wasting away in there for a week or so already. I spoke to Janks's lawyer and told him that I was scheduled to do a gig in Poughkeepsie the day after the live DVD taping, and since I was friends with the club owner we could make that the official Janks benefit. It seemed like a good idea—the venue and comics were already locked in. Like I said, it was my buddy's club, so I was only taking $5,000 from him for the night, but I told Janks's lawyer that I planned to donate my entire fee to the Free Janks Legal Fund. His lawyer was ecstatic, probably because he now knew he'd get paid.

That morning after *Jack and Coke*, I planned to take a helicopter upstate to the gig because driving there takes about two hours. And here is where we will start the tally of exactly how much this little adventure cost me. Don't worry, we will recap it at the end in case you lose count—I know I did at the time. Anyway, the helicopter ride cost $3,500 to take me, my buddy Timmy, and Adrienne there. Remember, I wasn't making anything on this gig, and remember that this was a conscious decision to do so on my part.

The three of us set out from my apartment in Hoboken in my Mercedes 4-door sedan, and since we were late and a helicopter sitting, waiting, hogging up the landing pad costs money, I drove to the private airport in Linden, New Jersey, as fast as I could. I was rushing, so when I got into the airport parking lot I managed to back my car smack into a cement block stanchion. I did it so well that the back of my car was completely destroyed, basically totaled. Mercedes are well built, so everyone was okay, but the trunk and rear end were history.

"Well, we've got to get out of here now," I said, staring at the wreckage. "I have to deal with this later."

We flew up to Poughkeepsie, no problem, and I did two crazy shows, both of them sold-out. The crowds were really into it, really loud, and really fun. After the show the club owner came over to me, and here we have the second entry in our tally.

"Hey, man," he said, all shrug-shouldered, "I know I'm supposed to give you five grand, but I only have two on me. Can I send you the other three in a couple of weeks?"

You don't have to be a lifelong stand-up comic to figure out that when a comedy club promoter says something like that, you'll never see the other $3,000.

"Yeah, whatever," I said.

Meanwhile I'd promised Janks's lawyer $5,000, and the guy was so excited by that I could tell they needed it, which added another $3,000 to my tab. I grabbed the $2,000, turned to my entourage, and said that I wanted to get the hell out of there.

"The last thing I want to do is get caught in Poughkeepsie tonight. This little outing is getting way too expensive."

Mike just stared at me for a second. "Well, Art, I've got some bad news," he said. "Obama is in town, so they've closed the airspace around New York City. We can't leave till morning."

I thought about Poughkeepsie for a second. "I've got to get out of here," I said.

I booked Mike into a $250-a-night room (which I found pretty excessive for the area), because he had to stay with the copter and fly it back the next day. Then I called a limo to take Adrienne, Timmy, and me back to Jersey. That cost me $350, and since I gave the guy a $150 tip, it came to $500. My tab for this gig was getting way out of hand.

The next day I went to pick up my car at Linden Airport and, as I expected, the thing was basically destroyed, but in the daylight it was truly grotesque. It was half a bumper away from being totaled, and it barely drove straight. By this point I had lost so much on Captain Janks that I wasn't going to pay someone to tow my Mercedes, so

I drove it to the dealer myself, and the thing was limping the whole way. I wasn't expecting good news, because it wasn't really that kind of week, but still, when the guy told me that none of the damage was covered under my service plan and that to get it back on the road it would cost $14,000, I started to wonder where the joke was in all of this, because there had to be one.

The only thing I could think to do was the math on this whole Captain Janks benefit, because I for one was pretty blown away. Here's my breakdown, and if I'm missing something, tweet me because if this story doesn't epitomize what I'm talking about when I talk about Quitter, I don't know what does.

Here we go. As predicted, I never got the other $3,000 promised in my performance fee, which meant that I had to put it up out of my own funds to give Janks's lawyer the $5,000 I promised him. The helicopter cost $3,500 and then $1,750 more, I think, because Mike had to stay over. Mike's hotel room, $250; limo home, $500; my Mercedes, $14,000 . . . This little favor for a friend cost me about $23,000. Captain Janks, I hope you're doing well.

Shit like that didn't make it easy to stay sober, that's for sure. And once we got into June, my schedule got even more hectic with all the book signings to promote the paperback and the endless stand-up gigs that I kept agreeing to. I didn't have a manager at the time, just a booker, which was probably not the wisest thing for me. He's a great guy, my booker, and he did his job well: offers would come in and he'd call me with the best ones. The problem was, I had no one to bounce anything off of, so, left to my own devices, I said yes to everything and spread myself thin once again. I started getting stressed, I started getting tired, and I started losing the armor I'd had when I was exercising and well rested. It didn't take too long for me to reach out for a familiar crutch once again.

———

It was sometime in early June, at a gig I don't remember, when I fell off the wagon. There was no big event or incident that caused it and I can't even remember the circumstances, just the fact that I had a drink, probably without even thinking about it. I didn't go on some drunken bender, I kept it under control, but I had another one to get me through the flight home the next day because I've always hated flying and it seemed like I could just drink casually. I was wrong, because as soon as I got back to Jersey from that road trip I drove my Mercedes into downtown Newark and scored a bag of painkillers off the first dealer I saw on the street. I went home, crushed them up, and snorted them chased with Jack Daniel's. Within a few days I was having bags of heroin delivered. I still looked pretty good, so I was able to fool everyone for a while, at least until my schedule got completely insane—and me along with it. My life was about to turn inside out as everything I'd done to get myself together came apart. I was about to step out of the eye of the hurricane and as usual I took everyone close to me along for a ride they'd never asked to be on.

In June, the paperback version of *Too Fat to Fish* was released and once again it hit the *New York Times* bestseller list, debuting at number nineteen and eventually rising to number six. I agreed to a new round of book signings, more gigs, and anything else to help promote the book, because truly, I can't say enough how proud I am of it. It was back to chaos for Artie: *Stern Show* during the week, everywhere from Pittsburgh to Cleveland to Philly to Vegas each weekend, with book signings for hours after every show. The book business has been good to me, by the way—much better than the DVD business. In the book business you see your royalty checks at regular intervals, and I remember one morning in late 2009 when I opened a check for $381,000 in book sales. I was so fucked up at the time that I just handed it to my mother and told her to deposit it.

In June I also appeared on the debut of Joe Buck's HBO show, *Joe Buck Live*. A lot has been made of that appearance in this book and just about everywhere else, so like Joe did so graciously in his foreword, I'm going to give my side of the story. Let me just say that Joe is a brilliant broadcaster, as his father, Jack, was before him, and that I was flattered to be asked to appear on his premier episode. The format was a live chat show covering the biggest events in sports that week but focusing on one major topic that a variety of guests would discuss. I was part of a comedian/actor panel that included Paul Rudd and *Saturday Night Live*'s Jason Sudeikis. The big sports stars of the evening were Brett Favre and Chad Ochocinco. The only thing I can say about what happened on that show was that, from the start, I had the wrong idea of what they wanted me to do. I blame myself, because I should have known better, but I have to say that the show's producers weren't very clear about their needs, which, trust me, is a surefire way to fuck up any relationship.

I figured that since this was HBO, anything went language-wise. Was that wrong? Last time I checked there's no censorship on cable, right? This is America, isn't it? My "material" that night was R-rated at best, and Joe did his best to keep me in line. But I'd completely misread the situation, so I came off obnoxious and took everyone to Awkward Town, and it was nobody's fault but mine. About four hours before the show I'd crushed up four ten-milligram Vicodin and snorted the entire pile, then chased it with liberal swallows of whiskey, so by the time I got to the studio I was what anyone would call "loopy." Video of my appearance has circulated widely on YouTube, so I'm sure you can still find it if you'd like to see this for yourself. For the most part HBO's lawyers have made it disappear, but the *Huffington Post* and a few other news websites have been able to keep it up thanks to a freedom of speech clause that allows them to deem it newsworthy. I believe that same clause allows people the freedom to buy celebrity sex tapes that have "gotten out." God bless America.

I'll give you a play-by-play of how my segment on Buck's show went. The first thing I said on what was, by design, a classy sports show, involved the phrase "sucking cock dot com." That's right, "sucking cock dot com." The audience, who'd had zero opportunities to laugh thanks to two painfully boring and egotistical guests (that would be Brett Favre and Chad Ochocinco), exploded. Ask any comedian, when an audience erupts at something you say, nothing else matters. It's like tossing a bucket of blood into the water when a hungry shark is around: once a comedian gets a taste for an audience's laughter, they'll hunt it down by whatever means necessary.

Here's how I got the laugh that triggered my feeding frenzy. Joe mentioned seeing something on his "favorite website," TMZ, which is a site that I actually really like and that's always been fair to me. I had nothing against TMZ or Joe, I was just being a wiseass. Besides, I saw an opportunity to say "sucking cock dot com" live on a major cable network, and what comic wouldn't want to do that?

That was just the start of me getting out of control, and Joe, being the consummate host that he is, did his best to be jovial while attempting to keep me in line, but I was getting out of control fast and dragging the show right into the gutter. I didn't leave Joe much choice other than to say I was being unprofessional and disrespectful, and to ask me to curb my "adult" language. Basically Paul Rudd and Jason Sudeikis sat there and watched this happen, because I wasn't letting anyone else take the focus off me, and the audience's laughter was all the affirmation I needed. During the break, Paul Rudd leaned in toward me.

"You realize that what you just did was legendary, right?" he said.

I've looked at the footage a lot and I have to say that the first half, the one Paul was talking about, is pretty incredible. I agree, it is legendary. Unfortunately I couldn't stop there and his encouragement inspired me to take things further. And that's where it all really went wrong because I completely lost the plot. When I watch the second half of that appearance all I think of is Robert De Niro as Jake La Motta in *Raging Bull*, all fat, trying to charm people in his nightclub in Miami. He's completely unaware that he's insulting everybody, spilling drinks on ladies, and making a spectacle of himself. He's an oblivious slob, which pretty much sums me up on that show.

During the fifteen-minute segment they recorded for the studio audience after we went off the air, I lit up a cigarette against Joe's wishes, and that was, as the French say, the coup de grâce, in which Joe lost it. He's usually a very controlled, well-spoken commentator, but if you listen to him at that moment in the show he sounds like a kid whose voice is about to crack as he yells, "Don't!" to the school bully stealing his lunch, which in this case would be me. I can't blame the guy! I had taken over his show, driven him crazy, and would not stop for anybody. The thing about me is, even if I weren't being paid to be funny, I'd be somewhere busting someone's balls the best I could if it made my friends laugh. That's just what I do; I'm lucky enough that I've found a way to make money off it.

I'm sad to say that this train wreck was the first of a very short run of *Joe Buck Live* shows, because the thing never really took off, and I feel bad for ruining that first episode for Joe. He didn't deserve it at all, that's for sure. I thought I was delivering the kind of performance they were after and since I was in a drug and booze cloud I didn't notice how wrong I was and how uncomfortable I was making everyone. In the moments when I caught a glimpse of it, I didn't even care because I was having one hell of a time! I'm serious: watch the video, I'm having a ball! The tension onstage is flying right over my head as what was supposed to be a civilized program becomes an out-of-control situation, while somewhere at least fifteen HBO executives regret their decision to let the show broadcast live. In any case, Joe, Jason, Paul, and show producer Ross Greenburg did their best to handle things in a very diplomatic way, but that didn't work because I was on a roll like the drunk uncle at the wedding who won't give up the microphone as he gives a speech that insults the groom's family and reveals that the bride was a slut in high school. Just like that asshole always does, I interpreted the crowd's attention to mean they loved my work.

I know a lot of my fans, plus people who don't like Joe Buck, still think this performance was fucking genius, and I suppose some of it was, but let's be honest, it's not an appearance on a talk show. It's a guy having a meltdown in an inappropriate way in the wrong place. I was in my own world that night and I overreacted, took no hints from anyone that I was going too far, and continued on, making everyone visibly uncomfortable. Joe even told me very clearly that I was doing this, but I didn't stop. I wish I could say that I had made a choice to deliberately create that awkwardness as some kind of tribute to the late, great Andy Kaufman, but I'd be lying. I swear to God I had no fucking idea that anything was wrong; I thought I was killing. I thought the producers and Joe would be grateful.

In my professional life, that appearance represents what drugs had become in my personal life. In the same way that I kept doing drugs while telling everyone I was quitting, I sat there on Joe's show saying whatever I wanted to, thinking it was funny and fine, even when I got very clear signs that it wasn't. I left the stage that night thinking I'd be a regular guest without a doubt. The next day I was literally the only person surprised to hear, via the *New York Post*, that HBO and Joe Buck were "dissatisfied" with my behavior on the show. The *Post* had a field day because they have much more fun reporting my mistakes than my successes, so they gave me a nice write-up explaining that I was banned from appearing on any HBO Sports program for the rest of my life. They also took great joy in describing just how tasteless and embarrassing I was to Joe on live television. What they failed to report—and this is true for any gossip website or column—was the follow-up story. Gossips never follow up, which is one of many reasons why I hate them—they'll never report anything that exposes them as being full of shit. Anyway, this whole Joe thing "went viral," as they say, and it got so much attention that two days later, the *Joe Buck Live* producers called me to ask if I'd film an intro piece for the second episode. Either they weren't as angry as everyone in the media let on or by then they just realized they needed ratings fast; whatever it was, everybody knows that controversy of any kind never hurts when it comes to publicity.

Of course I agreed, because, I'd like to say it once again, I never bore Joe any ill will. To be honest, once I got the memo that I'd really offended him and possibly hurt his show I was overjoyed to have the chance to make that right. He and I taped a funny little bit for the opening of the second episode where he's minding his own business, hanging out on the street when suddenly he sees me and runs full speed the other way. Clearly HBO hadn't banned me for life—I mean, I was on an HBO Sports show literally one week later, making this the shortest lifelong exile in history. Like I said, none of the gossips that covered my first appearance picked up that story at all, because they'd gone for it too hard in the first round to backtrack. Some of them even claimed I'd purposely tried to ruin Joe's show, without giving a reason for my so-called vendetta, by the way. That couldn't be further from the truth.

I was just being funny the way a wiseass from Jersey knows best: by busting balls. I was also very high, and looking back I'd say I treated the show as if it were a Comedy Central roast more than a sports talk show. I thought I was Don Rickles on *The Tonight Show* in the seventies. He used to make fun of Johnny Carson and every guest for the whole show—and everybody loved him! That's who I wanted to be that night. The only problem is, sober or wasted, I'm never as funny as Don Rickles. I didn't meant to hurt Joe or the show, so I'd like to officially apologize to him once again right now. Joe Buck and Ross Greenburg, I'm sorry for what happened, guys. I was busting balls and I went crazy, thinking we should push the envelope there on HBO, and also because, watching the interviews with Brett and Chad, as a fan, I was bored to tears. I was trying to "liven things up," but I went way overboard. It was a bad call on my part, and I'm very sorry about it. Can we be friends again?

A lot of people in comedy supported what I did, and still do, for various reasons. Some of them have something against Joe because he may not like their hometown football team, and that kind of thing goes a long way. Others just think it was cool and subversive, and comics love that shit. For the record, I'm not proud; I feel horrible about it, because whether you like his style or not, Joe Buck is a good guy and I regret putting him through those moments of awkwardness, because the guy really didn't know what to do. Imagine that happening on your first episode! I've done a bunch of sports-related comedy on *Conan* and *Letterman* where I had to be clean language-wise, and that's what they wanted, but instead they got Artie unleashed. One last time—sorry, guys.

CHAPTER 6

I'M GOING DOWN

In June 2009, the *Stern Show* went on its summer hiatus as usual and since I didn't know what to do with myself, I booked non-stop stand-up gigs. The Buck incident, regardless of how we patched it up, still weighed heavily on my mind. It was the start of an unraveling that had begun just after taping *Jack and Coke* and continued, gaining speed with every passing week as I started to lose my footing. Here is a list of my schedule that month:

6/1–6/3 stand-up and book signing in LA. *Stern Show* all week in NYC.

6/8–6/10 stand-up and book signing in Pittsburgh. *Stern Show* all week in NYC.

6/15–6/17 stand-up and book signing in Cleveland. *Stern Show* all week in NYC.

6/22–6/24 stand-up and book signing in Vegas.

6/25 fly to LA to meet Rick Rubin at his home near Malibu. *Stern Show* all week in NYC.

I insisted to everyone who asked that I was sober, because I'd had Joe and Mike on hand for so long. I'd let them go, by the way, in terms of paying them to keep me sober, but I kept them on the payroll as

my private transport. So to the outside world, meaning those closest to me who cared about my well-being, it looked as if I had those
two still in charge, still looking after me and keeping me away from
temptation. But like the Pope or the Queen of England, they were
only really there in theory; they were figureheads of my sobriety.
And like any figurehead, they had no real power. People close to me
had gotten so used to seeing me high that they had no real measure
of my sober-to-high ratio anymore. I had been high around them so
much that me being a little bit high seemed like me sober. They had
seen me so far gone that I was able to get away with being a little bit
high by that point.

Anyway, once Mike and Joe had been downgraded, I had a lot of
free time without them on my heels all the time, so I got into everything: booze, painkillers, heroin, and amphetamines occasionally. I'd
met a stripper a year or so before who shared my appetite for narcotics and she'd shot me up, just under the skin a few times. I had just
started seeing Adrienne, and we weren't completely together yet (it
was the very beginning of our relationship), so I took the opportunity
to see that stripper again when the occasion presented itself and she
and I got into everything. She always had a huge stash of pills, so I'd
steal her Adderall, her Oxys, and whatever else she wouldn't notice
missing whenever she'd leave me alone with her pill case. I didn't
even care what the pills were; I'd just crush them and snort them
the way normal people take Advil. I figured I'd find out what they
did soon enough, and I've always liked surprises. I'd do all of this
on my own time, late at night and on the road away from my family,
my employers, and everyone else in my life. I continued to tell them
I wasn't using drugs and for as long as I could I swore I hadn't been
drinking either, until they saw it with their own eyes.

The book signing in Cleveland that month was touch and go,
because I got more drunk than I had in a long time, on whiskey, as
usual. It was obvious to everyone by then that I was no longer sober,
but they did believe me when I said I was clean, and as if to prove

it, I managed to avoid taking any drugs in Cleveland, drunk as I was. This might not sound like much of an achievement, but it is. Any addict can tell you that once you indulge yourself in one of your appetites, the rest are not far behind, so I was proud that I managed to stay clean, at least for that one event.

That was short-lived, of course, because the next weekend in Vegas I dove back into being a mess on all levels with enthusiasm and gusto. After a week at *Stern* that came off without incident, I flew out there to do stand-up and a book signing, and I'd agreed to host a poolside beauty contest that would be filmed for Howard TV. It was going to be a long weekend: Adrienne was going to join me out there, we'd hang out for a couple of days, and then she'd accompany me to LA to meet Rick Rubin at his house in Malibu. She couldn't make it the night of my gig, so I had that night to myself, and being me, I got into plenty of trouble.

I was still trying to keep up a front, so I called ahead to a drug connection I'd had for years in Vegas and lined up (get it—lines?) some heroin. At the time the two cops were still traveling with me, which made everyone, including Adrienne, feel that I'd be all right out there alone for a night. I was staying at the Hard Rock and since I was being somewhat watched, the guy couldn't come to my room. That didn't matter; we figured out what to do.

My flight landed at five the morning of my show, so about that time my dealer left my heroin under a garbage can outside the hotel, just right there on the street. The plan was that he'd come to my gig as my guest, come backstage to say hello, and that's when I'd pay him. As soon as I said good night to the cops, I snuck down the hallway to the elevator and out to the street to get my stuff. I looked under the first garbage can I saw and found nothing. Second garbage can—nothing. Finally I went half a block down the sidewalk to the third garbage can and there it was, my goodie bag. Like anyone who's gone to that much effort to get anything I had to sample it right away, so I did a few lines and went to sleep.

The next morning I was still high—and loving it—and Mike and Joe could tell because I'd scored some really good shit. The cover was blown and they were pissed as hell at me to the degree that they threatened to call my agent and ask him to cancel the show. There was no way I was going to let that happen, not only because I'd be sued by the casino and lose a shitload of money, but because these guys worked for me, so I wasn't taking orders from them. Suggestions were fine, but not orders, not so much.

They were fuming, but they stood by me—literally—making sure I didn't go on a bender. The only problem was paying my dealer, but it turned out okay because there were about 100 people backstage, so he and I could have an inconspicuous conversation and make the exchange. By the way, I did go on a bender, because I'd bought a lot of heroin and I continued to do it all day. I did my show in a complete blackout, yet somehow got through my contracted hour and earned my check. Another crowd filled the backstage area after the show, which allowed me the chance to lose the cops and slip out. I partied the whole night away and even managed to get back to my room, thinking I was home free. Hardly—when I opened the door I saw them both sitting there. They got me into bed, making sure I was alone and safe, and they took my drugs. What they didn't know was that I'd stashed some just in case they busted me.

The next morning every fan I ran into in the hotel told me that I'd seemed fucked up onstage and that it was all over the Internet that I was back on drugs. Apparently I'd thrown out a kid in the front row for saying something I didn't like. I stopped my routine cold and yelled, "Get the fuck out of here," and was scary enough about it that the guy just got up and left. My after-party involved taking the Howard TV guys and many others to Nobu—a party of thirty in all. My friend Richie Notar, who is a co-owner of Nobu, gave me a break on a few things, but still, a party of thirty at Nobu? Am I Jerry Bruckheimer? I thought I was a billionaire because I made 100 grand on the show that night. My bill was upward of six thousand dollars with the tip. And then I went and gambled, and to this day have no idea how much I won or lost.

The next day Adrienne arrived just as I was waking up feeling like the bottom of a garbageman's work boot. She thought something was wrong, but I told her over and over that I was fine.

"How did the show go?" she asked suspiciously.

"It was fine; everything's fine, really. I just stayed up too late gambling."

The whole crew was at the pool for the beauty pageant I had to host. I looked like a newspaper that had been left in a puddle all night: my hair was all fucked up, I needed a shave, and I went down there wearing a T-shirt, shorts, and no shoes, just white socks. I looked like a photo of someone's grandfather, fresh off the boat in America in the '40s. I was totally out of place. We taped the show, which turned out pretty bad, and all of us spent the rest of the day and the next few days partying at the pool and in the casino.

The next day, Adrienne, Mike, Joe, and I flew to LA a day ahead of my meeting with Rick Rubin because my manager made it clear that Rick is an early riser so I couldn't be late. Adrienne and I checked into the Four Seasons and spent the night, and the next morning at seven we were on our way to Malibu to meet Rick just after he'd finished his morning meditation. We were driving along the Pacific Coast Highway, my agent, my manager, Adrienne and I, when I felt heroin withdrawals creeping into my muscles.

Along with the Joe Buck fiasco and the horrendous appearance that got me banned from *Conan* after ten years, my meeting with Rick Rubin is a moment I'll forever wish I would have been clean for. I was in withdrawal, but still—and this is all because Rick is one of the most special people anyone could hope to meet—the time I spent with him was as close as I'll probably ever get to what people mean when they talk about feeling enlightenment.

For those who don't know, Rick Rubin is probably the most important producer of the past twenty-five years. He started Def Jam records with Russell Simmons and is responsible for producing some of the greatest recordings from everyone from LL Cool J to Metallica to the Black Crowes to Slayer to Johnny Cash. He's only done comedy records for one guy, the one and only Andrew Dice Clay, so when my agent got a call that he wanted to meet me I jumped at the opportunity. I'd mentioned how much I respected him on the *Stern Show*, and I guess Rick's girlfriend had read *Too Fat to Fish* and really liked it and told Rick that he should meet me, even just to maybe help me out with my problems. Rick has never touched a drink or a drug in his life; he meditates and is very, very spiritual.

Rick's house is secluded so it took us a while to find it, which made me more and more anxious about being full-tilt sick in front of him. Finally we arrived at the most gorgeous place you can imagine, with the most beautiful view of the ocean. It was peaceful in every way. The door was answered by what I assumed was Rick's assistant, a real serious guy with a shaved head. From his monk-like appearance to the impossible tranquility of the place, everything was completely zen. My entourage was put into a living room area where they were served coffee and offered ice cream, while I was taken to a terrace overlooking the ocean. I sat there eating chocolate ice cream until Rick came out a few minutes later sipping some special health drink. He was thin and fit with a long gray beard and the most piercing blue eyes I'd ever seen.

He was very complimentary off the bat, which I could hardly believe because the guy is a hero of mine who has worked with people far more talented than I'll ever be. He told me how much he loved the *Stern Show* and how much he loved me particularly on the show, and then we started to talk about life. Rick Rubin loves Abbott & Costello as much as I do, so we went on about that, and then I asked him all about how he started Def Jam out of his dorm room at NYU.

"You know, I have to be honest, man," I said. "When I heard that first Beastie Boys record, my friends and I thought it was a comedy album."

"It's interesting that you say that," he said, "because that's kind of how I thought it would be taken in the beginning as well, but it turned into this art form."

We talked about various comedians and the records he'd done with Andrew Dice Clay, then he told me why he'd really wanted to meet me.

"My girlfriend really loves you on the show and she's read your book and she knows about your problem. I wanted to meet you because if you're open to it, I'd like to get you into meditating. It might help you out."

He told me about this woman in Beverly Hills who'd taught him meditation and who is probably the best in the country. He gave me her name and number and said that I should call her because she could help.

"Yeah, yeah, sounds great," I said. Just like I always did.

"I know you just put out a DVD," he said, "but I'd also like to say that if you ever have an hour of new material that you'd like to make into a record I'd love to maybe produce it."

"Really? That's unbelievable. That would be an honor, man, thank you."

Rick Rubin was so peaceful and full of energy that his vibe stopped my withdrawals. I'm not kidding in the least. It was weird. I'd felt sick until the moment I arrived, but I felt completely fine during our time together. We spoke for three hours and I felt like I was completely clean.

It didn't last, though, and by nighttime I really started to feel sick, and crashed out hard at the Four Seasons before catching a redeye back to Jersey. The *Stern Show* was starting back up, and I was in trouble. I'd need opiates immediately when I landed if I stood a chance of getting to work in anything close to good shape. I arranged for that and realized that I was on the train again and probably wouldn't ever get off this time.

When Adrienne and I landed in Jersey, I was pretty groggy because I'd taken some sleeping pills for the flight that I'd gotten from some guy on the plane. We pulled in bright and early and both Adrienne and I were both too tired to drive down to my shore house. My apartment was getting painted at the time and everything was covered in tarps, so I did the sensible thing and got us a $1,500-dollar-a-night room at the Mandarin Oriental. That was me—it couldn't be a fucking Sheraton even though we were both so exhausted all we needed was a bed. What can I say? I love that hotel.

I pulled in there in the black Mercedes SUV I was driving as my loaner car and left it with the valet. Our plan was to sleep there for the night and drive down to my beach house the next morning to prepare for the Fourth of July party I'd planned to have. As we got settled into our room and into bed, withdrawals started to kick in and I started to feel really sick. Adrienne was about to fall asleep, which meant I might be able to slip out without her wanting to come along.

"Oh my God!" I said in a dramatic whisper. "I just got a text from my buddy in Jersey; he needs my help. I've got to leave right now."

Let's just say she was pretty suspicious; as sleepy as she was, she gave me a sidelong look. "All right," she said slowly.

"Stay here, I'll be back in a few hours."

I got my black SUV out of the valet and drove into downtown Newark, New Jersey, where I scored heroin and some sleeping pills. The way I always have, as soon as I got the drugs, I did some: I pulled into a parking lot and snorted a couple of lines of heroin off the dashboard. That hit the spot and I started to feel okay. I did one more for the road then got back on the Turnpike heading toward the Holland Tunnel and Manhattan, where I drove straight into bumper-to-bumper traffic. There was no worse place I could possibly be. After a red-eye flight featuring a generous dose of sleeping pills to keep the withdrawals at bay and a few lines of heroin, sitting in traffic while behind the wheel was a recipe for disaster. I nodded out in no time, and when I did my foot slid off the brake, sending the truck forward, right into the back of a huge, brand-new BMW SUV.

The BMW didn't take much damage, but the front of the SUV I was in was wrecked—the hood was bent and the radiator cracked. The impact woke me up and I was coherent enough to realize what had happened. It was now about eleven a.m. and we were right in the middle of serious noontime Holland Tunnel traffic. I got out of the car and walked over to the window of the BMW. There was one guy in the front and a few in the back.

"Are you okay?" asked the guy in the driver's seat.

"Yeah, man, I'm fine. You guys okay?"

The guy in the passenger seat was pissed off. "What the fuck is your problem?" he asked.

"I don't know, I took a red-eye flight in this morning, and I'm really tired. I'm sorry," I said. "But more important, are you okay?"

That calmed him down a little bit. "Yeah, I'm fine, I'm fine," he said. "Wait a second . . . Artie?"

"Yeah, man, that's me."

It got a little awkward for a second because those kind of things can go either way, then he said, "I used to work with your publicist. He's a friend of mine."

"Oh, no way, really?"

Now I'm having this conversation in the middle of traffic with a nearly totaled loaner SUV on my hands. A minute later five cops showed up, and in case you forgot I was holding enough drugs to put me away for a while. Luckily every single one of them was a huge *Stern* fan. So before I knew it I'm signing autographs and telling stories but I can't help thinking how bad it had to look and what they were going to do about it. There was a totaled SUV driven by a known drug addict who probably still smelled like booze. And God help me if they searched my pockets.

Somehow none of this happened. I exchanged insurance info

with the BMW driver, charmed the cops as best I could, and tried to act casual. The other driver was really cool; he said he wouldn't sue, he just wanted money to fix the car, and he stayed true to his word. I can only imagine what my insurance company had to pay out, but that's what insurance is for. And the cops—I guess because they were fans—were so great. They didn't make me take a sobriety test, and they never even talked about searching my car. They were more concerned about how I would get back to my hotel.

"Is this thing running okay, Art?" one of them asked.

"I think I can drive it. Don't worry about it, man." This was a ridiculous thing to say because one wheel was completely bashed in and would barely move.

"Okay, man," they said. "Go ahead, we love you."

I'd dodged a huge bullet and once I got in the car and got it started I breathed easy. That could have been the end of so much for me. I started driving and immediately realized that this SUV wasn't going vary far because it was very screwed up. I made it through the Tunnel, past the West Side Highway, but at Tenth Avenue, the thing just stopped—completely dead, not moving at all. Cars whizzed by me as I triple-checked to make sure I had all of my drugs. I called a tow truck and twenty minutes later this amazing Puerto Rican guy showed up and helped me out. He called the rental company for me and took care of everything. Then I spoke to the girl there and they couldn't have been nicer: they sent another car out to meet me at the Mandarin, and I liked the girl on the phone so much I offered her tickets to my Beacon Theater show later in the year.

I can only imagine what the valet at the Mandarin Oriental was thinking when I pulled up: I'd arrived in a black SUV, I was returning in the cab of a tow truck with the SVU from before totaled on back, and just as I was about to go inside, my new car showed up, which was a Honda Civic.

"Hey, Mr. Lange, it's good to see you again," was all he said.

Up in our room Adrienne was taking a bath and she came out

and eyeballed me even more suspiciously than before. She could tell something was off.

"I'm gonna take a shower," I said, and that's what I did.

While I was in there she went through my pockets and found the sleeping pills, but thank God not the heroin. She got really mad and flushed all of the pills down the toilet, which would have made me furious if I didn't have some heroin. This started high-test tension between us.

"Forget it, Artie, let's try to get some sleep," she said.

I was pissed at her for taking my pills, so I wasn't going to just roll over. "No, I want to get out of here right now," I said. "I want to get down to the shore."

"Artie, what are you talking about?!" she said.

"I want to leave. I want to leave right now."

This kicked off a huge argument that ended with her agreeing to leave the hotel. There was no reason for it aside from my stubbornness, which caused me to pay $1,500 for an amazing room that we only stayed in for four hours. Adrienne didn't know what to think when she saw the car, and I can't imagine the doorman did either: he'd seen me get out of an SUV, a tow truck, and a Civic within four hours. Adrienne knew I was screwed up and now she knew that I'd screwed up.

"Are you even going to bother to explain this car and where you went?" she asked me.

This kicked off a huge screaming match as we drove from Manhattan to Hoboken, and that fight was all my fault. When I was busted I always got angry. We were no closer to resolving shit by the time we got to my apartment (where her car was), and I couldn't take it anymore.

"You know what?" I said, "I'm not taking this shit down to the shore. I'm not going to be fighting with you at my party. Go sleep in my apartment!"

It really wasn't the nicest thing to do because there may have been a bed there, but the whole place was covered in tarps and still smelled of paint. She was so exhausted that she just pulled the tarp back off the bed, crawled in, and got some rest.

I drove down to the shore in the Civic that night and wasted a perfect day the next day sleeping in a darkened room in my beautiful $2.5 million shore house (another great move—spending that much on a shore house in 2007, just before the real estate crash). Adrienne and I made up on the phone at some point and she ended up coming to the Fourth of July party a few days later and we were fine. But the drugs were taking their toll on our relationship and things between us were about to get worse.

After the *Stern Show* returned from vacation I didn't let up with the live gigs like I'd planned to, even though everyone in my life had told me to do otherwise. They all reminded me—Howard included—about the plan I'd agreed to with Don Buchwald. Like I'd done the last time this was brought up, I said I'd get through my current commitments with the book tour and stand-up and then I'd change everything.

As I started to slide back into drugs, I tried to keep alive the only positive thing I'd found by spending as much time as I could that summer with Adrienne. After we'd been together just a month she moved in with me and came to every road gig she could, which gave us the chance to have a lot of fun out on the road. It seemed like my personal life was going well, even as the amount of opiates I was consuming on the sly became larger and larger. Still, Adrienne and I developed real feelings for each other in a very short time, and she wasn't just there for the good times: she figured out what was going on with me and she did everything she could to help me, hoping of course that I'd get off drugs again. That was a fantasy, so the whole situation became pathetic after a while. Here was this sweet twenty-five-year-old suddenly put in charge of looking after an addict slipping back down the hill. It got to the point where my shrink put her in charge of my sleeping pills because as much as I've done opiates and downers and suffered depression, somehow the side effects have been that I can never sleep. I just lie there riddled with anxiety.

I'd been going to a shrink that Howard had suggested I see for a few months and I'd really enjoyed it, to be honest. He was an older Upper East Side guy and the days I'd see him I'd walk from the *Stern Show* through Central Park up to his office. He helped me a lot because he wasn't your typical shrink in any way. He wasn't controlling or judgmental; he wasn't traditional; he just talked to you and got to know you in an abstract way that I found very helpful. He got me to talk about things that I'd never talked about because he didn't go right at them, he found a way to approach them that worked for me.

He got me to talk about my father a lot and my obsession with his death. One day he did something that helped me more than I would have thought, even though at the time it was kind of crazy: he spent twenty-five minutes reading me a novella by James Joyce called "The Dead." The focus of the story is a guy who lost his first wife and how he was devastated without her even though he'd remarried. The guy was able to listen to a song that reminded him of her and go into his mind and basically spend time with her. He had to do this to deal with the loss and basically told his present wife that she had to deal with that and allow him that time. The shrink wanted me to do that with my dad, and I tried it, when I was sober at least. When I'd really miss him I'd lie back and relax and picture him and relive my best memories of him and it was a pleasant experience, it really was.

When I started drinking again I started lying to my shrink—he was just one more on the list—and who knows if he believed me or not. I didn't tell him about the drugs, of course, but I did tell him how stressed I was and how it was so hard for me to sleep, so he agreed to prescribe me some sleeping pills, but like I said, only under the condition that Adrienne held on to them and handed them out to me. She agreed to it because she was in love with me and she wanted to help. The two of us were trying to build a relationship; I was just dead set on fucking it up. Since she spent most weekdays with me and most weekends an hour or so away at her parents' house, she'd have to hide pills around my apartment when she left in case I had an anxiety attack and my prescribed dose wasn't enough to calm me down. As I got deeper into the opiates, this became a regular thing, because if the withdrawals didn't have me strung out, pretty often I'd cry wolf, just because I knew there were pills in my house and I wanted to do them. Adrienne was pretty creative: she'd tape them to the backs of pictures, put them inside books, you name it.

It was about this time in my crash that my performance on the *Stern Show* slid into the shit after eight solid years. Whether buzzed or not I never seemed to lose my sense of rhythm; I knew when to talk and when not to and I was always able to bring some laughs into whatever conversation was happening with a well-placed comment. Long before I was on the show I'd been a fan, so when I got the job I promised myself that I'd never lose sight of the fact that timing was everything. As I've already mentioned, all of that went way the hell out the fucking window. If you want to talk about a loss of timing, all I need to say is that falling asleep, on the air, with six million people listening, became my most consistent contribution. That is when I wasn't making nonsensical comments, interrupting Howard, or fighting with just about everyone.

One morning that sticks in my mind was the day we had Ben Stiller and Jimmy Kimmel on the show. At some point in the conversation Kimmel mentioned that he was friends with Tom Cruise and that he didn't believe the story in *Too Fat to Fish* where I talk about how rude Tom was to me on the set of *Jerry Maguire*. Jimmy was being friendly about it, just saying it didn't sound like Tom, but I didn't see it that way at all. I saw it as personal attack.

"Fuck you, Jimmy," I said. "Tom Cruise is a fucking asshole. He's a fucking creep."

"Calm down, Artie," Howard said.

I didn't calm down, of course. I kept at it to the detriment of the show and to my already sagging performance. That was the first time I really sucked, but it was far from the last.

In September Howard had to sit me down for a heart-to-heart, which he'd never had to do in my eight years on the show, no matter how crazy I'd ever gotten. He slipped me a note off the air that day and then he and our program director, Tim Sabean, cleared the studio and closed the door during a break.

"Listen, Art," Howard said. "We don't know if you've got something going on again, but you've not been doing your job on the air lately."

"Howard, I'm clean," I said. I was totally lying—I was high at the time.

"Art, if you've got something going on, we'll give you time to recover," Tim said. "Just tell us what's going on."

"We always had a rhythm, Art," Howard said. "You and Robin and I were always seamless, and that was great. But now you're sort of interrupting us and I'm worried about you. You get crazed over little things. I don't want to drug test you because that's none of my business, but I want you to be all right."

"Howard, I'm clean and I'm working on myself," I said. "I've gotten rid of the drugs, but I've got a lot of work to do on myself. I understand that."

"I don't want to fire you, Artie," Howard said. "It seemed like you were doing so good. Just work on that."

"I will, Howard, I promise."

"Do me a favor: when we have guests in, why don't you just not talk for a little while. Let me get things going before you comment at all."

"Okay, man. I can do that. I'm sorry. I'll work on it."

Yeah, right. I just got worse and worse. As the drug use increased, so did my interruptions, because I couldn't follow my own rule. I was going in and out of being on and off drugs with such abandon that most mornings by this point I had no idea whether I was coming or going. I so wanted to be doing my job well that I'd jump in too much, and I was either so high or so strung out that I had horrible ADD. I'd get distracted by one detail in a conversation or an interview Howard was conducting that I'd direct the entire flow of the show toward that. And since I was in my own world, that detail was often completely irrelevant to anyone else but me. I was either in or coming out of a daze that no one else was tuned into, so I became like Frosty the Snowman when the kids put the hat on him and he says, "Happy Birthday!" which in context doesn't make much sense. Later that year I'd find myself in my version of the greenhouse, where I'd melt, just like Frosty did. That's what it felt like when my mother and sister found me at my very lowest point: I felt like nothing but a puddle.

━ ━ ━ ━

Howard was getting really frustrated with me, because the last thing a perfectionist as busy as he is needed was my brand of unpredictable trouble on the air. Gary was in an even worse position because people in corporate started to ask him how he intended to handle me falling asleep, aggravating Howard, and missing work all the time. I'm glad I didn't know about that; I would have made a jihad out of harassing those desk jockeys.

Gary had my back. He'd tell them, "Artie's been with the show a decade; he's part of the family and we're all trying to help him through this. You've got to let us do it our way."

As I got worse, the awkwardness I felt from putting people who had done right by me through this drama began to weigh on me heavily. I began to suck everywhere, which pissed me off even more: my stand-up gigs became rambling diatribes, I fell asleep at work every morning, all because I needed to get higher and higher. And

I wouldn't stop taking on more work that did nothing but make it harder and harder for me to ever get any rest. For a guy who liked doing opiates and downers and then crashing out for hours, you'd think I'd have planned a little better.

Here's a perfect example: I'd bought a fantastic beach house, so I planned on having a huge Fourth of July party. That house I bought for $2.5 million is now probably worth eighty grand. Anyway, this party was the last thing I needed to do, but because we'd talked about it on the show, I invited everyone, though I really didn't need that kind of pressure. I had it catered by a local Italian chef, complete with everything. It was very lavish in every sense. It was worthy of the house, put it that way, and I'd invited my whole family, and that's where I introduced them to Adrienne for the first time. My nieces and nephews were riding up and down in the elevator, you name it, it was a real gathering. I even sprang for a fireworks display, right there off my dock, practically in the backyard. It was really beautiful. And I was coming down, hard, off of opiates and the rest of it, with no relief in sight.

To make things worse, months before, I'd agreed to appear in a film as a favor to my friend Maria Menounos, who is best known as a host on *Extra* and *Access Hollywood*. She writes, produces, and directs movies, and she'd said she'd only need me for a day. That day happened to be July 5, which I forgot all about (of course) until that week. Maria was great; she let me postpone my day of shooting until the sixth.

I slept in on the fifth, but I didn't want to get up at four a.m. to get to the shoot in Connecticut on time, so I drove the hour and a half to Manhattan and checked into the Mandarin Oriental, once again in a $1,500-a-night room. Adrienne went home and I told Maria to send a car at six a.m. to drive me the two hours to Connecticut. Maria is a sweetheart, but this was the last thing I wanted to do on a holiday weekend. So I locked myself in my hotel room and numbed out by snorting heroin all night. I didn't want to oversleep, because I was responsible, so I did the smart thing and stayed up all night. Makes sense, right? I then got up and had a healthy breakfast of Kit Kats from the mini bar, which cost around $800, and got in the town car Maria had sent, completely fucked up, with a bunch of heroin in my pocket to "get me through the day."

I slept all the way there and when I woke up did my best to pretend that I was okay. I went through hair and makeup and gave Maria a big hug when I saw her. I met the director, who explained the scene and what they wanted from me, which was great because I hadn't even looked at the script. My job was to play the older brother of a kid who goes on to become a serial killer, probably because of how often my character called him an asshole, which I did in every scene. I really don't know what the fuck that movie was and I barely remember doing it, but I love Maria and I hope it worked out. I tried to learn my lines, but I was all fucked up, and there was nowhere for me to get some privacy. There were no trailers; the best they had was a spare sedan, so I climbed there and, in the heat, dozed off in the middle of "rehearsing."

After a fourteen-hour shoot, the car took me back to the Mandarin Oriental, where I crashed for another night because I was too fucked up to do anything else, flushing away another $1,500. That night I had an out-of-body experience where I realized that my life had become a dream or something worse. It had become something I was watching as an audience member, and it no longer seemed real. I was on the biggest radio show in history, living the life I'd always wanted, but I was so detached from it all and I'd forgotten how to care.

I kept on and it got worse as my on-air "fatigue" became a regular feature of the show. It got so ridiculous that one day when Kathy Griffin was our guest, I fell asleep so deeply and snored into the microphone so loudly that Howard couldn't continue. He could only be heard between snores. Howard turned it into gold, of course, but after they'd finished laughing at me, they woke me up and suggested that I sleep it off (whatever "it" was for me that day).

"Art, why don't you just go into the dressing room and sleep," Howard said. "We don't need you for the Kathy Griffin interview."

"Fine," I said, so during the commercial break they kicked Kathy and her hair and makeup people out of her dressing room so I could get back to snoring.

"You're kicking me out so Artie can sleep?" she asked our producer, completely dumbfounded. "I have an Emmy."

I intended to doze through her interview and rejoin the show, but instead I slept there until two p.m., three hours after the show was over and everyone had left. I walked out the door, got myself home, ordered some pizza, snorted whatever I had left in my pocket, and went to bed. That was just another day at the office. The only reason I didn't lose my job was that Howard is so brilliant at making anything funny—even a fat addict sleeping—that I became a source of humor and a regular joke. My naps were a recurring theme because he turned it into a bit the way only he can, even though it was a huge burden for him to bear each day.

The top that was my life started really spinning out of control this time. I was so physically addicted, and it had happened so quickly and I really didn't care. It was horrifying to me: I'd hired guys to get me clean and I'd made such a show of it on the air on *Stern*, and even in my own stand-up DVD, that I was ashamed of what had happened. There was no way I was going to cop to the fact that I'd slipped. I was going to keep this front up no matter what.

I'd wire money to dealers who would leave me pills and powder wherever I was traveling, and I was back in that cycle again. Everyone started to pull away from me again: my mom, my sister, my friends, and Adrienne, who began to spend most of her time at her parents' house and fewer and fewer days with me. Because even though I wasn't admitting a thing, they could feel that I was lying. And it got very bad very quick. This wasn't a slow slide—this was a nosedive.

When *Stern* went on break for two weeks in July I stayed at my shore house doing nothing but getting high in my bedroom. The shame of failing at being sober was so heavy upon me that I couldn't even consider trying to fake it by being social. I hid out from everyone except the one person I couldn't avoid: my mother. She came down for a few days, and got sick with some kind of flu, probably because she was stressed out over me. Her doctor called in an antibiotic to the CVS a half mile from my house. The night before, I'd taken some sleeping pills, so that morning I was still groggy as I got into the car and drove to get my mother her medicine. I was pretty out of it, so some woman who saw me swerving called 911, and before I knew it the cops were following me. That didn't help my concentration any, and by accident I bumped the car in front of me while coming to a stop just a few blocks from my house. No one was hurt and there was no damage, in fact the two teenage kids in the car got out and recognized me and asked for autographs and pictures as if nothing had happened.

The cops behind me decided to give me a sobriety test, however, which became an unscheduled improv show, because the whole time they made me walk the line and touch my nose, people were pulling over to take pictures and watch. Thank God I didn't have any drugs in the car, because they weren't satisfied with my performance and decided to arrest me on suspicion of DUI. Thankfully the cop agreed to take my mother's antibiotics to the house before taking me in to be arrested. My poor mother. She thought her son was going out to get her antibiotics until a cop showed up to deliver them and told her I'd been arrested for DUI.

My mother was my one phone call. She then called my buddy Al, who is one of my best friends from childhood—Al's father was the guy who got me my job at Port Newark back in the day. It took him a few hours, but eventually Al bailed me out. For the record, I blew a 0.0 on the Breathalyzer because I wasn't drinking, and when they took my urine sample I told them the truth.

"Listen, I have a prescription for sleeping pills and I took them last night, so that's all you're going to find," I said.

"That's great," the cop said. "Get a lawyer, because you're gonna need one."

They took my mug shot and threw me in a cell and about twenty minutes later one of the detectives who'd booked me came back all smiles.

"Looks like you made TMZ, congratulations."

Really? I'm not sure what is more nauseating, how giddy the guy was about it or the fact that it took TMZ something like fourteen minutes to report that I'd been arrested for DUI but CNN still can't find the weapons of mass destruction.

"That's great."

I tried to sleep on the floor until Al showed up, but that didn't work out too well, because, contrary to what you might have been told, jail cells aren't very comfortable.

When I got home my mom was crying, and it looked like she'd been at it for a while.

"Ma, don't worry about this, it's nothing. I wasn't drinking, I was just sleepy from my medicine," I said. "I'm calling my lawyer and this whole thing will be gone."

It was the truth, but it didn't put her at ease one bit.

My lawyer said later that day. "You blew a zero; they'll never be able to convict you. This whole thing is bullshit. They're just out to make some money."

What he didn't count on was the small-time prosecutor in the seaside town where my house is thinking he'd make a name for himself off of whatever little fame I have. The guy told my lawyer in no uncertain terms that he planned to prosecute this case to the end.

"I plan to read his book in the courtroom," the guy said. "The public needs to know how much of a drug abuser he is. I'm going to subpoena tapes from *The Howard Stern Show*, I'm going to subpoena his mother and his friends. Artie Lange is a public menace."

My lawyer knew we could beat it, but we would have to go through with a trial.

"If we go to trial, he says he's going to subpoena *Stern Show* tapes and my mother will be called as a witness?"

"Yeah, I'm afraid so, Art."

"Fuck it, I'm not going through all that. I'll plead guilty."

That's what I did, and the judge suspended my license for six months.

One night during those months when it was clear that I wasn't all right I came home to my apartment and found my mom sitting there in tears. She came right up to me and got in my face as soon as I got through the door.

"Artie, I love you," she said. "I'm afraid you're going to die and I don't want to go to your funeral." She had to pause to catch her breath. "Artie . . . I don't want to bury you."

I'll never forget that moment, but as poignant as it was—and it was one of the most poignant moments of my life—it didn't slow me down. I couldn't slow down, but I knew I had to do something, so I promised her I'd quit stand-up because the road was to blame, I said. I wasn't entirely lying; touring had always been my trigger, but the problem was, I enjoyed pulling it. I hated flying, so I'd medicate; to deal with the crowds at an all-night book signing, I'd medicate. I had so many reasons to take my medicine that I was always on it. In an effort to remove the stress of air travel and to keep a better eye on me, Mike began to book me a tour bus. That way there was no hotel room for me to hide in and get up to no good. This worked out well because I liked the bus. The rocking movement actually helped me sleep. I liked it so much that I booked even more live gigs. Besides, I'd found ways to bring drugs around: I began to carry a small bag full of papers that I said were my notes for stand-up and I forbade Mike,

Joe, or anyone from looking in it. I wasn't completely lying; there were ideas on notepads in there. But usually there was also a stash of as many pills as I could get my hands on.

Listen, even I knew this party couldn't last, because I'd lost my edge—I just didn't want to admit it, and I sure as hell didn't want to do anything about it. I just wanted to bullshit my way out of trouble, hoping I'd make up for it the next time. But that wasn't happening. I continued to make a fool of myself and a fool of the *Stern Show* every morning because I'd become the weird guy in the corner shouting nonsense—and that was a good day for me. I kept telling myself I'd get off the road but kept accepting offers I thought I couldn't refuse. I didn't even know what motivated me anymore, because as much as I was greedy and felt like I should get all I could before it all fell apart, I kept doing things that made no sense and I kept wasting my time and money.

That September I got a fan letter from a kid in Detroit whose brother was a quadriplegic, asking me to do a charity gig at the Detroit Opera House to raise money to buy the special equipment he said his brother desperately needed. Any extra money raised would benefit quadriplegic care facilities at their local hospital. I'd done a few things like this before because my father was a quadriplegic and shit like this moves me, so I got in touch with him and agreed to do the gig.

The moment I got off the plane I realized I'd been duped because it was clear to me that these people had money and didn't need a handout. What sucks is that I would have hung out with them or done something else for them that didn't involve me coming to do a gig, because that was literally the last thing I needed on my plate, since I was already under so much pressure and being watched so closely. I only did it because they said they needed the money. That said, the kid was an inspiration. He was doing everything he could possibly do in life and not letting his condition hold him back. He had the most positive attitude that you can imagine and I kept wishing that my father had shared this kid's point of view. If he had, he and I could have enjoyed a few more years together.

I put this whole trip together myself, so I flew up to Detroit solo. I'm sure Joe and Helicopter Mike were fine with that, because they'd gotten sick of my shit by then and were taking a big step back, even from just flying me around. My whole circle was coming apart—I'd even fired my driver of eight years, whom I'm going to call Alice Cooper, for no good reason at all by then. Alice Cooper had been so good to me and always looked out for me and kept me safe, but because of that very quality, Mike and Joe felt that he was a weak link in the chain and pushed me to let him go. Alice was almost too nice, they said, so he was the kind of guy that could be manipulated by me. They weren't wrong, but they also weren't exactly right: if I'd told Alice Cooper not to get me drugs no matter how much I begged or tried to bribe him with cash, he would have done that for me too. Alice was loyal above all, and he got me to work as on time as best he could every day for eight years.

I don't want to get off track, but I do need to say that I feel horribly guilty about the way I let Alice Cooper go. The last morning he came to pick me up I was really late—I think I had about eight minutes to get from Hoboken to Sixth Avenue and Forty-Ninth Street in midtown Manhattan. I was under a lot of pressure and a lot of scrutiny and I couldn't be late, so I insisted that Alice let me drive. My license hadn't officially been suspended because my court case was pending, so technically this wasn't illegal. I was, however, high on pills and booze at the time.

"Alice Cooper, you gotta let me drive," I said.

"Why?" he asked.

"Because we need to run red lights and speed, and I'm willing to do that," I said. "I don't want you to get a ticket, so if we get one, let me be the one who gets it."

I drove to work, high, like a man possessed. I ran every red light.

I passed garbage trucks on the shoulder and crossed into the on-coming lane whenever I needed to.

"Art, you're fucking nuts!" Alice shouted.

I was swerving and I sideswiped a bus, breaking the mirror off of Alice's car on the driver's side.

"What are you doing? You're crazy! What the fuck are you doing?"

I made it just in time, which must be some kind of record, but it was the last trip to work Alice Cooper and I took together. The next day we fired him and he'd done absolutely nothing wrong. About a year and a half later I saw Alice in front of a pizza place in Hoboken and we hugged and talked it out and I explained everything that was going on with Mike and Joe trying to control me. Alice understood, but I still feel like shit about it. Anyway Mike and Joe replaced him with some driver they knew from Long Island I'm going to call Sebastian Bach. I drove his car a number of times too, by the way, always when I was high and late to the show. I'd swerve in and out of traffic and pass in the space between lanes if I saw an opening. I actually broke Sebastian's mirror getting there one morning, which I dealt with by giving him $800 when we got there.

To give you an idea of how bad I'd become, my sister, Stacey, insisted on coming along with me on this trip to Detroit, and she had long ago reached the end of her rope with me. But she loves me and I'm her brother and she knew that I was in very deep trouble, no matter what I said. So she came along, taking a break from her job as a clothing designer at American Eagle to do so.

When we landed in Detroit I realized that these people weren't hard up at all. It was the weekend of October 11, which was my forty-second birthday, and I'd been flying high on opiates for two days when Stacey and I checked into The Townsend Hotel in Birmingham, which is just outside of Detroit. That place is a beautiful, kind of stuffy four-star hotel with generic hallways that look like the pictures you see of the inside of the White House. The people that hang out there, however, are not stuffy: the bar was always happening. I would have warmed up there with a drink, but withdrawals had kicked in, so there was no way I could be social. Besides, Stacey was with me, so I had to play it cool. I went to my room, realized that I didn't have nearly enough painkillers to get me through the weekend, and cursed myself to high heaven. I didn't know what to do—I knew no one in Detroit, and the measly number of pills in my hand weren't going to mean shit in about eight hours. I took them all, knowing I was in trouble, and did the only thing that made sense: I downed half the booze in the minibar, tipping back one little bottle after another, straight with no chaser, in about forty-five minutes. I remember thinking that was taking it easy, telling myself, *Okay, let's not get crazy here.* I wanted to drink all of it, but the other half was my backup plan in case I couldn't find pills at the gig. And it was the best I could do: with Stacey just next door I couldn't order booze from room service or sneak out to the bar.

I feel bad about it now because my minibar spree probably cost the kid and his family a mint. I usually pay for my excesses, so I feel guilty because this was the type of hotel where a bag of cashews costs twenty-five bucks and I'm pretty sure the minibar was the kind where moving anything incurs a charge. I'm guessing my bill was in the high hundreds because every time I went for another bottle I'd move the Diet Cokes and Toblerones I had no use for, which probably charged the room again. I also kept taking bottles out and looking at them, deciding which to drink first, then putting them back before I'd take them out again and drink them. By the end of this tour through the minibar I felt as decent as I was going to, which was great because it was showtime.

I met Stacey in the lobby and she took one look at me and just shook her head because she knew what was up.

My performance totally sucked, by the way. I was sluggish, out of it, and slurring—just bad. The audience could see that I was wasted, and so could I, but it seemed to me like they were cutting me slack since they knew this gig was a benefit. They were forgiving . . . well, all except for that one guy.

He weighed about four hundred pounds and he was sitting right up in front wearing a Detroit Tigers jersey that looked like he'd bought it new in 1979. He had a Windbreaker on over that, as if he'd just jogged a few miles to the show, along with some shorts, even though it was winter in Detroit, which isn't what one might call balmy. The guy had long hair and the kind of face that would look pissed off even when he was happy. I'd bet ten grand he had the same look on his face when Kirk Gibson hit that second home run in game five of the '84 World Series. Despite being born looking angry, I'm still pretty sure that the guy fucking hated me because from the start of my set he stared me down like a gang member gearing up for a knife fight. He didn't laugh at anything I said and he didn't frown at anything either; he didn't react to anything I did in any way at all. He just sat there, huge, looking like he wanted to fight the world, starting with me—and it drove me crazy.

Ask any comedian, it only takes one person like that in a crowd to throw them off for the night, and they don't even have to look like John Wayne Gacy in his clown suit. When you have one of those unwavering lumps in your sight line, they become all you focus on and nothing else matters but them. If you can't get them to laugh, you're a failure, and trust me, memories of them stay with you forever. Anyway, as shitty as my performance was that night, I had people laughing, but that meant nothing because I couldn't get to this guy in any way. I tried everything: jokes that always killed, stupid sight gags, making fun of myself more than I usually did, but it was useless. After a while I gave up trying to get a laugh and just started staring at him because he was a fucking freak show. I figured I'd try to return the favor by freaking him out the way he was freaking me out. Still, nothing.

About halfway through my set I repeated a joke I'd done ten minutes earlier—like I said, it was not my best night. And there it was, when I least expected it—I got a reaction from the guy. I was looking right at him at the time, so I know this for sure. As I started in on the joke, he began to scowl, and a look of pure disgust came over his face. This didn't tip me off because in my mind I'd won, so I kept going. Once I was too far into the joke to stop it or change direction, the guy crossed his arms and shouted, real loud, in this deadpan voice, "DID IT!" That's all: "DID IT!" He barked it out the way someone heckling a baseball player up at bat would yell it: "DID IT!"

I gotta hand it to him, that was funny—funnier than I was at that point. I stopped dead in my tracks, started laughing, and almost thanked him, because honestly he made my night. I thought he wasn't paying any attention at all, but apparently he'd been logging in my every word, keeping a box score of my stand-up routine. The guy had the focus that Jerry Sandusky would at a small-town Little League game. Now that I think of it the guy was wearing the same kind of shorts I could see those guys wearing. You know the kind I'm talking about? Those baggy beige cargo shorts worn by every deviant? I think they just pass the same pair around. The phone calls come in at the end of the week: "Hey, Gacy, can I get the shorts this weekend? I've got something lined up."

"Sorry, Sandusky, can't do it."

"You're fucking kidding me—really?"

"Relax, I don't even have them. Dahmer said he'd FedEx them from Milwaukee, but they're not here yet. You know what he's like; he never washes them. I'll have them to you by Tuesday, okay?"

That guy being the highlight of the evening, it's easy to see how this gig was pretty much a disaster, so I got out of there as fast as I could, went back to my room, and passed out. I hadn't scored pills, so I knew the morning would be terrible. I woke up at seven a.m. feeling like my skin was covered in fire ants. I was sweating, I started scratching uncontrollably, and I would have done anything to just get out of my body. The booze had worn off hours ago and there was no masking my screaming need for opiates. I half crawled my way to the minibar and started drinking the other half of it, trying to numb the pain. I never thought the day would come when I'd be excited to see mini bottles of Drambuie and Kahlúa. I don't remember much of the flight, but I kept myself pretty boozed up, desperate to keep the nausea at bay.

When we landed in Newark, I wasn't home free, because Stacey and I were meeting my mother, my uncles, and Adrienne at a birthday dinner for me. I insisted we stop by my apartment first because I had a stash of heroin there, but at that point I was too far gone into the withdrawals to straighten up and fly right. Withdrawals aren't some puddle you can clean up with the right-sized paper towel. What happens when you slip into them is that the further along you go, meaning the longer you go without opiates, the more incapacitated you get, so by the time I flew home, got to my apartment, and snorted four fat lines of heroin, it was too late. They helped but they weren't getting me anywhere close to normal; all I could hope for was arriving just outside of "functional," which hopefully was good enough to get me through dinner. Believe me, food was the last thing on my mind, because another thing that happens with withdrawals is that the physical need doesn't go away quietly, so even once you get the drugs in you, the sick feeling takes its time. I wasn't going to feel well, let alone high, that night unless I stayed home doing bag after bag of dope until I was out of my mind.

I was on the verge of breaking down through the entire meal. I was so uncomfortable I could have screamed and so miserable I wanted to cry. I wasn't kidding anyone, because I could barely keep up a conversation or enjoy any of the food. I sat there looking nervous and sick, just holding on for dear life until the meal was over. Afterward I went home and did some more dope, but it was too late: by the next morning I was so sick with withdrawals that I had to miss work. I woke up shivering and so nauseous that I couldn't move. I felt desperate, pinned to my sheets, soaked in sweat, and paralyzed as if I'd been nailed into an invisible coffin. Nothing could take away my chills or stop the sweats, and there was no way I'd be able to fake it through five hours on the air. I had no choice but to call in sick. Adrienne had stayed at my place that night, but as she usually did when I started snoring real bad, she went to sleep on the couch. When she woke up around seven and realized I was still in bed, she came running in telling me I was late—and saw what kind of shape I was in.

A few hours later my agent called and told me that the folks at *Stern* were being lenient, but they knew I'd been out of town doing stand-up and if I were going to book weekend gigs, I couldn't miss work. It wasn't cool and I knew it, but I had painted myself into a corner that weekend.

"Listen," I said to him. "I promise I'll stop traveling for live gigs next month after I do the last few I'm committed to." I'd been saying this for over a year.

I don't know why I kept doing it, I really don't. I've had a lot of time to think about this, and I know the greed had a lot to do with it—the greed for the money, the greed for the attention. And so did the drugs, but the upsides weren't greater than the hell I faced every Monday morning trying to resurrect myself to get to *Stern* on time. Those mornings were literally a living hell for me because of my withdrawals and exhaustion. When we were still living together, Adrienne would sleep on the couch when I went to work because she didn't want me waking her up at four thirty, and on those Sunday nights she knew I'd be even worse than usual by the time I got home from the road. She didn't know how to help me by this point, so she was just going crazy.

One of the last gigs I had on my list was playing the Beacon Theater in November, sold out, as part of the New York Comedy Festival. Once again, this was a big fucking achievement for me—one of the biggest. I remember Adrienne taking a picture of the marquee: ARTIE LANGE, SOLD OUT. I wanted that show to be special, so I hired two guys to play acoustic guitar as I sang the Allman Brothers' "Midnight Rider" as a tribute to the many years that band has done weeklong stands at the Beacon. My act was whatever at best—I know this because I was completely lit and don't remember it—so the only consolation I have when I think of this milestone is the fact that I got to sing that song on that stage no matter how good or bad my version was. My uncles were there and I had great openers—Nick DiPaolo, Joe Matarese, and Pete Dominick—so even if I sucked, I know the show was quality thanks to them. Like so many other things I wish I could go back and cherish, I couldn't even enjoy the after-party; I went home right afterward and passed out.

That year, somehow I actually made it to Thanksgiving at my mother's house for the first time in three years. It wasn't saying much, because this had been my second time in about six. Considering how close we live to each other, my stats were pathetic. There I sat, smiling, proud, claiming I was better, fitter, and happier than ever. I said I was booking no more stand-up gigs and would stay off the road for six months because I had to get my life in order. My mom and sister had heard this rap from me so many times that they didn't even react. They had gotten so fed up with it that they said nothing because they didn't know what to do. My sister was starting to worry about my mother's health because all of my antics were taking such a toll on her. My sister had started to talk to my mother about the fact that she was being dragged down with me and that maybe I wasn't capable of being saved. She didn't like facing that reality, but from her point of view it looked like she might lose both of us. Stacey was preparing herself for the worst and thinking that she could probably save our mom. My mother is made from different stuff: she is a true giver, a true nurturer, and she would attach herself to a sinking ship and go down with it to save one of her kids. When counselors told her to turn her back on me because that's what would help me the most, it made no sense to her, and she didn't do it. But she didn't know what to say either. So that's where our family was, emotionally, that holiday. To say that it was an awkward family meal is like saying that Vietnam was just a military exercise.

Adrienne wasn't with me that day; she was at her parents' house, and I really missed her. I was starting to fall deeper in love with her, experiencing feelings I'd never had with anyone in my entire life. I'd had a seven-year relationship with Dana, but the way I felt for Adrienne was in a different league altogether. I can't explain it, but that love began to take over everything else in my life. It was a new relationship and when we met she knew nothing about me, which was something that I really liked about her. She didn't know me from the *Stern Show*; she didn't know me at all. I was just Artie, and that was nice. She also didn't know anything about my problems with drugs, aside from what I told her. I warned her, but those words didn't do the reality justice. And when you fall in love, warnings like that are usually dismissed anyway, which I think is how Adrienne entered into things as we got more serious. She had no idea about me or my world and we came from very different backgrounds, and even though I told her that she was walking into a hurricane she went in anyway. I told her that if she ever wanted to drop out, I'd understand. I kept her in the dark about how tragic my life had been in the past when it came to the drugs. I think she saw me as a guy in showbiz who traveled a lot, but we had a lot of fun and it seemed like I had my issues under control. And for a while I did, but that didn't last, and when it all came apart, she saw the reality. She didn't know my drug patterns, so it was easy to keep it from her for quite some time. But Adrienne figured it out once we started living together, which began in the fall. There was nowhere to hide in a two-bedroom apartment. She forgave a lot, she excused a lot, until she couldn't anymore.

Somehow I stumbled into December, looking down the barrel of my last few gigs. Little did I know they'd be my last gigs for a very long time. I played the Wellmont Theatre in Montclair, New Jersey, on December 5, and don't remember one single detail about it. I really need to start a blackout library of all the gigs and appearances I don't remember. By my estimate it would be longer than the *Twilight* series. After the gig I went to dinner with my family at this Italian place in Newark because Montclair is next to Bloomfield and Newark, where I grew up. And that was that: I got the check that night, gave it to my mom to deposit, and told everyone at the table, "That's it, guys, I'm done with stand-up."

I planned to quit the road for at least a year to focus on *Stern*, on writing the sequel to *Too Fat to Fish*, and on getting off drugs for good. Stand-up money wasn't worth it if I was dead, and since I'd come to blame stand-up (and convinced my family of this too) for my drug abuse, this seemed like a huge step forward. The truth was that I was an addict and I'd be doing drugs regardless, but I didn't need to admit that out loud, did I?

The holidays were nearly upon me again, which has proven to be a critical time for me when it comes to drug abuse. I can't help getting caught up in the spirit of the season; I just have a different way of celebrating is all. This year, in honor of my vow to quit the road, I seemed intent to bring the road to me by upping my intake a notch. I was no longer into heroin because I'd become deeply paranoid and thought that it was safer to stick to pills. I worried that the heroin dealers might be talking to the cops and that I'd be the victim of a setup of some kind. I thought that the cops were staking me out and started hearing footsteps in the hallway and voices outside my door. After my DUI I thought I was being framed. Basically I started to act like Ray Liotta in the last half of *Goodfellas*, thinking every helicopter and every black car I saw was following me.

I was an addict—a bad one—and in December of 2009, despite my paranoia, I pushed my limits further than I ever had before, which if you've read this far you know is saying a lot. I combined everything I could get my hands on: all kinds of prescription pills, booze, even over-the-counter sleep medicine. Some nights I had terrors from these combinations that were beyond anything I'd even thought possible. I had been using drugs for so long that I felt like I could handle anything at anytime, plus I had a high tolerance, so I had to take a lot of whatever I was taking just to feel it. It was a recipe for disaster. I wasn't bigger and badder than the drugs, just fatter and more arrogant.

Adrienne didn't know what to do. She had moved in full-time because she was worried. And she had reason to be: I blacked out a bunch of times that month and I'd wake up in the bathroom or in the middle of the living room floor and she'd tell me that I'd been doing the craziest shit. One time I told her I was going to take the trash out and instead of taking it down the hall I put it in my bathtub, where she found it when she went to take a shower the next morning. That kind of shit became ordinary. I became so freaked out from mixing and matching all these drugs that I started really scaring the hell out of her. She hadn't asked Santa Claus for a paranoid addict for Christmas that year. She didn't like being around me, but she was afraid not to be around me. She cared for me and was convinced I'd die if she wasn't there to make sure I didn't overdose.

She tried to curb my abuse by hiding whatever pills or powders she found in the apartment or in my jacket, but I always had more stashed because there was no stopping me. I had regular appointments with various dealers, so I'd leave every morning about seven a.m. then again at seven p.m. for a few days in a row until I was good and stocked up. I'd make some dumb excuse about where I was going that I shouldn't have bothered with because Adrienne knew exactly what I was up to. One night when I guess she'd had enough she insisted on searching my pockets when I came back. When she found my drugs it didn't go over so well and we got into a huge fight that ended in a wrestling match over the drugs. It's embarrassing, but it's true, because at that point nothing mattered more to me than what was in that bag. I ended up getting the bag from her in the end.

"Look," she said, watching me gripping my stash the same way

Earl Campbell gripped a football whenever he dove for a first down, "I can't do this by myself anymore. If I find drugs on you again I'm calling your mother or Helicopter Mike or somebody else and they're going to come over and you're going to have to go away."

"You're right," I said. "I know. But I can't fucking do that now. I'll do it in the new year."

As I always had, I reacted by procrastinating and getting angry. I'd say I knew what had to be done but people had to let me do it my way and if they didn't want to they could fuck off. The truth was that "I'll do it in the new year" had been my excuse for years, and everyone who knew me was getting pretty fucking tired of hearing it.

CHAPTER 7

THIS IS THE END

I can say without any hesitation that December 9, 2009, was and will always be one of the saddest days of my life. I spent the early morning of that day drinking whiskey and snorting twenty painkillers over the course of seven hours before going into work at the *Stern Show*—and making it there on time. It was yet another instance where the lights were on but no one was home because I was in a full blackout on the air. I'd started making my driver stop at this deli down the street from the studio where I'd buy a few bottles of Smirnoff Ice that I'd put into plastic cups and pass off for soda that I'd drink all through the show. So I'd basically resigned myself to being drunk at work, live on the air, which I'd top off by taking whatever pills I had on me every time I went to the bathroom.

That's how I was operating that morning and I was pretty far gone when I got there. But I kept at it, getting progressively sloppier over the first few hours of the show. I spilled drinks and ate an eight-thousand-calorie breakfast burrito and a few cupcakes. I yelled, I interrupted everybody, I acted crazier and with less sense than ever. Benjy Bronk, my friend and *Stern Show* writer, sat next to me the whole time trying his best to contain the collateral damage. He kept saying, "Art, are you okay, man? You've got to calm down and just get through this day. Get through it, get home, and get some sleep."

This was, I can say without hesitation, the worst in a long line of bad shows. "Art, come on, man. Get it together, brother; you're ruining this," Scott DePace, the director of Howard TV, said to me during a commercial break. Scott was one of my very favorite people in the *Stern* family and he would have understood if I'd been honest, but why would I ever do that?

"Scott, I know, I'll get it together." I was bullshitting wildly, just looking to get into the next conversation. It could be about anything, it could be with anyone in earshot so long as it wasn't about me and my behavior.

Howard didn't know how to handle me that day and neither did Gary or Robin because I'd gone to another level. Everyone just kept shaking their heads because I was that far gone. Then, in the middle of the show, Tim Sabean asked me to leave.

"Art, just go home and get some sleep—you need it," he said.

The only time I'd ever been asked to leave was after the fight with Teddy. I understood it then, but I didn't see what the problem was today. And since I didn't leave after the fight with Teddy there was no way I was going anywhere. I just really hate being told what to do, especially when I'm fucked up.

"No, man, I'm fine," I said, slurring a bit. "I'm staying here for the whole show. That's what I get paid to do, so that's what I'm going to do. I'll sleep after."

I stayed for the whole show and I felt like I'd won a victory; I felt like I'd proved something. All that I'd done was seal my fate by confirming everyone's suspicion that I was in desperate need of help. My family had heard me that morning too, and so did most of my friends. After the show ended I went to Newark to get more pills, probably at the same time that the *Stern* producers were on the phone with my mother and sister, all of them very concerned and unsure what to do about me.

I got back to my apartment, snorted a bunch of whatever I'd gotten, so I was good and buzzed when Tim Sabean called.

"Art, why don't you take a week off and consider going to rehab again," he said. "We want you to be okay more than we care about having you on the show."

"Okay," I said reluctantly. "Is this an order? I've been fine. I was on time today."

"It's not an ultimatum, Artie, but it's what we'd like you to do."

"That's fine."

My mother's call came in next, and only when I heard how upset she was did I realize that yes, finally I really needed to get some help. I told her I'd check myself in somewhere, then called the *Stern Show* and told them I was doing it, I was definitely going to rehab, which they were thrilled to hear. I was really disappointed that I was going to miss Howard's Christmas party, though, because he was throwing a big one, which he'd never done before. I'd bought Adrienne a dress for it and now, because I wasn't able to hold it together, I'd be in rehab instead of there with her in that beautiful dress. I kept telling myself that it would all be okay, though, because this would be a quick trip. I'd do what I'd done in the past, just get clean while making a lame pass at participating in the program. I'd return and be better than ever, as if I'd spent a long weekend away in the Poconos. Hopefully this place would have colonics like the "spa" in Florida I'd detoxed in. Instead, December 9, 2009, was my last day on the *Howard Stern Show*, and that quick vacation? It lasted two and a half years.

I've thought a lot about how to explain just how much my time on *Stern* means to me, but I still can't find the right words to do it justice. There are so many memories, so many upsides, that the way I left was even more of a fuckup. It was also just so me. It reminds me of a Springsteen lyric from the song "The Wrestler": "You know me, I always leave with less than I had before." I've always been self-destructive and most of the time I have left with less than I had before, whether we're talking about a relationship, a job, or chips at the blackjack table. I left a decade of being a lead cohost on the greatest radio show ever made in the worst way I could imagine. It's up there with the day my father died as one of the two worst days of my life. I miss everyone at the *Stern Show* so much. I miss having fun and I miss the fans. And I thank God for those fans too. It's because of them that I still have a career. It's because of them that I'm still alive, because having people out there, in need of entertainment, keeps me going. And I'll never take it for granted.

––– ––– ––– –––

I'd agreed to go to rehab, but like all of my other promises, I had no intention of following through. I loved talking about rehab, I loved talking about making changes—all that talk was so exciting that I didn't feel I had to actually do anything. This was great because I might have been lying to everyone else, but I'd come to a conclusion, once and for all, that I kept to myself: I was never going to rehab—ever! I didn't need that shit, because I didn't want to be clean—ever! I would keep bullshitting people forever! I'd agree to everything and never do it! This wasn't much of a plan, but I was enthusiastic about sticking with it.

That kept things the way they were until the night Adrienne found drugs on me while I was passed out and called in the cavalry. When I woke up, my mother and sister, along with Helicopter Mike and Joe the Cop, were there and they took me to a rehab on Long Island. I claimed that I had no problem with this, but it was inconvenient because it was happening earlier than I'd planned to go—yeah, because I never planned to go. That same day, on December 12, 2009, Adrienne packed her things and moved out of my apartment for good. We blew a kiss to each other as the front door closed and I didn't know it at the time but I wouldn't see her again for over two years. That moment and that image of her is always on my mind, and it makes me sad every time I think about it, much more than all of the tragic moments that lay in store for me put together. Adrienne was such a positive light in my life and things between us ended in a truly awful way. I dragged her down into the shit I was determined to make of my life. It's something she didn't deserve and something I couldn't help.

The rehab was in eastern Long Island and if I'd wanted to be there, even just a little, it would have been a nice place to be. But I didn't, so I fucking hated everything about it, nearly as much as I hated everything about my life at that moment, from me to the people who cared enough to bring me there. My roommate was a cool enough guy, probably because he wasn't really an addict. He'd gotten a DUI and was headed to court and thought that it would look good to the judge if he checked himself into a rehab facility. He was such a positive dude in addition to being one of the most organized people I've ever met in my life. He was the kind of guy who would see you making your bed and come over and help you, showing you how to do it better, but never in a bossy or superior way. Trust me, most people you meet in rehab aren't like that.

Most people you meet in rehab are a lot like me: addicts who haven't grown up, who can't control themselves, and who have fucked up their lives so much that getting sober is their only hope. I met a lot of guys there who I understood immediately and we shared a lot of laughs, usually at the expense of other people in our group therapy sessions. There was one girl who bore the brunt of it more than anyone else. She was probably about forty years old and I swear to God, she looked exactly like Flavor Flav. I remember sitting there thinking that the first time she got up and spoke in group, but before that thought was even complete, two of the guys next to me shouted out, in perfect homage to the guy: "Flavor Flaaaav!" I felt like an asshole but I couldn't contain my laughter, and I busted up for about two minutes straight while the poor girl told us how she'd lost her babies to the state foster system. The release I got from laughing at pretty much the most juvenile joke anyone could have made at her expense was definitely the most constructive thing I got out of group that day. The problem was that the joke didn't die because this girl liked to get up and talk about the many horrible things that had happened to her because of drugs at every opportunity she got. It didn't matter how bad her confessions ever were: the moment she stood up, just like clockwork (*clock*work—get it? Flavor Flav wore a clock!) me and the two other guys would shout, "Flavor Flaaaav!"

That was about as entertaining as things got there, which didn't ease the pain of being in rehab when I could have been at Howard Stern's Christmas party. My first night was terrible and sleepless, because when you come out of a drug haze you start to see how all of your actions caused reactions. I'd disrespected the *Stern Show*, and I'd disrespected what was becoming a very loving, real relationship and managed to fuck myself out of everything good in my life once again. The worst part about this realization was that I still had no idea why I had done those things and why I kept doing them over and over. I had no answers, only questions—and more feelings than I could handle. I couldn't stop my thoughts from coming, so I curled myself into a ball and cried as hard as I ever have. My body shook and tears ran down my cheeks as I tried in vain to hold it all in. I didn't want my roommate to hear me, but it was no use, so I pulled the covers over my head and stuffed my face into the pillow and sobbed harder than a mama's boy does on his first night at sleepaway camp.

At least I was consistent: after the physical detox was over for me eight days later, I checked myself out of there, because I considered rehab a detox where you were given free pajamas with the price of admission. For those who don't know, if you voluntarily check yourself into a rehab you can voluntarily check yourself out at any time. If you're committed to one by your family, legal guardian, or the state, however, it's a whole other story. Once I decided I was done, I was back home in Hoboken by December 23, and within an hour of my arrival was taking healthy swallows from a liter of Jack Daniel's. Soon enough I remembered that I'd stashed a handful of Vicodin where Adrienne would never find them and in no time they were smashed up into lines, ready to be snorted up my nose. I did everything I had at once, and boy, did I feel fucking fantastic—sad, pathetic, and lonely, but fucking fantastic.

I missed Christmas Eve and I missed Christmas Day because I spent both of them locked up in my apartment by myself, getting high on pills and booze. I didn't shower and I barely ate. I didn't have to—I got most of my calories by drinking, as the days slipped by, carrying me away on an ocean of whiskey.

My shrink—the same one I had been seeing for a while—had put me on an antidepressant called Lexapro back in September, and I'd started abusing that as well, because for some reason I thought taking them in high quantities would get me high. Since antidepressants regulate serotonin you're supposed to be careful about mixing them with drugs and alcohol and you're supposed to monitor how they make you feel on a regular basis. I didn't do any of that; I just treated them like another pill despite the fact that I'd never heard (and still haven't) that they get you high when abused.

By the time I ran out of Vicodin on New Year's Eve I'd lost all reason, so it made sense to me that a handful of Lexapro, rather than the one a day I was supposed to take, would make me sleepy—which was the only effect I was trying to achieve. I couldn't bear the thought of just getting tired, or even worse, having my thoughts keep me awake until the sickness of the drug withdrawals took over. I had to lose consciousness and give my exhausted, wired mind a rest because I'd had enough of this holiday binge I'd arranged for myself. I hoped that I'd sleep for a week, I *wanted* to sleep for a week. By New Year's I'd had enough of my own binge. I could only keep a bender up so long before reality seeped in. I hated that so much: even if I was still getting a high from the drugs on day five, my mind would be so filled up with all of the thoughts and feelings I'd been trying to escape because, like anything else, you can run but you can't hide. That's where I was by New Year's, so at that point the only escape from what I didn't want to face was sleep.

Like I said, sleep wasn't going to come easy because opiates, in addition to satisfying my addiction, also made me peppy and perky. It didn't help that I was stressed out and depressed, both of which also kept me awake, just staring at the ceiling at night. It was torture to be that exhausted and miserable, knowing withdrawals were coming a few hours later, and unable to just fade to black. Heroin was always so great for that: it gives you the most incredible feeling of falling into an abyss. Nothing else matters, all your problems are gone and you're on your way to passing out into blissful sleep before you know it.

I didn't have any, so I figured that twenty-three antidepressants washed down with whiskey would do the trick. That's exactly what I took, then lay back on my couch, waiting for that sway to come over me and take me off to dreamland. I wanted that knocked-out opiate rush and was willing to get something close to it however I could. Well, here's what I found out: ingesting twenty-three Lexapro does not make you sleepy, not one bit. It makes you fucking psychotic. I started twitching, hallucinating, got incredibly paranoid, and heard strange sounds including a high-pitched ringing in my ears. Not long before this I'd gotten so paranoid that I believed—truly believed— that people were out to get me. I'm not talking about my family coming over for an intervention, I'm talking about people coming to murder me. I had gotten so sloppy with gambling that I wasn't sure if I owed people money and I started believing that I did and that a few bookies would be sending hit men to collect. Whenever I heard someone in the hallway I'd get down on the floor and peek through the crack at the bottom of the door trying to see who it was while trying to be as quiet as possible. I started keeping a bat near the door, convinced, every day, that today would be the day it might save my life from the murderers in the hall

I spent New Year's Eve in bed, in the dark for the most part, shaking, believing I heard someone in the living room every five minutes. My apartment has a beautiful view of New York City, and I remember looking out at it as the clock struck midnight thinking about the people having fun over there as I sat cooped up and alone, by choice. New Year's Day is also Adrienne's birthday, which made me feel five thousand times worse. I was so sad that we weren't together, and I missed her so much that I began to shudder uncontrollably all over my body. It felt like every inch of my body, inside and out, was whimpering and crying. The events of the last year kept spinning through my mind and as I went over them, I became so desperate, realizing that I'd had it all and had let it go simply because I had no self-control and seemed to like tearing things down more than I did building them up.

I remembered that I had another bottle of Jack stashed in a closet, so I went and got it and started chugging. I started scouring the place for extra pills, and when I found more antidepressants and a few sleeping pills I threw all of them down my throat at once. After half the whiskey was gone I finally got sleepy. Eventually I passed out.

I slept through most of the next day, straight through to four a.m. on January 2, 2010, when I awoke completely and sat bolt upright in bed because I realized that I was out of booze and drugs of any kind. Ingesting anything else would have been like throwing gas on a bonfire because the ludicrous mix of drugs I already had in my body was making me acutely anxious. My thoughts were a mess: just a stream of consciousness that I couldn't stop, most of it terrible. I realized very clearly that I was a lost cause, just like my high school guidance counselor predicted. No matter how successful I'd ever be, no matter how many impossible goals I achieved, I thought to myself, I'll always be a loser. I'll never get off drugs anyway, so there is no point in trying to stop ever again. It made more sense to me to keep at it until it killed me. The way I was living was no way to live. It was a ride with only one way out. That's what was going through my mind.

Thoughts of my father came to me too, over and over, as did the fact that I was exactly the same age he had been when he'd fallen off that roof and become a quadriplegic. I'd always feared turning forty-two because of what happened to him, as if the same thing lay in store for me just because I'd turned forty-two. In my mind, the fact that all of my struggles were coming to a head was a sign. I'd become a self-fulfilling prophecy in a way, because I could still walk around, but in every practical way I was as crippled and incapable of changing myself as my father had been when he'd become a quadriplegic.

I sat on my couch, unable to sleep, unable to make my mind stop, wishing I could just feel high. I wanted heroin. I wanted to forget life and nod in and out until I found some rest. As I watched the sun rise over Manhattan, I started shaking (it had to be the antidepressants) like a leaf in a hurricane. My entire body was vibrating uncontrollably and there was nothing at all I could do to stop it. I wasn't hot, I wasn't cold, I was just uncomfortable and trembling. I lit a cigarette and watched the smoke rise from my shaky hand. I stared out the window at the most beautiful view, not knowing what to do with myself. I figured I'd need to go to the hospital to get the nodded-out feeling I was after; I'd need to be admitted for something in order to get an IV of downers.

I didn't want to die; that thought never crossed my mind. I just wanted to feel. I wanted to float away on a high and fall asleep, away from the thoughts that wouldn't leave me alone. That is the seduction of opiates: a false sense of security and the promise of a good night's rest. I wanted that bliss—not the shakes, not the comedown or withdrawal, just the high and a long day's sleep. I started to think about how I could simulate it since I didn't have the drugs to make it happen and could in no way leave the house to get them. I didn't check the bottle of Lexapro, but I'm pretty sure it didn't advise taking twenty-three at once under any circumstances.

What I'm about to tell you is going to sound psychotic. Believe me, I've gone over it many, many times and it still makes no sense. It's the most insane thing I've ever done or ever even heard of, but trust me when I tell you that it made sense to me at the time. In that moment, that moment of desperate need, I logically believed that what I did next would get me where I needed to be. I believed that my actions would make the physical discomfort stop and that they would also give me a brief sense of escape followed by the peace of sleep I was desperate for.

I got up off my couch, went to the closet where my maid keeps her supplies, and got a bottle of Clorox bleach. I went back to the couch, sat down, removed the cap, and took a swig. I did this four times, thinking that bleach was so toxic it would get me high then make me pass out. Yeah . . . not exactly. Instead I threw up violently, everywhere. I vomited like a fountain, all over the couch, all over the carpet, and all over myself. I fell to the floor and kept vomiting. I got up, slipping and sliding in the puddle of puke, as I stumbled to my terrace to get some fresh air. I vomited all over the terrace and terrace door as bleach, blood, booze, pills, and whatever food I'd eaten in the last twenty-four hours came out of me.

I fell again, hitting my head so hard on the living room floor that I almost passed out. My body stopped convulsing once there was nothing left to throw up and for a moment I came close to sleep, until one involuntary jerk woke me again. I couldn't take it because I felt sicker and more horrible than ever. I had to get that passed-out feeling but I didn't know what else to do. I was too sick to run into a wall or try to knock myself out (but I thought about it), so the only thing I could think of that would make me faint was losing blood. I didn't want to die, I just wanted to lose enough to lower my blood pressure. Then I'd faint, fall asleep, and finally get some rest. This seemed like a logical thing to do at the time. I didn't even consider what would have happened after I fell asleep, after losing that much blood. None of that mattered, only finding the falling feeling. What can I say, I've never been good at planning ahead.

I went to the kitchen and got the biggest chef's knife I had. Then I lay down on the couch and cut into my stomach. I'd stab it a bit, then slice into it, and then squeeze the wounds to make the blood run out faster. I continued to do this—a stab followed by a cut—as my blood flowed. I watched it run down my legs, onto the couch and floor, just staring at the color of it. I didn't feel any pain after the first few cuts, just the strange invasion of the knife, but after a few rounds of stabbing I got used to it. I started to dig the knife in deeper and slice into myself harder. In the hospital they counted a total of nine wounds, three of them deep enough to really make the red run. I started to feel light-headed and woozy, which made me want to lie down in my bed. I'd get some sleep after all.

I got up, my head spinning, and shuffled through the pool of blood, vomit, and bleach on the floor. My hand left a trail of red along the wall as I made my way to the bedroom and since my blood had been running out at a steady rate for some time, I began to feel faint. I made it to the bed, lay down, and began to nod in and out of consciousness. It was what I'd wanted to do for hours.

Sometime around nine a.m. my mother called me to say that she wanted to come over and talk. I vaguely remember this.

"I guess," I said. "Whatever, I don't care, come over."

"Art, are you okay?" she asked.

"Yeah, yeah, I'm fine, I can answer a call." Whatever that meant.

I lay in my bed watching the red puddle spread slowly across the sheets. As I went to put the phone back on the nightstand I fell out of bed onto the floor but was too weak to get up. I lay there watching my blood—and my life—stream out of me, lost, detached, feeling myself starting to slip away.

I only remember a few more things. I heard the door open when my mother arrived. And I heard her screaming as soon as she saw the blood. I remember seeing her face above me, which is a horrifying image that I will never forget, and one that causes me more guilt than I can ever express.

"Artie! Stay with me, Artie!" my mother shouted. Her face went blurry and her voice sounded very faraway. "Don't you go away from me, Artie! Don't you go!" She was crying, sobbing, pleading. It looked like I was seeing her through water, as if she were in another world.

I reached up and she grabbed my hand as she dialed 911 with her other hand, and I remember the frantic tone in her voice as she yelled into the phone.

"My son has stabbed himself! Please hurry, he's stabbed himself!"

That's what I've put my poor mother through. That's how I've taken care of her. I may have given her money, a house, and a car, but nothing material can take that pain away.

My sister came running into the room at that point, which I remember thinking was odd, because she should have been at work. What I found out later was that they had planned a formal, full-court-press intervention featuring Colin Quinn, my two uncles, a cousin, and another close friend, all of whom were waiting downstairs in the lobby of my building. My sister and my mother held me in their arms, stopped the bleeding the best they could, and made sure I stayed awake. I went in and out of consciousness, but I remember my sister calling Colin downstairs to tell him how they'd found me. Then she turned to me with tears in her eyes.

"Artie, why do you want to die so badly?" she asked me. "Why are you so sad? You can't die! We love you too much."

The simplest of sentiments are the most true, and Stacey had said it all. How could I ever forget that? How could I ever go back? How did I ever let it come to this?

I heard the sirens in the distance and I heard a group of official-sounding people come into my apartment. The paranoia was still with me, so my first thought was that they were cops, but I didn't worry because I knew I'd done every single drug in the house by then. The EMTs stopped the bleeding and put me on a stretcher. And as they wheeled me out I saw my mother and sister crying, holding hands, hovering over me.

"Don't leave us, Artie," my mother said.

"Don't close your eyes, okay?" my sister said. "Stay awake."

I tried to do that as long as I could, but my eyelids weighed a ton. I let them drop, and as the noise faded away and I slipped into the black, I finally found some kind of peace.

CHAPTER 8

BED, BED, AND BEYOND

After I stabbed myself and my mother found me, saving me once again, I lost consciousness and woke up three days later in the Intensive Care Unit of New Jersey Medical Center. The first people I saw were Robin Quivers and *Stern Show* producer Tim Sabean, who were sitting right next to my bed. They had been there for hours and had visited every day hoping I'd come out of it, hoping they'd get a chance to talk to me and thinking at times, I'm sure, that it might be the last time they'd see me alive.

"We're here," they said. "We're so sorry. We love you. We miss you, Artie. Please get better."

By the time I came to for good I'd gone through surgery, where a great surgeon had stitched up my wounds. Physically I was fine, aside from being sore and not being able to move much without causing blood to leak from the wounds. I'm lucky that I didn't hit any major arteries or any organs because I would have bled to death immediately. I'd cut into my skin and muscle pretty badly, though, and I'd lost so much blood all over my living room and bedroom that I needed blood transfusions. I'd find out later that I'd disturbed the balance in my bloodstream so much that I had become anemic. I was on an IV to keep me hydrated and another to keep me sedated and I had bloody bandages on my stomach and a catheter tube in me, which is just a horrible thing. It wasn't my first time either: I've had catheters in my dick four times in my life, all of them due to being so fucked up on drugs that I needed to be hospitalized.

My mind was foggy and I was confused when I saw Robin and Tim and everyone at my bedside, but I was coherent enough to realize that I wasn't going to die and that I'd lived through whatever I'd done. My memory of the events weren't crystal clear, but I knew that I hadn't meant to die. . . . At the same time I wasn't sure how happy I was that I hadn't died. I know it's confusing, but put it this way: I knew that I hadn't meant to kill myself and only then did I begin to understand how little I'd thought about what would have happened if I had fallen asleep the way I wanted to when I started stabbing myself (I would have died). I didn't mean to die and I wasn't trying to, but at the same time I wouldn't really have been disappointed if I had died. Like I said, all I wanted was to go to sleep, and if I'd woken up dead—whatever that means—I wouldn't have been disappointed.

I remember lying there in my hospital bed looking at all the faces in the room thinking, *Who knows? Maybe I* am *dead.* I was on a morphine drip, which probably had something to do with how detached I felt, but then again, I was so used to opiates maybe that's the only reason I was coherent at all. It was foggy; it was all a bad dream. I was floating there, just staring at everyone, feeling like a zombie. I had no idea what to say, so I said nothing. Maybe I was still alive according to this universe, but maybe this is what it means to be dead, sitting here in a hospital room being visited by people who wish you were still alive. Maybe that is what we experience before we truly leave the earth. I didn't know and I didn't know who the fuck *would* know, because there's not really a buzzer for that kind of question on the hospital bed remote. And so the confusion set in. And it made my head explode. "Maybe I'm in hell, maybe I'm in heaven, maybe I'm in purgatory—I don't know." All I did know was that I was still here somehow, and there wasn't anyone who could tell me what the fuck to do next.

My mother and sister put on a brave face for Robin and Tim, but they had been crying and they had been sleeping there in my room on a cot together for two and a half days. They never left my side and all I could think about was how much suffering I'd caused them once again. I was insanely embarrassed and didn't know what to say, so I just lay there in silence mostly. I realized that Tim and Robin weren't just people I worked with; they were friends, and I felt guilty for troubling them.

I spent a total of four days in the hospital, checked in under the name Brian Carter in an effort to duck the media. Unfortunately there was more interest in me than I expected, so it was just insanity, none of which was helped by the *Post* when they ran the headline "Lange Stabs Himself" with a very flattering picture of me looking completely inhuman and out of it. I didn't see that piece when it came out, but I did later on when I was in somewhat better shape. And I'd say that little piece of print set me back ten steps in my recovery because it made me feel lower than shit on a shoe. I got so upset when I saw it because they'd dug up an old interview and recycled the quotes, taking things out of context to make it look like the signs had always been there and the *Post* had seen them first.

There was no hiding from the world finding out, but Brian Carter tried his best. That alias, by the way, came courtesy of the hospital, who made it up to sound generic. A few months later when I'd started to piece together the events of those first few days and had become capable of talking about them with Colin Quinn, he wouldn't let it go because the name cracked him up.

"Who chose Brian Carter?" he said. "He sounds like a member of a boy band, and since he was you, obviously he's the one with the problems who doesn't get invited to the reunion tour."

"Yeah, I know," I said, "and I don't really look like a Brian, but

I think that name was the right choice. Maybe it got me more respect because there had to be some nurse in there who thought I was a former Backstreet Boy who'd really gone downhill. A name like that made me want to get thinner, that's for sure."

The thing about Brian Carter is that the guy stuck with me through every institutionalization that followed (and there were a few) because whenever I was admitted, that was the name at the top of my file, so that's what they used. He was like Vanilla Ice if I were Rob Van Winkle, except I really didn't hate the guy. Anyway, since I'd attempted suicide, I was required by law to spend time under surveillance in a mental hospital after my stay in Intensive Care. I was Brian Carter there too, and after that, over the course of the next two years, I was in and out of a few rehabs, and each time I was admitted they asked if I wanted to be Brian Carter or Artie Lange. A few times I took them up on the offer not only because I felt like I'd gotten to know this guy Brian pretty well, but also just in case a paparazzi or an ambulance-chasing gossip columnist hack happened to be roaming the halls looking for Artie Lange's room that night. Brian Carter . . . he sounds like he must be a born-again Christian, but to me he's always been a second cousin of Lil Wayne.

The first few days I spent awake in Intensive Care while my wounds healed were also a complete daze because I was given morphine, at first by IV then by shots administered every two hours. That was fine by me—in fact I really, really enjoyed it, because I had no desire to feel anything clearly at all. A bunch of great people came to visit me, including my hero Colin Quinn, my uncles, my aunts, my cousins, my mother and sister, of course, and Nick DiPaolo. Nick was one of the few comics (I can count them on one hand and have already named two of them) who came to see me. I understand it and I'm not mad, because I'm sure a lot of them wanted to come see me but just couldn't do it because it would have been too difficult for them. Seeing me would have brought up their own issues in a way they wouldn't be able to ignore.

As the reality of what I'd done that morning came into focus for me, an overwhelming sense of paranoia came with it and nothing could keep that under wraps. I knew there were reporters outside, but I thought I saw them everywhere. If my door was opened a crack, I'd swear I saw a guy with a pad or a camera walk by and eyeball me. I was convinced that the nurses who came to take care of me knew something I didn't know, or maybe they were on the take, telling the spies in the hall what I was doing so they could write it up in tomorrow's paper. I wanted to see the papers but I was too scared; I was smart enough to know I couldn't handle that shit yet. My mother would tell me that she was impressed with how Howard was defending me, because she was. The King of All Media was telling everyone to leave her son alone, and she was impressed by that. Still, I'd ask my family about what had been written about me and no matter what they said I was always convinced that they'd lied. My shame was that enormous. I was convinced they were too scared to tell me the truth. One time they even brought me a paper with a big headline that said "Stern Defends Lange." The article was great, but it didn't calm me down at all because I was convinced it wasn't real. I figured they'd had it printed up somewhere.

My biggest worry once I'd "come to" was how Howard had taken the news and what his reaction was. I'd stabbed myself a day before the show returned from its holiday break and I couldn't imagine how hard it had been for him to deal with that and all the publicity. My mother and sister told me over and over how nice Howard had been on the air during that first week after I'd stabbed myself. They'd tell me how he defended me to every fan that called in to say something negative about me. I was so paranoid that I didn't believe them, but I did get some kind of comfort from the thought that maybe, just maybe, there was some truth to what they were saying. I was just so paranoid about public opinion of me, what some crazy caller would say on the air, and the fact that Howard would have to deal with that. The idea of all that happening out there and me not being able to do anything started to make me feel smothered, and after four days in the ICU I was completely claustrophobic. I just had to get out, back to the world somehow, even though I wasn't anywhere close to ready. I was only in that place four days, but thank God I had insurance, because the stay still cost me something like eighty-six grand.

So it was out of the frying pan and into the fire, because the next stop on my crazy train was the psych ward. Like I said, by law I had to spend at least seventy-two hours under observation in a state facility because I'd deliberately hurt myself. This was no surprise to me because I'd been through it before back when I was on MADtv in 1995 and overdosed on pills in a misguided suicide attempt. My family and I tried to pick a psych ward in the area, and let me tell you, if you haven't had the chance to bond with your loved ones, try choosing a psych ward together. It will bring you a lot closer than debating what you'd all like to have on the next pizza you share. It was one of the strangest conversations we've ever had, but we all agreed that one not too far away with a good reputation was what we were after. But to take it back to pizza, if you're in a strange town, how well do you know the local pizzerias anyway?

The administrator at Jersey City Medical Center was honest with us: she said that the psych ward in their facility was pretty intense and that I should go elsewhere, so we found a place in central Jersey, but didn't fare much better. Put it this way, I won't name the place because I don't have very nice things to say about it and I do plan to say them. The day I was transferred all of my relatives came to see me off, and they were crying—my mother, my aunts, my sister. My mother and sister had been sleeping in my hospital room every night, so they were completely exhausted. I put them through so much: one of those four nights I woke up miserable because the morphine had worn off and I needed more and seeing my sixty-eight-year-old mother curled up in a ball in her sweatpants, with my little sister next to her on that cot next to me, tore me up inside. My poor sister had to get up at six a.m. to get to work on time, but there she was. Because of those two strong women I'm still alive, and there's a level of guilt inside me that I'll never get over. It's hard for me to think about it, even still, even in passing.

The hospital I was transferred to looked great online, so much so that I'd made a joke about picking up a pair of sandals in the gift shop downstairs because apparently I was going to the Caribbean! The pictures in the brochure promised flat-screen TVs in the rooms and there was a shot of a nice gym area. Basically the place looked like a resort. What they should have, in my humble opinion, are pictures of a guy playing Scrabble while his opponent stares blankly into space, or maybe a patient eating another patient's throw-up. Those images would convey the feeling of what it's like to spend time there. I would even go for something more bold, like a picture of one patient trying to cram another patient's head into a blender in the TV lounge beneath the beautifully tranquil landscape paintings you'll find on the premises. Let's face it, when you're going to a psych ward, how great can it ever be? This place took my insurance, and that's what decided it, but I should have known the day was going to suck the second my catheter came out. That is never a good time, but this one was just awful because the morphine had worn off completely, and boy, how I missed it. The removal of a catheter, which any man who has experienced it can tell you, is one of the worst sensations a guy can have. Going in is smooth but coming out sure as hell isn't, and if I can give anyone in that situation a piece of advice it's this: don't look down. You don't want to see how long that fucking thing is, because if you do, you'll want to die if you're not dead already.

I was loaded onto a stretcher and strapped in like a mental patient, which technically I was. Now let me preface my next statement by saying I have a lot of respect for the guys who drive ambulances, because that job is no picnic, but the ones I've met, particularly during that week of my life, weren't the brightest bulbs on the tree—any tree. Here's an example. This is the conversation I had with one of them as we were getting ready to leave Jersey City Medical Center for the psych ward.

"There's a guy with a pad outside," he said. "He's downstairs."

"Excuse me?" I said.

"There's a guy with a pad asking questions downstairs," he said.

"A guy with a pad . . . you mean a notepad? Like a pad where you write things down?" I asked.

"Yeah," he said, "a pad like that. It's like a little book."

"So there's a guy with a notepad and he's writing things down and he's down there asking questions," I said.

"Yeah."

"That's a reporter."

"Yeah, that's what he was," the guy said. "He was, yeah, a reporter."

"He was, yeah, a reporter, huh? And you talked to him?"

"Yeah, he was talking to everyone."

"So what did you say?" I couldn't believe this shit.

"When I saw him in the lobby I didn't say anything," the guy said.

"Well, that's good."

"But then he asked me who I was going to pick up and I said that when I came back down he'd find out. He was guessing you, but I didn't tell him that. I told him he'd have to wait and find out. So he doesn't know."

"Oh, perfect! That's great. Thanks for that."

I can't tell you how much anxiety rushed into my veins at that moment. I'd been picturing the press as a pack of wolves waiting to attack me the moment I left my hospital room and this genius made those fears a reality. The guy did realize how pissed I was so he did me a solid and rushed me through the parking lot. It was a scene: me, the ambulance guys, and a pack of reporters running across the parking lot to an ambulance while my poor family jogged behind us. The reporters were relentless, asking when I'd be back on *Howard*, why I'd stabbed myself, and just about everything else you can imagine.

"The show?" I managed to say. "Yeah, I'll be back on tomorrow for the news."

The guys loaded me into the ambulance and my mom and sister followed us to the psych ward of the hospital I won't name. It was nighttime and the idiots in the ambulance ran a red light, causing us to lose my mom, so I yelled at them to pull over. Being a backseat driver was the last thing I felt up to, but that's how bad these guys were at their job.

When we arrived, the place wasn't open and the night guard wasn't around, which wasn't a good sign. By the time someone showed up, about an hour and a half later, to let me in, it was three a.m., which didn't help the place look any better. I tried to tell myself that it only looked like the set of *Hostel* because it was so late and dimly lit. I found out the next day that the place was grotesque in any light. There were mice running around, and I can't imagine what the rehab unit must have looked like because the psych ward made LA County Jail look like the Four Seasons. The place was so bad that I wasn't going to stay there one minute longer than I had to. The problem was that I wasn't legally allowed to leave for at least one night, then it would probably be another day before my poor mother and sister could arrange to get me into another facility. I wanted out immediately, but as the doctor explained to us, if he committed me I could end up there indefinitely, but if I admitted myself I would be able to leave voluntarily the next day, so that's what I did.

I had to go through processing, which involved a complete shakedown. An orderly was assigned to me and he went through my bag, removing everything that could be construed as a weapon and other potentially harmful objects like toothpaste, my toothbrush, and my roll-on deodorant. It was worse than jail, and here's why: when you end up in jail, it's likely you didn't intend to go there, but in the psych ward you've willingly surrounded yourself with insane people. Since insane people have invisible triggers no one can predict, most of your stuff has to go, including clothing with logos—but as you'll see, their judgment on what constitutes a logo was very subjective. A psych ward is the kind of place where wearing a Yankees shirt might get you killed if you end up sitting next to a psychotic Red Sox fan, although the term "psychotic Red Sox fan" is redundant. Everything you wear in the psych ward has to be pretty plain and unexciting so that even something that mentions beer (like the *Beer League* shirt I never got back) was illegal. Basically I entered the place with nothing more than a couple of plain white undershirts, my gray *Jimmy Kimmel Live!* shirt (a logo that was apparently acceptable), and one pair of gray sweatpants. I wasn't done, though, because after my bag was empty and my clothes were taken away, I had a strip search to look forward to. I was in a place with people so crazy that some of them didn't know what year it was and others thought they were from another planet, but when I got my shirt off, the orderly freaked out over my scars and stitches.

"What is all that?" he asked.

"They're stab wounds," I said.

"Who did that to you?"

I almost came out with a story. I wanted to tell him I was in a gang fight because I was so embarrassed, but I didn't do that. I was too exhausted to be a wiseass. Besides, I had to learn to tell the truth and I had to get used to it, so for the first time, I said it out loud.

"No one did that to me," I said. "I did it to myself."

The guy got quiet because he was really taken aback. It was the same as punching out the biggest con on the cell block—from then on I was considered the king of the nuts by the orderlies. I went to my room after the strip search and met my roommate, who was an Asian kid. I didn't plan on making friends, but he was nice enough and very quiet. Until about 5:30 a.m., that is, when he woke up screaming bloody murder because the Thorazine and Methadone he was unaware of being addicted to had worn off and left him in a living hell.

"My ears are bleeding!" he yelled. "My ears!" He wasn't lying either; blood was running from both of his ears, all over the sheets.

I got up and grabbed one of the T-shirts I'd been allowed to keep and tried to stop the bleeding while I yelled for help. The nurses and two guards came into the room and strapped the kid down as one of the guards got in my face.

"Go to sleep; don't worry about this," he said.

Oh, no problem, I thought to myself. *I'll just go over to my little corner of heaven and drift off to dreamland.* What, did the guy think I had a cabin with a fireplace waiting for me over there in my bed? Did he think the Asian kid's screaming sounded like an angel's harp?

I finally got to sleep sometime around 6:30 a.m., after spending an hour staring into the abyss. I also stared at the drawings that the former lunatics who had been there had done on the wall, and I kept running my hands over my stitches and scars as one question repeated itself over and over in my head: *What the fuck did I do?* I knew I only had two hours of sleep ahead of me because my wounds were still so raw that the nurses had to change my bandages that often. Every time one of them came in I watched their eyes when they saw my stomach. These were nurses on a psych ward—they had seen everything, every desperate thing people can do to each other or themselves, but each and every one could barely hide their shock.

I didn't care how much I stayed up, sitting there in my bed during my stay there because I love the middle of the night. I'm not Dracula or anything, it's just that in the middle of the night no one expects anything from you. You can't possibly do anything in the middle of the night, that's why it's the best excuse in the world for doing nothing. Let's say it's three a.m. and someone calls you and asks you to do something. They can't question you if you say, "Sure, of course I'll do it—but I can't possibly do it right now because it's three o'clock in the morning." Anyone who insists that you do it anyway is an idiot. At three a.m. you're off scot-free, but try to pull that shit at two in the afternoon because you'd rather be sleeping and you'll look ridiculous. In many lines of work that kind of shit will get you fired. But if it's three a.m., the other person becomes the asshole.

Anyway, after I made it through that first night, breakfast was served early and when it was I got up and went to eat. I'd started to feel a little sick because I'd been on morphine for four days in the ICU and now I was withdrawing from that, plus all the pills I'd been taking on my own, which isn't something they cared to address on the psych ward. It was the kind of place where you had to wait on line to get a toothbrush and toothpaste, so making patients completely comfortable wasn't priority one. In my experience, without a doubt, prison had better amenities. I remember looking around in jail thinking that these people had stories, that they had done things like steal cars because they had to. Not so on the psych ward. I only had one thought: all of these people are crazy. Then I remembered that I was the one who'd drunk bleach and stabbed himself nine times.

I hoped I'd find something to eat at breakfast that might take my mind off the withdrawal fever that was starting up inside me. I wasn't up to showering once I caught sight of the little jail shower across the room. This brand of shower has a button that spits out water for about thirty seconds before shutting off to keep you from flooding the place, because in case you forgot, you're a lunatic if you're in there in the first place. At breakfast, as I was about to shovel powdered eggs into my mouth, I noticed two mice running back and forth along the baseboard in the corner of the room. I almost threw up, and after that I couldn't eat a bite. When I brought it up to the guards they laughed at me.

"We're in the woods, man," one of them said. "Animals are everywhere here. And those two weren't even bad."

I was stuck in that zoo for three days, and aside from getting personal with more mice I learned a few things about the residents.

First, there seems to be a way that all crazy people wear their pants. They hike them up too high, way above the ankle, and usually they have them on crooked, like half-twisted around so that their zipper is on their hip. At first I thought it was just the guy I happened to notice it on, but soon I realized that this was like a uniform in there, one that said loud and clear, from a distance, *Hello there! I'm nuts.* As I started to notice this over and I over I thought to myself that maybe the crooked pants were how they got by in society for a while because from a distance you might mistake them for being retarded. That's until you got close enough to realize that these were no retards. It's like there's a regulation height for retards' pants that's somewhere just above the belly button, but these guys were at regulation nuts' height, which is another three inches above that. It's like they had a convention and all agreed to this. It doesn't look comfortable at all, by the way, but comfort isn't much of a priority when you're crazy.

I wasn't completely antisocial. I made a friend named Teddy in that place. It wasn't my idea, but when a three-hundred-pound black man decided he wanted to talk to me on a psych ward, I figured being friendly was the right way to play it. This guy was so huge and intimidating that the guards would let him roam the halls all night from one to six in the morning because he just wanted to walk, and there were not enough of them to restrain this guy if he lost it. I don't know what landed Teddy in there in the first place, but all I saw of him was a gentle giant who was a bit scarier than the Indian in *One Flew Over the Cuckoo's Nest.* He'd spend those late-night hours walking the halls, reading his Qur'ān and yelling out passages whenever the spirit moved him, which was kind of a lot.

Teddy and I met because one of the few shirts they let me keep was a *Jimmy Kimmel Live!* T-shirt, which I wore on my second day there. By then withdrawals had gotten so bad that when the Asian kid started snoring that night, I couldn't stay in the room anymore, so I went for a walk in the hallway, where I ran into Teddy, who had been eyeballing me earlier that day while I was watching TV in the lounge.

"You're famous," he said.

"No, I'm not, man, not really," I said.

"You're famous. You were in the film *Dirty Work*," he said.

I was surprised at that point. I mean, he was right: I was. I guess he kind of knew who I was, so I went with it. He was also twice my size. I'd have said I was in *Beaches* if that's what he'd wanted to hear.

"Yeah, I was in *Dirty Work*. Did you like the movie?"

"Yes, it was very good. You're very famous." Then he took a long look at my shirt. "You're Jimmy Kimmel!" he said.

"No, man, I'm not Jimmy Kimmel, my name is—"

"You're Jimmy Kimmel!" He started to get really excited, which was alarming because there wasn't anyone else around. "Jimmy Kimmel is here! I saw your show tonight. You're Jimmy Kimmel!"

"Really, man, my name is Artie, I'm—"

"No, Jimmy! You're Jimmy Kimmel!"

After five tries, I gave up. I mean, fuck it, why not? "You know what, man?" I said. "You're right, that's me. I am Jimmy Kimmel."

"I knew it! I knew you were Jimmy Kimmel! Hey! Everybody! This is Jimmy Kimmel!"

He'd gotten so loud that the crazies started wandering out of their rooms to see what the fuss was about, and he greeted them like a publicist telling all of them I was Jimmy Kimmel and that I was on TV earlier and now I was here.

"This is Jimmy! He's famous!"

I was Jimmy for the rest of my stay, and I consider myself lucky because there are so many worse people to be. Teddy and I became best friends from that moment on, whether I liked it or not, and starting the next morning when he wasn't reading the Qur'ān, he told everybody in earshot that Jimmy Kimmel was his friend as he pointed me out. It got really interesting when he and I watched

Jimmy Kimmel Live! together the next night. I'm not sure what his theory on someone being in two places at the same time was, but I wasn't going to bring it up. I was happy to have him turn to me and say, "I love your show, Jimmy," after it was over. Thanks, Teddy, we try to do a good show for our fans every night.

After two days I wanted a shower, and that's when I found out that my shower didn't work. I guess the Asian kid hadn't tried it, and who could blame him; the kid was either zombied out on Methadone and Thorazine or strapped down and screaming for more Methadone and Thorazine. Smelling fresh wasn't really on his mind. I let the guards know that my shower was busted and they decided to take me to the other wing on the floor, which was the children's wing, by the way. It's not something I'd ever had the misfortune to think about, but they have wings on psych wards for kids who are so mental (or so their parents claim) that they are brought to institutional hellholes like the one I was in and left there. On my way to a functional shower I passed a few rooms, where the most sullen, angry children I've ever seen sat on the floor drawing. I can't imagine what kind of parent would leave their child someplace like that.

I also passed the communal lounge on my ward, where Teddy and a few of our "peers" were doing whatever it was they did. When Teddy saw me walking with the guards, who were carrying a towel, soap, and shampoo for me, he couldn't contain himself.

"Oh yeah!" he shouted. "I see how you roll, Jimmy! Look at Jimmy, everybody! He's showering in a special shower!"

This got the crazies all up in arms. They started making noises and turning to look. Some of them even started shouting at me, because none of them seemed happy about this.

"Teddy, man, no. My shower is just broken," I said.

"No way, Jimmy! You see how Jimmy roll? He ain't gonna shower with all you motherfuckers—that's Jimmy Kimmel, man! Jimmy can't shower like all you regular people. He know! He gonna use a special shower!"

I got my shower in, but for the rest of my stay, which wasn't much longer (thank God!), literally everyone else there hated me. Not one of them, by the way, ever questioned whether or not I was actually Jimmy Kimmel.

The guards started to let Teddy hang around me whenever he wanted, which got weird because he'd come and grab me and drag me around the floor to show people that I was Jimmy Kimmel and his friend. It sucked; the guards would basically say, "Teddy, don't do that to Artie," as if he were a harmless child instead of a three-hundred-pound schizophrenic. They didn't bat an eye when Teddy came and grabbed me out of my room on my last day there.

He pulled out a piece of paper and asked for my autograph. Who was I to say no? I took his pen and wrote: "All my best, Jimmy Kimmel."

But that wasn't it. "Pray with me, Jimmy," he said, pulling out his Qur'ān.

"Okay."

We put our hands on the book and closed our eyes. I squinted a bit to see what he was doing, which was standing there in silence. This went on for a painful amount of time, probably something like three minutes. Then Teddy mumbled a few things to himself before saying, "Jimmy?"

"Yeah?"

He started me right in the eye for a long moment without blinking and said: "I'll see you in heaven, Jimmy Kimmel."

Then he took the book and his autograph and walked away.

———

After four days and three nights, with the help of my lawyer, my mom and sister got me transferred to a nicer place in New Canaan, Connecticut, called Silver Hill. Once again my poor mother followed the same ambulance through another freezing January night to this minimum-security psych ward. I had to pass an evaluation to be able to stay there, since the doctors in the ICU had understandably recommended that I be admitted to a maximum-security institution. I passed the interview because they could tell I wasn't fully nuts, just a strung-out drug addict who was a little bit crazy. I could have told them that, but my vote didn't count.

Unlike the place I'd just left, Silver Hill turned out to be exactly how it looks in its brochures and online: it's a gorgeous old mansion that happens to have been a successful mental institution for the past eighty years. I was there for a month and lived on a floor with about twenty-five other patients. And I saw the Super Bowl there that year because I had a TV in my room, so I watched the Packers beat the Steelers. I knew people going to the game, I knew who was going to play the halftime show, and all I kept thinking about was how I'd be there and all the fun I'd be having if I hadn't fucked up and landed myself in this place. I was so depressed watching the game in a mental hospital that I couldn't even finish it. I think I had one eye open for the first half, but by the second I was so depressed about the mess I'd made of my life that I said I'd never watch another one. I hadn't missed a Super Bowl since I was ten years old.

I had the room to myself for a week, which was cool, and then I had a roommate for the remaining four weeks I was there. The doctors at Silver Hill were very, very good and also very, very cynical, but still they didn't know what to make of me because what I'd done was so severe. Ultimately they were good doctors because they basically told me off the bat, "Okay, you stabbed yourself, so you're not leaving here until we tell you that you can leave because we're not going to have you try that again." They weren't what I'd call sensitive; they'd pretty much tell patients like me who had a grip on reality that we were nuts. To be honest, I don't think it took a degree to figure that one out, I just wonder if they used the opposite approach on the patients who were so nuts that they thought they were Napoleon or Cleopatra. I'd love to hear how those sessions went. That place cost me $1,500 a day, by the way.

There was a community phone on the ward, and one of the kids who was a very depressed, very bad heroin addict (which is what they call a dual diagnosis) used to enjoy answering the phone all the time. God only knows why. He also recognized me from the *Stern Show* right off the bat because he was a big fan of the show—and he wasn't the only one. Let me tell you, trying to get my mind back and make sense of what I'd done and what I'd have to do to get back to normal was hard enough to comprehend without *Stern* fans on the mental ward. Just think for a minute of what *Stern* fans who have actually been committed to a mental ward are like! To say that getting recognized in that situation was awkward is the understatement of the century because the last thing I felt like doing was answering questions about anything in my so-called celebrity life. Just imagine what it was like talking about my role in the movie *Elf* to someone who thought it was a documentary.

I couldn't even retreat into being Brian Carter because word spread around the ward pretty quickly, and once my stand-up special *Jack and Coke* aired on Comedy Central for the first time on January 22, my fate was sealed because the staff allowed it to be aired on the TV in the communal lounge. Show business can be downright creepy, and strange things happen every day, but the fact that I earned $150,000 when that special aired and was in a mental hospital bed listening to it, too depressed to even open my eyes and watch, takes the cake for me. To be honest I'd completely forgotten I'd sold it, and so had my mother. The next time I talked to her, she asked me what the check was for. It all worked out—that check paid for Silver Hill.

I did keep my ears open to tune in to what got laughs out in the lounge because they may have been lunatics, but they were an audience. It was like free market research for future routines, because I figured if I kept things up, the only places that would book me in the future would be places like this. Comedy Central aired a censored and uncensored version of my special the same night and they showed both on the ward. The good news is that both killed. The lunatics loved it! Lying in my bed, in the dark, listening to the other patients laughing their crazy asses off to my stand-up act was . . . something else. It's something I both wish and also never wish happens to my closest comedian friends.

When I went to breakfast the next day I was bombarded with questions: "How did you do that?" "How do you make people laugh?" "Can I eat your Jell-O?" "Who taught you to be funny?" "Can you teach me to be funny?" "What is it like to be inside the TV?"

I wanted to jump out the nearest window (and if they weren't locked I might have) because it was like walking into a focus group run by the Manson Family. I hadn't wanted to die before, but I sure did then: when I first got up at a comedy club never did I expect to end up explaining how I do stand-up to a bunch of lunatics. And they wouldn't take no for an answer! Eventually I stopped the madness because someone had to.

"Guys! I don't know what the fuck you want from me!" I said "It's not like tying your shoes or something. I can't just tell you how to do it. It's something you do if you can do it. Go try writing jokes in your rooms, okay? If they're funny you can be just like me."

That got a whole lot of grumbles and most of them started wandering away. I should also mention that I didn't impress all of my peers at Silver Hill. There were a few older women who I gathered had been long-term residents who apparently really didn't like it. It's not like they were going out of their way to welcome me with cookies before, but boy, did they shoot daggers at me every time we crossed paths after that. There's nothing worse than somebody's grandma hating the hell out of you, even if she's nuttier than a peanut farm.

The kid I mentioned before, the heroin addict and huge Stern fan who liked to answer the phone, happened to be the one who answered it when Howard called me. It freaked him out so much that he didn't even tell me about it. I found out as I casually passed by the message board a full day later and saw a note that said "Artie, Howard called, 2:30 p.m." It was six p.m. the next day at the time. Howard is a busy guy and though he was very concerned about me, anyone who knows him at all could tell you that calling a mental institution was a big deal for him. Conversely, the kid in question was a patient in a mental hospital with relatively few patients and besides his therapy sessions he had very little to do. Plus he had no problem talking to me every time he saw me, so I couldn't believe that this kid hadn't hunted me down. He'd spent hours hounding me about Howard, but now that he'd actually spoken to him, suddenly he wasn't interested? It made no sense, but then again, we are talking about a mental patient.

I went and found the kid right away because I wanted to make sure it wasn't a joke—crazy people like to prank each other, you know. "Dude," I said, "did you write this note to me?"

"Yeah, I did."

"Okay. Did Howard call?"

"Yeah, he did," he said with the enthusiasm of a postal worker three months from retirement.

"What did you say to him?"

"I asked him if he was Howard Stern."

"No, you didn't! You're not supposed to do that! That's violating my privacy and his, man!"

"How was I supposed to know it was him? You might know more than one Howard."

This kid was impossible.

"Let me ask you something, why didn't you come find me and tell me I had a call from some guy named Howard? You know where I am if I'm not out here watching TV. I'm always in my room sleeping."

"Yeah," he said. "But you probably needed your sleep."

"Yeah, thanks. So what did you tell him?"

"I said, 'He's not here.'"

"My God. And what did Howard say?"

"He said he'd call back."

I had steam coming out of my ears. "Listen, man, if he calls back, come and get me no matter where I am, okay? Wake me up if I'm sleeping. I only know one fucking Howard."

A few days later Howard called back and the kid answered and this time he came to find me. I was in the lounge watching *The Golden Girls* and he came shuffling in, shaking like a leaf.

"Artie . . . um . . . Howard is on the phone again."

Howard and I had an unbelievable forty-five-minute conversation that changed my life and really saved me in many ways. He told me about how he'd been thinking of me and rooting for me, and that made me feel so guilty. I love Howard so much and he's such a busy guy that I hated the fact that I'd taken all that energy from him and disturbed his life and career that way. He said he was there for me and would give me whatever I needed to get better, I just had to say the word. It was a lifeline; his words were what I needed to hear, because I was in such a surreal location and my mind was in such a clouded place that his voice brought me back to reality for a while. The combination of medication and not knowing what was going to happen to me had my mind on a constant merry-go-round. Was I going to spend the rest of my life in places like this? Unless I was heavily sedated I thought that was the case. There was no way I could sustain this financially and hope to take care of my mother. I didn't want her to die poor because of me. All of these things occupied my every waking hour. Howard's voice cut through all of that; it was a friend and a dose of what I used to have as my life. It was a wake-up call, and also a reminder of what got me into the business in the first place, because it was the same voice I'd heard on the radio all those years ago.

The doctors at Silver Hill prescribed me a list of medications: mood stabilizers, tranquilizers, and antidepressants, plus the steady diet of iron supplements I had to maintain because, as I mentioned, I'd lost so much blood that I was anemic. Those supplements replaced the missing iron, but they also turned my shits New York Jets green, which was disturbing; it was like shitting the remains of a leprechaun every morning. The anemia made me weak, but after three weeks I wasn't anemic anymore, so I couldn't use it as an excuse to skip group therapy, which I'd done my best to avoid from day one. When I was too weak and too tired to leave my bed they didn't push me hard, but after a while those excuses didn't cut it anymore.

Once I could no longer avoid group, I committed myself to faking it, because that really was the only way out. Step one was leaving my bed each day because if I didn't do a certain number of hours in group therapy I'd never be allowed to leave. Antisocial behavior, you see, was an indication that I was still suicidal and should not be left unsupervised. I understood that well enough, but what really motivated me after I felt better physically was the fact that I realized I was more or less just sleeping there at a rate of $1,500 a day. I wasn't even showering and I was barely eating, so it was time to get with the program.

I started getting up, I started showering, and after a while I even shaved. I started attending group meetings and taking it all in. After a while I even started raising my hand and saying things like: "That means you're on drugs, Counselor. And drugs are bad." The worst thing about rehab or mental institutions if you're a marginal nut like I am is that once you figure out how to fake it and learn to tell them what they want to hear, you have the system beat. And once you're there you're halfway home, whether you give a shit about changing your ways or not. The really good doctors can tell when you're faking it, but I find them to be few and far between.

I did a month there and all I can say is that if you're planning to go nuts and you have both money and good insurance, definitely go nuts at Silver Hill. The place is clean and the setting couldn't be a better backdrop to lose your marbles and maybe even find them again. By February 1, I was ready to leave, but my friends and family weren't so sure. Silver Hill has a rehab program that is completely separate in every way and that's where they wanted me to go, and so another intervention happened, there at Silver Hill, involving Colin Quinn, my cousin Jeff, my uncles Bruce and Tommy, my mother, my sister, and an intervention guy. The intervention guy seemed nice, which is what I thought until I learned that he charged my mother $10,000 to mediate this little meeting that day. I'd love to see a breakdown on his costs: "Interrupting Artie fee: $2,000; Nodding sympathetically: $3,000; Follow-up two-line e-mail six months later asking how you are doing: $5,000."

The truth is, my suicide attempt and a month in a mental hospital hadn't put a dent in my stubborn pride. I wasn't ready to give it up and I still thought I knew what was best for me. There's no reason I should have felt this way—none at all. I mean, really, what was I thinking? That I'd be fine just heading back home and putting the pieces together on my own? I made every excuse to my family. I said that I'd seen the rehab facilities and didn't like them, that the doctors there weren't any good. I found every reason I could to refuse to go and I kept repeating myself, saying I wanted to be at home, so that's where I was going. This went on for four hours because I wouldn't budge (I'm sure intervention guy billed for overtime). I had no valid argument, I had no leg to stand on, I just kept saying that I didn't want to go. Because I didn't! Who would ever want to go to rehab after a month in a mental hospital? No one!

The sad truth is that no matter how much my family and friends begged and cried, as of February 1, 2010, once the mental institution said I was fit to be free, there was nothing they could do about it. That day was the twentieth anniversary of my father's death, which was one more reason I refused to go to rehab that day. So after trying as best they could, the next day, February 2, my mother and my uncle Tommy picked me up, and since my mother wasn't going to abandon me, she insisted that I come and live in her house for a while. She was afraid that if I was left at my own place I'd jump off my terrace, and she had every right to think that. I agreed, thinking it would be for a week at most.

Driving down to Jersey I heard the *Stern Show* for the first time and it felt like it had been a year. I listened to Howard go through his Oscar predictions and as depressed as I was, instinctually I thought of jokes to play off him, and how I'd jump in and complement the conversation if I'd been sitting at my microphone in the studio. At that moment I realized just how much I missed it and how badly I missed all of them. It took exactly two minutes of hearing the show to clear my fog, to break my heart in two, and to remind me of the life I'd had just over a month ago. At the same time it all seemed so far away; it was like looking at a life that existed behind glass, that I could observe but couldn't touch. I closed my eyes and imagined myself in my chair making jokes with Howard about the Oscars. And when I opened them I saw that my chair was only the front seat of my mother's car. My heart dropped lower than I'd thought possible and a wave of incredible sadness came over me. I stared out the window and said nothing for the rest of the ride. I didn't even hear the show anymore, I was caught up in my head. When we got to my mom's house she made me a big Italian meal to make me feel welcome, to nourish me, and to celebrate the fact that I'd come home. I was happy to have it and it was delicious. After I ate all that I could I got into bed. And I stayed there from that day, February 2, 2010, until April 3, 2011.

———

I came up for air every once in a while because I wanted to give my poor mother a break, but that never lasted long. I was supposed to go to several outpatient facilities, but I refused. I was supposed to see doctors regularly, but I didn't do that. I didn't do anything. I wasn't open to anything and I was still suicidal. I could barely sit up straight in bed most days because I was paralyzed with depression, guilt, and embarrassment. I refused all help. I didn't want to see daylight, I wanted to be invisible, and after a while it became hard for me to feel comfortable when the sun was up. I'd sleep a lot but I never felt rested. I had no appetite and I always felt weak. It was all in my head, but sometimes I couldn't even lift my arm to drink a glass of water. I lay there, unable to shower or do anything, tossing and turning for fourteen months, just thinking about how I'd fucked up for good, and about how my life was over. I'd gotten everything I'd always wanted and then I'd destroyed it, over and over again.

The drugs had beat me, which was something I had a really hard time with. I kept thinking about the first time I'd gotten drunk as a fourteen-year-old kid and how that moment had led me to this. I thought about how I started getting drunk every single day once my father became a quadriplegic and how I'd always told myself that booze would never beat me. I remembered how, as I got older and started doing drugs and saw friends from high school die from them, I told myself that drugs would never beat me either. All I thought about there in that dark for fourteen months was how wrong I'd been and how long I'd been wrong. Drugs and booze hadn't just beat me, they'd made a fool of me.

And they weren't done with me either, because I wasn't done with them, which is what I hated about myself most of all. Even while living at my mother's house spending all my time in bed, I still found a way to call dealers and buy pills and arrange for them to leave them outside of the house. My mom would be thrilled when I'd find the energy to go for a walk in the yard, thinking I was coming around, meanwhile I was picking up Ziploc bags full of painkillers that I'd hide in my underwear until I got back to my room. I'd stay in bed getting high until they were gone, then I'd find a way to make a call and order more. When anxiety and shame had kept me up for four days straight, a doctor would write me a prescription so that I'd get some real sleep. He was a guy who had always been generous with me, and he felt that if I couldn't sleep I'd never get over my anxiety. So on occasion he'd write me a prescription for sleeping pills, but they were few and far between. And those were the only times I was happy, taking them all at once, getting high. Nothing seemed worth living for anymore. I wanted to get back to my apartment in Hoboken so I could jump off of the terrace, just take a nose-dive into the pavement after making sure there was no one down there for me to land on. That's how I wanted to end it; that's how I wanted to make a final statement. I just didn't want to wake up alive. My apartment is high up enough, but I had one worry, that I'd hit someone else's balcony on the way down. In the end I decided that going headfirst was the only way. That's what I thought about when I was high.

Eventually my mother noticed that I was high, but she didn't know how I was getting drugs into the house and she got very frustrated. There was a lot of crying and there was no rational talk. Taking care of me was a huge burden on her, because I was still on drugs and depressed and suicidal, every single day. Sometimes, in the middle of the night, I'd start screaming so loud that I'd wake myself up. I just wanted to wake up dead and I hoped for it every time I managed to fall asleep. The depression, the anxiety, and the drugs became this constant weight crushing me. I'd have nightmares where I was being buried alive, and they were so real that when my mother would wake me from them I'd be more confused than ever. I wouldn't know who I was or what was happening, I couldn't breathe and I couldn't calm down. My poor mother would have to lie in bed next to her forty-three-year-old son and cry with him until he couldn't cry anymore.

"Let's die together," she'd say, crying. "Let's die. That's what you want, so let's die."

She was trying to snap me out of it. One time we had a crazy argument about it, when she told me that she wanted to kill herself. That affected me because I didn't want to be the cause of her death and in that moment I realized that if I didn't try to change I very well might be. For once I was calming her down, telling her not to talk like that, even though I felt that way every single day.

My sister became the backbone of our family because I was a mess and it took all my mother's strength just to keep me afloat. We were fine financially because of my book royalties and the residuals from my DVD sales and film roles, but even though it's hard for me to admit it, money isn't everything. No dollar amount could relieve the pressure on my family and without a doubt these were the darkest hours for Stacey. I will never be able to thank her enough for keeping us together all on her own. She did all of it while holding down her job, which is amazing to me.

The room I lived in for all those months was down the hall from my mom, above the garage. To this day I've not been able to go back in there not only because I traveled to the darkest depths of my own soul in that bed, within those four walls, but because I know seeing that room again will remind me too clearly of just how much suffering I brought upon my poor mother. I'd bought her this town house— all cash—to pay her back for raising me, but then I went and ruined that by using it to exorcise my demons. Under my room in the garage was the Range Rover I'd bought her too, but she couldn't enjoy it any more than she could enjoy her house because she could barely leave, too worried about what I'd do if she left me alone. My mother began to wither way from sadness and exhaustion as I got high and numbed myself into oblivion.

I was powerless and when I wasn't high I was shaken to the core by anxiety attacks so intense that I had to be rushed to the hospital a few times. They'd give me a shot or an IV of Valium to calm me down, then send me home. After my third trip, one doctor gave it to my mother straight as I sat there staring into space.

"You need to put him in a home somewhere. If you don't he's going to die," he said. "Your son can't help himself. If you don't take

a stand you're going to continue taking care of him, which will probably kill you too. And if that happens and you're not here for him,
they'll put him in a home anyway."

The doctor was harsh but he was right, and I knew it. I had a solution, which was getting out of my mother's hair long enough to return to my place in Hoboken and jump off my terrace. I saw myself as
a hopeless case and I didn't want to be a burden anymore. I didn't see
any other way out for me. But there was no way my mother would let
me live alone at that point, and there was no fooling her the way I'd
fooled the doctors in rehab. So after each of these emergency room
visits she'd take me back home, refusing to give up on me.

Every once in a while I'd go out late at night and walk around
trying to think, enjoying the emptiness and silence and the fact that
no one would see me. I isolated myself as hard as I could, but a few
people wouldn't let me. Colin Quinn, the city kid, would take two
buses to come down to my mom's place in central Jersey to visit,
just to get me outside. Those were the only times I got any kind of
fresh air during the daylight hours, and every time after I had, I felt
so strange and vulnerable that I'd seclude myself more than ever for
the next few days.

Whenever I saw Colin I tried to hide my darkness and seem so
much better than I was, and the effort that took exhausted me. He
didn't give up on me at all—one day he even got me to play basketball. My mom lives in a nice gated complex, so as we were walking
by the courts he suggested we go play a game of twenty-one with
some college kid who was out there shooting free throws. I've gotta
say, even though I'd been in bed for eight months, I won the game.
Somehow I hadn't lost my outside shot, and it's a memory Colin still
jokes about. As great as that made me feel, after Colin left, I took a
shower and got in bed and wanted to die all over again—worse than
ever. It was so bad that when my mother had to leave the house the
next day, she called one of my uncles to come over and keep an eye
on me. She was able to tell when I was at my darkest, even though

she was powerless to stop it. Of all the friends in my life, Colin Quinn was my savior. He kept calling, even when I wouldn't take his calls. He did what my closest family members did, from my uncles to the cousins I consider my closest friends—he never deserted me.

Around this time my hero, Bruce Springsteen, called me too. He and I had met at a funeral of a mutual friend who'd died of a heroin overdose five months before. At the funeral I got a moment to talk to Bruce because I was supposed to be clean at the time—though I wasn't—and I told Bruce in the ten minutes we spoke that I had a lot of the same issues as the deceased and that I was trying my best to work them out. He wished me well and we shared some stories about the kid who had died, who really was the sweetest guy. I miss him a lot.

I'd had no contact with Springsteen since, until my mother came into my room one night and in the same way she used to tell me my friends were at the door asking if I could come out and play stickball when I was twelve, she said, "Bruce Springsteen is on the phone for you."

I couldn't believe it, but it was true. Bruce had heard about what had happened, and he'd actually called—twice! The first time my mother didn't wake me up!

"Well, just call him back," she said.

"Ma, that's not how it works," I said. "You don't call someone like that back. You wait for them to call you. I mean, he didn't leave a number, did he?"

"No, but it's on the Caller ID."

"Ma, no, believe me, I can't do that. There's an unspoken rule—you wait for the famous person to call you. They do it when they have the time; you don't call them back."

Anyway, the second time Bruce called, we ended up speaking for over an hour and he couldn't have been cooler.

"I'm thinking about you, just want to make sure you're taking care of yourself, you know," he said. "There's a lot of guys who have gone through what you're dealing with and you can reach out and get help from a lot of people. There's a lot of good people out there that can help you."

I asked Bruce what he was doing at the time and he said he was home writing new music (which would become the amazing album *Wrecking Ball*) and then he told me how he'd taken his fifteen-year-old son to a concert the night before, because the kid had wanted to see some new rock band whose name I'm forgetting.

"And you know, Artie, I got him backstage at his first non-Daddy rock concert and he was so impressed I could do that," Bruce said.

As deep into my own hole as I was I still appreciated the surreal gift of that phone call, except for the fact that I was forty-three and living with my mother. To be sitting in that bedroom in central Jersey and have my mom come in and say that Bruce Springsteen was on the phone helped me in such a profound way I can barely express it. I was sixteen when *Born in the U.S.A.* came out and he was instantly my hero, as he is today. To be there at forty-three getting a call that sincere from him was an insanely amazing moment and I remember thinking how much I hoped I lived long enough to be able to thank him in person for it one day. It was the first time I'd thought about living for something in months. Bruce was so genuinely concerned that I wasn't sure what I had ever done in life to deserve such earnest attention from one of my heroes. He ended the conversation by giving me his number and telling me that I could call him anytime. The next morning I woke up feeling lighter, thinking about just how unpredictable my life is. Then I thought about how funny it would be if I started calling him every day, saying things like, "Hey, Bruce, Artie here, do you want to play volleyball today?" or "Dude, what are you doing? Let's get ice cream!"

— — — — —

In September 2010, Greg Giraldo died, and when I heard the news it sent me into a deeper depression because I admired and liked Greg very much. I heard this at a time when I actually had been making some headway, but I was fragile and that news sent me into a tailspin. Greg Giraldo was a great comedian, plain and simple, and saddest of all, he was on the cusp of becoming recognized for his talent when he lost his fight with drugs and alcohol. Greg's stand-up was an extension of who he was, which was an acerbic, insanely smart comic who had great observations about life and everything in it. Like every great comic he could also be insanely mean in a funny way. Comics are one of two things: they're either funny when they whine or they're funny when they're mean. Jerry Seinfeld is basically a guy who bitches about shit, but he's funny when he does it. Greg, and I mean this in the best way, was at his best when he was mean and scathing. And I enjoyed his company immensely, because the conversation was always just perfect.

Greg made a name for himself on Comedy Central's roasts because Greg, more than anyone else I knew, was amazing at taking someone down to nothing with just one line. And nowhere did I get a better exhibition of this than when he and I both took part in the Comedy Central roast of William Shatner in 2006.

I also knew firsthand that Greg and I shared the same enthusiasm for drugs and had the same brand of dark self-deprecation inside us because we'd partied together. We'd get high, we'd get wasted, and every time we did, at some point in the night we'd start talking about how fucked up we were and how we hated it. We'd talk about how we wanted to get clean because both of us knew we had to. We weren't talking about it only as a path to improving our careers, and I know we never mentioned it (God forbid!) as the obvious improvement it would be to our health. No, both of us realized very clearly that we were so far gone that getting clean was the only way we'd stay alive. Greg had a wife and children and he spoke of them in the highest regard, never as a burden or a nag the way so many guys with and without problems like ours do. Greg loved his family, he truly did, just as he knew that his habit would eventually cause him to

lose them. I couldn't relate to how he felt because I don't have anyone in my life and I'm lucky enough that I never had any accidental
kids, but I've put more than a few very nice girls who made the
grave mistake of getting seriously involved with me through hell, so
I could appreciate the guilt he felt for hurting his wife and children
with his behavior.

Giraldo and I traveled together to that Shatner roast, and it's a
flight I'll never forget, first of all because I wasn't too fucked up to
forget, and second of all because for the first time I had to take care
of someone on a level that I'd never had to before. Sure, I'd gotten
friends home before but this was different—I was holding this guy's
hand, keeping him from the abyss on a minute-to-minute basis. Let
me just say very clearly that I'm not judging at all, nor was I then.
It was simple: I was the one taking care of someone too fucked up
to handle themselves, which was something I could relate to pretty
well, having been that guy so many times myself. That day I finally
got a taste of what I'd put so many people, from my castmates at
MADtv, to my family, to my girlfriends, through.

Greg and I were booked on a first-class flight from JFK to LAX
on a Saturday, the day before the taping. I got to the airport nice and
early and was enjoying a cocktail in the club lounge of whatever
airline it was. I wasn't sober at the time, in fact I had a pocket full
of Vicodin, but I was nowhere near the depths and darkness that lay
in store for me. This was the same year I played Carnegie Hall and
did *Beer League*, so I was holding things together relatively well,
still fooling the people in my life most of the time (or so I thought).
I mean, no one considered me an angel, but I'm pretty sure they had
no idea just how serious my intake was shaping up to be. Put it this
way, by 2006, I never got on an airplane sober. I was in training for
my crash and burn.

That day I was sipping a Jack and water about half an hour before
boarding time when Giraldo barreled in like a tornado out of west
Kansas. The guy's energy was crazy; he couldn't stand still, he was

nearly spinning in place, all jacked up and totally manic. He was moving so frantically that everyone else in the lounge walking or talking at a normal pace looked like statues compared to him. His eyes darted around in every direction until he zeroed in on me and he basically ran over to where I was sitting.

"Art!" he said. "Art, I fucked up. I fell off the wagon and my wife is pissed."

"Greg, it's okay, calm down," I said.

"No, Art, you don't understand. I'm really fucked up and anxious. I've been up all night partying. . . . I don't think I can do this, man. I don't think I'm gonna make it through this flight. I don't think I can get on that fucking plane, Art."

I had a pocket full of Vicodin, which, being a painkiller, takes all your pain away, but it also has that opiate quality that gives you a sense of well-being, even when you have no reason at all to feel that way.

"Dude, c'mon, sit down for a minute," I said. "You've got to get on this flight, so you've got to try to relax. If you don't go out there and do this you'll fuck up your whole career. I'm gonna help you. Here, take a couple of Vicodin. These will calm you down."

The poor guy's eyes were so wild. "I'll try, man," he said. "But I don't know."

The pills numbed him out enough to get him sitting down and I kept him talking so by the time they were doing last call for the flight, Greg was well behaved enough to get on board. Now I only gave him Vicodin, but when he told the story on Pete Dominick's Sirius radio show not too long afterward, Greg insisted that I gave him Ecstasy. I wish! Both of us would have been much more cheerful if I'd had a pocket full of that! We sat next to each other in first class and basically I held Greg's hand for the entire six-hour flight because the Vicodin I kept handing him may have kept him from getting out of his seat, but the guy was still a raw nerve, just pure anxiety. When he had to go to the bathroom I went with him and waited outside because I was worried that he'd get claustrophobic in there and freak out. Thanks to me we made it to LA without incident, but I have to be honest: just short of diapers and a bottle, I took care of the guy as if he were a baby. You know what? He couldn't have had a better chaperone because I've been that baby more times than I care to remember (and even more that I don't remember). I was paying a karmic debt to all of those who had done the same for me and I was happy to do so, because I knew what someone in his mind state of mind needed.

Like I said, when Greg told this story he claimed that I had given him Ecstasy, and here's further proof that he was wrong: the two of us sat through *Alex and Emma*, the worst movie of Kate Hudson's career, with no problem. If we were on Ecstasy we would have loved it, but we didn't. We hated it, we just didn't care enough to look away. That's what painkillers like Vicodin do: they make you lazy and complacent enough to let crap like that wash over you, even when all you'd have to do to avoid it is just look away.

We had a pretty tight schedule to keep when we landed, the first stop being rehearsal at CBS Studios. A car took us there straight from the airport, and since Greg was still pretty touch-and-go, I made sure I stayed close to him during the run-through. We were lucky enough to end up standing next to Farrah Fawcett (who was still a grade-A fox, by the way!), and I remember Greg freaking out about that, like, every five minutes.

"Art, she's an Angel," he kept whispering in my ear. "She is one of Charlie's Angels. Artie, look at her! You remember that poster, right?"

"Yeah, man, of course, keep it down."

"The one with the mesh bathing suit?"

"Greg, yeah, I remember. I had one. Be cool, man."

"She's still fucking hot."

"Yeah, she is."

I got him through the proceedings and I'm pretty sure Farrah, rest in peace, didn't hear us recalling all of our adolescent fantasies that involved her. When rehearsal ended I got Greg to the hotel, up to his room, and into his bed without a problem. I didn't see him until the next day at the studio, and by then he seemed fine.

"Artie, thank you so much," he said. "I can't thank you enough. I really can't. You saved my ass. I fucked up, but it would have been so much worse if I didn't get here and do this."

"No big deal, man, you'd do the same for me."

"No, Artie, you don't know how bad I was yesterday."

"Greg, stop, it's okay, don't think anything of it."

He was so ashamed about what he'd done that he thanked me over and over like crazy all day, but he would have done the same for me, end of story. And if his behavior had been noticed by the producers during the rehearsal, they forgot all about it the next day when Andy Dick showed up. That guy was so fucked up and unmanageable that it took every spare handler on set to keep him in line.

I remember sitting in the greenroom with Greg and my friend Lisa Lampanelli, and Joe Francis, the Girls Gone Wild guy, was there doing his thing, which involved boozing up a barely legal broad while trying to seem relevant. Anyway, Andy came in there too, and by then he'd decided, against everyone's wishes, to do a spoof instead of a monologue. Andy is a funny motherfucker, I don't care what anyone says, and he could have done a roast as well as he can do sketches, stand-up, you name it. He should have gone out there and just done a bunch of killer jokes but instead he chose to put on a sketch where he played Mister Spock in a bad wig and delivered a list of stupid dick jokes. It didn't work at all; it was just awkward.

During the roast I sat next to Greg and Lisa and George Takei and as much as I wanted to support Greg—who was staying sober—and lead by example, I indulged in the two bars they had set up on the stage for us. How could I not? They were on the stage! There were also hot girls dressed in green everywhere, as an homage to Captain Kirk's prowess with alien pussy.

I was good and loaded throughout that taping, so much so that I made a point of insulting Kevin Pollak, who is a great stand-up comic and actor. I said something like, "Kevin Pollak is here. And the only reason he's here is because he does William Shatner and every other hokey imitation you can imagine. Get your fill because you're not going to see Kevin on this show again unless Comedy Central decides to roast Peter Falk."

Kevin got genuinely mad at me for that, by the way. Every single person—I mean every single one—made a joke about me being a drug addict who would probably be dead in a year, and that was fine, but Kevin got mad at a Peter Falk joke. Betty White got up and made a joke about outliving me, for Christ's sake! Anyway, here's what Pollak came back at me with when he got his time at the podium:

"I'm sorry, Artie, for insulting you with my impressions. It's something you might not be familiar with. It's called a career."

Thank you, Kevin, for letting me know what you do for a living.

The best part of the night was Greg's turn at the podium—he was first, by the way. He started with a few cursory remarks, then he looked over, directly at me, and apropos of nothing said, "Artie Lange, you fat fucking drug addict," then he continued with his roast. It was hilarious and I started laughing hard along with everybody else in the house. Greg was always a sweetheart, though, he made sure to shoot me a look just after that that said, *It's a roast, man, don't take it personal.* Like I ever would! How could I when it was so funny and on the nose?

The shoot was on a Sunday so I had to take an early flight to make it to *Stern* on time the next day, and it's a good thing I did because the roast was really fun and things were heating up to be a good night. I think Andy Dick got into trouble for pissing on the girl Joe Francis was hanging out with or at least I read something like that in the tabloids, and I bet I would have done something inappropriate or illegal or both with one of the green girls if I were given half the chance. I can't say because I wasn't there, but I'm pretty sure Greg didn't stay clean that night.

I saw Greg quite a bit when we were both in New York because Greg was a Comedy Cellar guy. He'd do sets there but more often than not, he'd spend his evenings upstairs in the restaurant with his fellow comics, just shooting the shit. At this time in my life I was at the Cellar at the very least a few times a month, usually more often than that, and I always ended up at a table catching up with him for a few hours. And every time I saw him he thanked me once again for taking care of him. It got to be silly because I know in my heart he would have done the same thing, if not more, for me.

There's a store downtown called Lazaro run by a guy who designs his own jewelry and clothes. I used to go there with Adrienne a lot, but the place always did and always will remind me of Greg because he was the one who told me about it and he always wore Lazaro's stuff. It's very rock-and-roll and very cool and when I see someone wearing it or read about Lazaro I think of Greg. Whenever I walk into the Comedy Cellar I think of Greg. And whenever I see a roast I think of Greg because he'd perfected it; he was the best roaster I've ever seen. It makes me very somber when I think about Greg and what he struggled through. He loved his family so much and he didn't want to be what he was—a true addict. He was brilliant, but just like me, he was a true drug addict. If you want to call it a disease, that's one he and I both shared.

Greg died on September 29, 2010, after a gig, in his room at the Hyatt in New Brunswick, New Jersey, of an overdose of prescription pills. At the time I was at my mom's house in a bed I hadn't left in months, truly at the bottom of my well of depression. I didn't know how to react to it, except for the fact that I had just, for the first time in over a year, stepped foot in the Comedy Cellar. I was far from returning to functional, but for a moment there I was able to rejoin the world. It was the first time I'd appeared in public in ten months and I did a short set at the Cellar. I'd been in a vacuum, completely out of touch with everything that existed outside of my head and the room I'd been hiding in. I'd never forgotten my friends, but that night, being in the Cellar, I remembered just how great it was to be around Dave Attell and Greg and all the guys I'd shared so many laughs with. So I started asking about them, hoping they'd come in that night. All of them were on the road, so I didn't see them, but that was fine.

I went back to my house in Hoboken for a short period of time after that because I thought I would get back into stand-up and I thought I was out of the woods. My mom was going to monitor me and my sister lived very close by. For the first time I actually thought I could begin to rejoin society. And that's when I heard that Greg had died and I was devastated. I'd just gotten up the balls to do some new material at the Cellar, the place I associated with him more than anyone else I knew, and within a week I heard he died. That sent me into a deep depression once again. So I retreated back to my mother's house, back to that room above her garage, because once more I became completely incapable of taking care of myself, just like that.

I wish I could have been with Greg that night, I really do. Even in the state I was in, I think I could have found the words that would have kept him alive, or at least gotten him through to the morning. When you've got demons you're trying to beat, those long lonely nights are endless; it's something only someone who's been there can understand.

Greg's death reminded me of another genius who left us too soon, Mitch Hedberg, and when I returned to bed, completely paralyzed again, I thought about him often. I began to think that there are some souls that aren't meant to endure this life—and that maybe I was one of them.

To me, Mitch Hedberg is the bar for modern comedy by which all others should be judged. People who get him understand what is truly funny and those who don't are pretty much losers. Mitch was a genius and a loving, warm human being. He was also a raging drug addict who died of a heroin overdose on March 30, 2005. I've never met anybody quite like Mitch, because he was one of a kind. Talking to him was just so fucking relaxing because, I'm telling you, the guy was a sedative in human form. He'd do anything for you, even things as boring as giving you a ride somewhere when you could have gotten one yourself. Mitch was a brilliant guy and a truly beautiful person; he was never patronizing. When he said the kind of things people say all the time and don't mean like, *Hey, don't worry, it'll be all right*, he actually meant them. That's unusual anywhere, but in comedy, everyone is so sarcastic and dark it's unheard of.

Basically Mitch was a mellow, long-haired angel from the seventies who cared about making people happy and making people laugh and nothing else. He was the comic of this generation, in my opinion, and I can only imagine what he would have done if he'd been able to stay alive. Another thing that was great about Mitch was his honesty: he knew his strengths as a comic and never wanted to do anything but perfect them. He was a master joke teller; he didn't want to act, and he didn't want to host a show or ever be a celebrity. He had this great bit about it where he talked about all the money he had been given to be in pilots that were being developed for him that he'd told the agents and network executives pushing them that he couldn't do the first time they met because what he does is tell jokes. The same way that Mitch told jokes and stories, he went along for the ride, all the while asking the simple questions that revealed just how dumb these pilot concepts were. The funniest one he mentioned, by the way, was Mitch Hedberg starring as a tennis instructor in a suburban town, which is ridiculous.

Here's how sweet of a man Mitch Hedberg was. One night way back, in the late '90s or early 2000s, we were at the Comedy Cellar in Greenwich Village, sitting upstairs where the comics gather whether they're doing sets downstairs or not. I was at a table with Dave Attell, Greg Rogell, Keith Robinson, and a few other guys, and Mitch was there that night too. He did stand-up that night but I didn't see him because as anyone who has been to the Cellar knows, it's a pretty tight room down there.

Anyway, we were all hanging out upstairs and at some point the conversation turned to the Aspen Laff Festival, which was a few weeks away. Most of us, like me, Attell, and Mitch, were going, and so was one of the nonregulars present—some douche bag who used to write for *Frasier*. The guy was "having a go at stand-up" and he couldn't have been easier to hate: the guy had an assistant with him and some hot chick he was probably paying to be on his arm all night before she fucked him and went home to her studio apartment. I'll give him this—the chick was really fucking hot. All of us were staring at her and trying to talk to her. Anyway, when we started talking about who was going to Aspen, the guy piped up.

"You guys are all going to Aspen, huh?" he said.

"Yeah," I said.

"Me too," he said.

Being a wiseass, I said, "How you getting out there?"

"I'm taking a plane," he said.

"That's good," I said. "Good way to get there."

"You could drive," Mitch said.

"No, I'm taking a plane," the guy said.

"So am I," Mitch said. "Wouldn't it be cool if we were on the same plane?"

"I don't think so," the guy said, with the most stuck-up arrogance you can imagine. "I'm flying privately."

And without a beat, Mitch said: "Oh . . . that does bring the odds down."

The guy then turned to the chick and started talking to her, so he didn't see this, but Mitch turned to the rest of us, shrugged, and quietly said, "Out of my league." I nearly fell on the floor.

I didn't know Mitch nearly as well as I knew Greg, but I will always feel guilty about not doing more for him when I could have.

He was on the *Stern Show* two weeks before he died to promote an upcoming show of his at Caroline's and he looked terrible. His teeth had turned black from neglect—that's how into shooting up he was. He just didn't brush his teeth, and let me tell you that when you're on drugs all the time you don't eat well either. He'd show up for gigs with blood on his sleeve from shooting up and it had gotten so bad that he'd developed gangrene in his foot from shooting up in his ankle so often. By then he and his wife, who was a serious addict as well and died shortly after Mitch, were living in an RV. They would drive to each of his shows, eat at truck stops, and do drugs until they nodded out in the mobile home or in whatever hotel room they'd booked for the night. After a gig in Atlantic City, the two of them were bedded down in a hotel in south Jersey and when his wife woke up in the morning, Mitch was dead. It was right around April 1, and I remember people thinking that his death was an April Fool's joke because the guy was only thirty-seven.

That last time I saw him at *Stern* I was really fucked up, because I was getting to the top of my own roller coaster. I'll never forget how he looked when he came in: nervous, hunched over, tinted glasses on, just foggy, frail, and stumbling a bit. I remember Howard asking him right away about his drug problem and the fact that he claimed he'd cleaned up.

"Yeah, I've got that under control," Mitch said. "I only use drugs for creative purposes."

Everyone laughed.

"I know what you mean, Mitch," I said. "That's one of the reasons I use drugs too."

It was a pretty awkward interview and none of it was really very funny, but there's another reason why I'll never forget that day: it was Saint Patrick's Day, which was my father's birthday. Seeing Mitch that day did something to me, because for the first time in five years, right after the show, I went to my father's grave and I cried my eyes out. Something about seeing Mitch that way, knowing I was heading down the same path if I didn't make some changes and realizing that, in the blink of an eye, it had been thirty-seven years since my father died, all hit me like a bat to the head. I walked out of the studio knowing what I should have done—I should have grabbed Mitch by the back of his neck and taken him to a hospital. I should have yelled at him, *Fuck this radio show, fuck your gig at Caroline's, you need to stay alive!* I didn't do that and he was dead fourteen days later. He and I were the same age.

I know the truth now, from experience. I could have dragged Mitch kicking and screaming out of the studio to a rehab program. I could have tied him down and stayed with him (this would have been weird seeing as we didn't know each other too well) or found some other way to get him under lock and key, but you know what? It wouldn't have changed anything. It wouldn't have made a difference. He probably still wouldn't be here. Because if someone isn't ready, there's nothing in this world anyone can do to help them. I know it all would have been useless, but I can't help it—the thoughts of what I could have done still haunt me.

—— —— —— ——

I was in bed again. All of my limbs worked, but I was just as much of a cripple as my father had been after his accident, and at the time I was the same age he had been when he'd died. These facts swirled around my brain like shit in a toilet, but they never got flushed. I couldn't help but feel sorry for my mother having to take care of me day in and day out, another handicapped man on her watch after she'd spent years taking care of my father. She didn't deserve it and she hadn't signed up for it: my father was one thing, but I'd brought this on her and on our family all by myself. I'd dug such a deep pit that there was no ladder tall enough and no rope long enough to reach me. My mother stayed strong, and she always told me: "This too shall pass. It will be okay; you'll get out of this." But I didn't believe her, not for a minute.

"Not this time, Ma," I'd say, and I'd usually start crying, because I didn't want things to be that way but I didn't see any other path for me. "I'm so sorry. I've gotten out of it a couple of times but not this time. I'm too far gone. There's no hope."

I couldn't live with the guilt of what I'd done without being high and I couldn't be high anymore and be able to function and work, and if I couldn't work, I didn't want to live anymore. That's how I saw things, and it was all very simple to me, to the point that I wondered why I was the only one who saw it this clearly. My mother and friends talked about other options but in my mind they knew nothing.

Every time my mother would leave the house I'd hear the garage door go up because it was below the bed where I'd chosen to try to sleep my life away. Like I said, she rarely left, and if it was for more than half an hour, she'd leave a chaperone of some kind in the house to watch out for me. Usually her short trips were for me—most often she'd be going to the pharmacy to pick up some pills that a doctor I'd found in Virginia would prescribe me to keep my benzo and opiate withdrawals from kicking in. I told my mother I was trying to wean myself off of them, but I wasn't, I was getting as high as I could.

If that wasn't bad enough—having your own mother be your drug runner—Christmas 2010 was a whole new low for me when it came to guilt. There was a blizzard that year and about a foot and a half of snow fell in central Jersey in just two days. That whole week I'd been pretty bad, just so dark and depressed and hopeless that I had my mother worried sick. I kept thinking I was on the verge of a seizure from the benzo withdrawals and I was so bad that my mother called the doctor and got me a prescription. In a white-out blizzard, my poor sixty-nine-year-old ma shoveled enough snow out of the way that she could get her car out to go pick up drugs for me. I remember hearing her down there and when I went to the window and looked outside, I saw all five feet nothing of her crying, in the cold, shoveling. The storm was so bad that the news had advised everyone to stay inside and she had to drive so slowly that going half a mile down the road to Walgreens and back took her an hour. She kept calling me every five minutes.

"Are you okay?" she'd ask me, crying the whole time.

"Yeah, Ma," I'd say. "I'm sorry."

She got back all right, and she gave me my medication and I didn't have a seizure, I just fell asleep. I must have seemed so ungrateful. The truth is, I was devastated. How could I not be after subjecting my mother to that? She was almost seventy; I'd worked hard to give her a house and car so that she could relax and retire, not take care of me. I should have been taking her on vacation for the holidays, not ruining her life.

Every morning around eleven a.m. my mother would come into my room as if it were 1975 and I were still eight years old and nothing bad had ever happened to our family.

"Come on, Art, get up!" she'd say. "I'll make you breakfast. Come on, it's a beautiful day."

Just about every single morning I'd hardly respond. She'd try again a couple of hours later, all morning, into the afternoon—one o'clock, two o'clock. I'd try my best for her, but most of the time I couldn't do it. When one o'clock hit I'd feel like it was okay, because now I was into the day. One o'clock meant it was afternoon, which meant everyone was already out living their life, so if I were too depressed to get up, I'd be given a pass. That idea also usually made me even more depressed, so you can see how there was no winning for me. Being in bed on a beautiful May day, hearing my uncles come by to help my mom with one thing or another or hearing her on the phone scheduling stuff the way normal people do all the time—those simple everyday things were torture to me. I began to believe that I'd die forty feet from my mother, in that bed, in that house, if she didn't die forty feet from me first. One of us was going in the next fifteen years if we continued living that way. We'd leave my sister to clean up the mess and then die without any family, all alone in this world. And all of it would be because of me.

My mother would sit on the edge of my bed each night and tell me how she prayed for me every day because what I'd done was forgivable, so God wasn't going to punish me. I just had to be strong and get through this trial.

"There will be people who will always be upset with you, Artie, but that's life," she said. "Your friends will always be there, your business will always be there, and that's because you're talented. You have so much more to do."

She said things like this over and over again; it was the constant sound track to my fourteen months in bed, and mostly I believed none of it. There's an old saying that you hear in AA meetings, that alcoholics love to wallow in their misery. They say that if a normal person falls down a large hole they start screaming for a ladder, but if an addict falls down a large hole they scream for an interior decorator because they plan on staying awhile.

— — —

Entertainment media is so powerful and strange that I guess I shouldn't be surprised that the story I'm about to tell you happened, but I still am. One night my sister came to the house to eat dinner with my mom and me, so I managed to get out of bed. I doubt that I showered or shaved; it was hard enough just to show up. My sister had brought a guest with her whom I hadn't known about, a girl named Christine who was Robert Downey Jr.'s assistant. Christine had read *Too Fat to Fish* and in the extra material in the paperback we actually mentioned Robert as someone who had beaten his demons and bounced back better than ever. He and Christine had met when Robert was in recovery and she had been an essential influence in keeping him clean and helping him take his career to the incredible heights he's achieved since then. When she read my book she got in touch with my sister because she wanted to help me out, almost as if it were a mission for her. She had been a lifelong *Stern* fan, but what struck her the most and what Robert felt after he read the book was that they both really felt like they knew me. It was more than just being familiar with the substance addiction side, it was that they felt like they understood me and could help.

I was really touched because no one had made more enemies, fucked more people over, or gotten more far gone than Robert Downey Jr. in his heyday. Christine really believed, and Robert apparently agreed, that she could get me on track. I guess the timing was right, plus the fact that these two people who were a part of a career so far from and so much more important than my little world, would take the time, or even care about me in any way, really moved me. I can't pinpoint it better than that, but for the first time what Christine was saying seemed like an option to me. Anything was better than what I was doing with my life, that was for sure. I agreed to try, that was the best I could do. A week later Robert called my sister to give her a pep talk because he said it was going to be a long road. I thought that was awesome of him to do because God knows she needed it. My wanting to try may have been a ray of light, but it was so far from the end of the tunnel. Christine had lit a path for me to follow, but I was still too fucked up to make any real kind of life change. I hadn't even tackled the real problem of still being very much on drugs. But that's when the great Colin Quinn stepped in.

On April 3, 2011, Colin and two huge Irish guys straight out of Brooklyn (and Central Casting) came over and got right to the point.

"Hey, Art," he said. "So you're going to detox, you're going right now, and there's no discussion unless you think you can take these two on."

"Oh, is that how it's gonna be?" I was stubborn to the end.

He'd brought a guy named John Moriarity from Sunrise Detox Center in Stirling, New Jersey, with him, and everything was already arranged. This wasn't an intervention, it was an ultimatum. Actually it was an abduction, which was exactly what I needed. My mom started crying as they dragged me, literally kicking and screaming, out to a big Cadillac and stuffed me in the backseat. I kept thinking about *The Godfather: Part II*, *Goodfellas*, and every mob movie where a guy gets into the back of a Cadillac and never returns. I was too pissed off to make jokes about leaving the gun and taking the cannoli.

I was also so far past my expiration date when it came to drugs that the seven days the doctors predicted it would take to get me fully detoxed stretched to twenty-two days, which must be some kind of record at that place. I needed it so badly. I was so miserable, sick, and desperate, but the staff at Sunrise saw me through and were unbelievable. I walked through those doors bitter, hating everyone, talking shit nonstop, not wanting to be there, as I'd suddenly decided that the dark and my bed were a much better life, but no matter what I said or did, they were all amazingly patient with me. Their dedication and compassion led me to do what I'd never even come close to doing before: I surrendered, and this time I meant it. They got me off the shit physically and then, when the mental part had to begin, I was able, for the first time in my life, to take it seriously. There was a lot of work to do, so after twenty-one days, once I was physically clean, they moved me over to Sunrise's partner facility, Ambrosia, where I started working on my mental health and facing things I'd barely been able to wrap my head around before. The name of that place is very misleading, by the way, because Ambrosia, though it's on Singer Island, about thirty minutes from Miami, Florida, is one hell of a hard-core rehab program. Ambrosia is supposed to be the food of the mythological gods, and I'm pretty sure this place is not what they had in mind. I hated the hot, humid climate and I hated the fact that I had so much left to work on, so I made a huge fuss, pulled whatever celebrity card I had, and managed to get my own room. And still, the people there could not have been nicer.

Now, like I said, considering that I blew past the seven-day prediction, it should be clear that not one step of this process was easy or pleasant. And when I say that I was dragged there, I really was dragged there. As much as I liked the idea and was inspired by Christine and Robert's influence, that didn't mean I was ready to really do the work in any way, shape, or form. I only went to get everyone to stop nagging me, and I intended to do what I'd always done: get somewhat clean then fake my way out of there. Not this time.

I had a counselor named Danny, who was a solid guy who let me spend my first two weeks in bed, basically in protest that I was there at all. I remained depressed and uncooperative, just completely stubborn in every way I could find. I'd committed to two weeks in the program, but in the end, I stayed two and a half months, because they got under my skin and figured me out. The staff were such good counselors that they broke down my walls and got through my bullshit and found a way to help me finally help myself, which no one else had ever been able to do.

Here's what they showed me. It wasn't anything groundbreaking or radical. It was just honesty, and honestly it was just me being ready. But if I can boil it down to one simple fact that can not be denied it is this: the more time you spend away from the drug the more you will understand who you are. Also that you can't do that in a vacuum. They made me realize that every day that I got further from opiates and the rest of it was what I needed to do, but I couldn't do it in isolation. I needed time away from the drug, but doing that in my mother's house—if I'd been able to do that completely—wasn't going to be enough. I needed to be out in the world and to realize that I could exist socially without the drugs. I needed to be around people who were sober too, because only then would I realize that there was a world out there to experience. It makes sense—if you're not used to being in the world sober, how do you know that that world even exists? The longer I was drug-free and interacting, the better I became. It was that simple. Even though I was stubborn as hell, eventually in an environment like that, one day I just got better.

After I got through my first two weeks of detox I was given a roommate we'll call Tommy, who was a great guy in a lot of ways. He was a cop, and though I didn't think of him this way at all at first, looking back, the guy was a godsend. He motivated me, he kept me from retreating into my darkness, and he got me out to meetings, which I did very reluctantly at first. But then something clicked in me and I don't know what it was, but I started engaging and I started getting better. I started *wanting* to engage and get better, and that's what it really takes to change. After a little over a month I just woke up and felt different. Everyone there told me that the longer I stayed away from opiates the better I'd become; the depression would lift and I'd be able to think clearly. That really is what happened, and I was in an environment that supported that and also reinforced it with positive experiences. What had seemed too depressing to comprehend wasn't so bad anymore. All of my mistakes weren't erased but for the first time I felt like maybe I could do something to make up for them. I wasn't just going through the motions at Sunrise and Ambrosia. I wasn't just trying to get the hell out of there so I could get to the first liquor store, then the first drug dealer I could find. I wanted to be there. I was doing it because I wanted to. Tommy was a huge part in getting me social again, getting me out of the room and to meetings. All of these people and all that happened there worked to get me to realize that my life is worth living.

It's a no-brainer that I'd never thought applied to me, but I began to think more and more clearly the longer I was off dope. And I liked it! I did worry about what came next, though, because I had a support system at Ambrosia, but what was I going to do on the outside? I began to make a list of the comics and friends I knew who were either sober or had never had a problem with drinking and drugs, and they were all right there: Colin Quinn, obviously, and Dave Attell were sober and close friends I didn't have to feel funny in front of, and Nick DiPaolo was a guy who had been there for me through all of this. I just had to reach out to them and for the first time in a year and a half I wanted to. I started to think that maybe my career would still be there if I got myself back out into the world, and I started to think I could handle the pressure without the crutch of booze and drugs, maybe if I had guys like that in my corner in one way or another.

Ambrosia is an institution very much based in the Alcoholics Anonymous program and a big part of participating in your rehabilitation is going to group meetings every night. I started to go, for the first time by choice, and during my time there I really understood the ritual, the enjoyment, and the support you can find there. I got the feeling for it and realized that would be a big part of my socializing when I left, and it didn't feel shameful to me at all. I was finally able to admit to myself that it was what I had to do. I realized and was able to vocalize to myself that if I wanted to live my life to the fullest that I could, I'd have to fight, every single day, to stay sober. That was the only way for me if I planned to never let those gifts life has given me get away again.

The night I met Bruce Springsteen at that funeral, I also met a guy named Don Reo who was working with Clarence Clemons on his book, *Big Man*. Don knew how much of a fan I was of Clarence and Bruce and the band, so he asked me to write a blurb for the book jacket. I was beyond honored, because I was in what I'd call very good company under any circumstances, the other two blurbs being by Bill Clinton and Chris Rock. How could I not do it? The biggest problem I had was having so much to say about Clarence and limiting myself to a paragraph. I thought about it for weeks, and then it came to me clear as day when I was at the Four Seasons in LA, getting ready to jump into a car to go promote the *Too Fat to Fish* paperback on *Jimmy Kimmel*. Here it is: "The feeling I get watching Clarence Clemons slowly walking to the center of the stage to play saxophone must be close to the feeling a Yankees fan got in the 1920s watching the Babe slowly walk from the batter's circle to home plate. A Big Man was about to do something to make you cheer louder than you ever had before."

Clarence loved the blurb so much that he wanted to have dinner with me, and I was overjoyed because I'd met a few members of the E Street Band, but never him. We made a plan, set a date, everything, but I was too fucked up at the time to show up, so I made some stupid excuse. It was worse than that: I told a mutual friend that I'd gotten into a car accident and asked him to tell Clarence. A car accident is hands-down the worst excuse you can make, because how the fuck do you fake that? That's the kind of excuse you make when you're a drug addict, because drug addicts just lie. We lie and we don't care how big or how often we do it, because that's just what we do. And usually we think we're getting away with it and always act like we have no matter how extravagant the lie, because see the sentence above where I mention that we just don't care.

Clarence had a home on Singer Island, where he lived most of the year, less than a quarter mile from Ambrosia, which is where I was the day that he died, June 18, 2011. It is a small community down there and Clarence was by far the biggest celebrity resident, so you can imagine how big of a deal it was. As a part of the program we didn't see too many newspapers in rehab, but somehow I spotted a headline that he'd passed away. To say the least my heart cracked in two. I went to group meetings all day, until every single person in the place heard how sad I was that drugs had prevented me from meeting him. I'd had the chance, I'd fucked it up, and Clarence had died while I was in rehab, so that was a chance I'd never get again.

A few months before, a setback like this would have triggered a return to bedridden darkness. Instead, for the first time, it did the opposite: it became a reason to never let drugs stop me from missing out on the kind of experience I would have cherished for the rest of my life. That was my moment, that was when I made up my mind: Clarence had died nearly across the street and drugs had kept me from meeting him. It made me mad at the drugs I craved—more mad than any other feeling, which was a first for me. Anger became the emotion that pushed me forward because I'd needed to get mad at my addiction in order to step into the light.

Three weeks later they released me from rehab because by then they were satisfied with my progress. I'd gladly participated in every group meeting. I'd done my chores, from picking up garbage to cleaning bathrooms, to making breakfast. I'd become social; I'd help wake people up in the morning, making friends and greeting new patients. I made a friend named Gary, and he and I became pretty tight during the last part of my time there. About four months ago I found out that after he left Gary relapsed and died of an overdose. Rest in peace, man.

Heroin and opiates have taken so much from me: money, love, women, friends, family. Heroin took the *Howard Stern Show* from me and nearly lost me Howard's friendship; heroin kept me from Clarence Clemons. I'd started to think that heroin would take me too—and that it deserved to. But after my detox and rehab, after four institutions in fourteen months, for once I thought my mother was right. Maybe the past could be the past. Maybe everything would be okay. I didn't know what the future held for me career-wise, but at least I was back. I felt like a human being, and it had been years since I'd been able to say that. I knew I had more to offer as an entertainer, and for the first time in over a year I wanted to. I really wanted to. And I knew that all of the people who had come together and gathered around me would be there for me. I needed them to still be there if I stood a shot at doing this. Because most of all, more than anything else I didn't want to let them down again.

CHAPTER 9

UP FROM THE DEPTHS

If I ever needed proof that God exists, and there have been plenty of those times, I don't anymore. All my doubts are gone. The fact that I made it out of my mother's house alive, the fact that she didn't die from worry while caring for me, the fact that I'm here, still in show business, functioning the best I can and living as normal of a life as I'm capable of isn't the parting of the Red Sea, but it's a miracle in my book. Alcoholics Anonymous's program is based on a fundamental belief in a higher power, and all that talk sounded cheesy and corny to me in the beginning when I didn't want to hear it, but once I got over myself, once I got my mind clear and less self-involved, it didn't sound so cheesy anymore. A lot of intellectuals that I truly respect love AA with all of their hearts, and that went a long way with me. Once I took the program seriously and started to get into it and really engage, I began to ask those same friends about it, and all of them more or less told me the same thing: none of them know why AA works, they just know that it does if you give yourself over to it. That doesn't mean it's for everyone or that it's the only solution, but if you have issues even remotely like mine and anything about the AA philosophy appeals to you at all, it will improve your life if you let it. AA preaches a higher power and a twelve-step path to sobriety, and that's the path I followed out of the darkness. And it worked, it really did. So I'll never indulge in a crass moment of cynical disbelief about it again because I know there's a higher power in this world. Don't worry, that doesn't mean I won't be crass and cynical about everything here on earth. I'm not sure I'm capable of that kind of control. I'm only human.

Rebuilding myself from the mind up was a slow process, but I kept at it, because something had changed in me and I no longer wanted to be down there in that deluxe pit I'd spent so long building. For once I got with the program once I was out of the institution: I started going to meetings every day, first just sitting in the back, trying to be invisible, but after a while I got comfortable and eventually I participated. Around the same time I started reaching out to the people who had been there for me every step of the way during the time I'd spent hidden away from the world. I made a few social plans to see them and just talking about life again was like achieving something new to me because I hadn't done anything like that in what felt like a century. I also couldn't remember the last time I just hung out with people and not been on drugs or drunk or a combination of the two. This was more than a second chance: it was a rebirth.

Nick DiPaolo was one of the guys who'd called me every week, no matter what, even when I didn't call him back multiple times. One day in late June 2011, just after I returned home I called him to shoot the shit and he had unbelievable news.

"Art, I can't believe you're calling me right now," he said. "I just got off the phone with a guy named Chris Crane, who is an executive at DirecTV."

"Okay, that's great, man."

"They put radio shows on the air now, like the Dan Patrick show, and they want me to take over for a guy named Tony Bruno and do a test show with a partner. It would be a late-night sports comedy radio show. . . . Would you want to do that with me?"

"This really just happened?" I asked.

"I literally just hung up the phone, no shit."

It was another sign from God, if you ask me. "Really? That's incredible. I'm definitely interested, man. And, well, you know I'm available."

"Yeah, I heard about that," he said.

I'd just found out officially from Gary Dell'Abate, but not too long before, just after Howard's new Sirius deal was announced in March 2012, he told *Rolling Stone* that I'd not be returning to the show. It was for all the right reasons too: Howard loved me and wished me the best but he was too worried to have me back. He'd said that the Artie years were over and that fans had to get that idea through their heads. It was clear that he'd support me in whatever I did (and he sure has), but I couldn't return to the show. I'd been listening one morning that week and even heard Howard say the same thing to a guy who called in. Howard's instincts were right; the show wouldn't have been a good environment for me to return to at all. It was coming from a really good place because Howard genuinely wanted me to be okay. I'm not going to lie, I'd held on to a glimmer of hope that I'd return and work with all of my friends there, but looking back now, I'm glad I didn't get the chance, especially then. Howard was right, I wasn't ready for that—it was time for everybody, including me, to move on.

One door closed as another one opened, because there was Nick, a guy I love, with an opportunity for me to do something completely new. It was sports, it was comedy—and it wasn't happening at six a.m.! It was a dream come true for me. Nick set up a lunch with Chris Crane; James Crittenden, another DirecTV executive; and my agent, Tony Burton, who works for Howard's agent, Don Buchwald. We all had a great lunch and by the end of it the DirecTV guys agreed to let Nick and me do a test show on July 6, 2011. This was just a month after I'd gotten clean and left Ambrosia, so the timing was crazy, but I felt strong and I knew I had a solid support group around me. I even felt fine enough to do a few unannounced sets at the Comedy Cellar, because through rehab and AA I'd started putting together some stand-up routines based on the hell I'd managed to live through.

When we did the test show, we didn't tell anyone I'd be on the air with Nick—no mention of it on the show's website or anywhere else. I just went live with him when the ON AIR light when on. Word spread fast, much faster than I would have ever guessed, and I'm still incredibly touched by this: within ten minutes I was trending worldwide on Twitter. Reading all of those comments from excited fans really moved me. I hadn't been forgotten; people cared and there were a lot of people out there who wanted to hear what I had to say. The phone lines lit up like crazy when we started taking calls, all of them from people telling me how happy they were that I was alive and how great it was to hear me doing live radio again. Nick and I had fun, we really did. We were funny, we picked on each other—having a built-in Boston vs. New York rivalry doesn't hurt—and the show was a success. The executives loved it too, and took an edited sample of it to their board of directors in LA, who then decided to let us have a regular slot from ten p.m. to one a.m. every weeknight.

This was incredibly exciting and for me proof that the changes I was making in AA were having an effect at every level of my life. Around the same time I got back in touch with my cowriter on *Too Fat to Fish* and this book, the great Anthony Bozza, and we got to work on what you are now reading. Anthony and I started getting together and going over preliminary notes and just talking, because I wasn't sure I could actually do this book. I didn't know if I could put all of these experiences out there but in time, as the two of us spent more time together, slowly, I realized I could. I knew that this book would be the most personal and honest thing I'd ever do, and being that vulnerable scared me, but what drove me on was the thought that if sharing my stories helped even just one person avoid going through what I had and inspired them to make some changes in their life then it was all worth it.

My whole team was still there for me: my manager, Dave Becky;

my stand-up agent, Rich Super; my agent, Tony Burton; my great lawyer, Jared Levine. Everyone stuck with me through those two years of hell. I found that the stand-up world was there too, ready to embrace me when I returned. *Letterman* called almost immediately. Piers Morgan, all these different talk shows wanted to book me. I was a guest of both Jimmys: Kimmel and Fallon, who in my opinion are a new generation's version of Letterman and Leno. When the radio show went on the air and became a reality, Conan O'Brien called and they had me back on. It wasn't all good news, though, because I'd destroyed relationships too. Some people fell by the wayside because of my bullshit and I don't blame them for it. If there's one thing you can say about heroin without hesitation it's that it takes away a lot, from money to belongings to friends, but a lot of amazing people stuck with me, including my cowriter, who is sitting here right now. And I'm very happy to be here working with him again.

———

When we got off the air at the end of our trial show I went for a walk, because I wanted to savor how great I was feeling before heading home. I walked uptown, taking in all the lights and buildings. It was about 1:30 a.m. when I stopped in front of Radio City Music Hall, just a few blocks from the studio where we did the show, and my phone rang. I had already been thinking about her, standing where I was, but the last name I expected to see on my Caller ID was ADRIENNE, my old girlfriend's. Drugs had ruined the two of us the way they'd ruined everything else in my life, and I'd realized since I'd gotten sober that it was all my fault things had ended so horribly. The girl had tried; she thought she could handle hurricane Artie, but he was too much for her.

"Adrienne, guess where I'm standing right now," I said.

"Where?"

"Right in front of Radio City, the exact spot where I picked you up for our first date. Can you believe that?"

It was the first time I'd talked to her in over a year; she'd contacted me once or twice while I was caught in the doldrums and barely able to muster a hello, so we hadn't really talked. That night she'd heard about the show and she'd tuned in to the last hour, then decided to call me.

"I just heard you on the radio," she said. "I can't believe you're doing so well . . . you sounded great! I'm so happy for you. I was up studying and you just popped into my mind. I decided to Google you and saw you were live on the radio, so I tuned in and listened."

"And you called me right now as I'm standing in front of Radio City. See, I told you we're like *When Harry Met Sally.*"

Adrienne was living at home with her parents at the time, taking classes at a college because she wanted to try to get into medical school but needed a bunch of science and premed credits before she could apply. That was how we reconnected, and two days later she came to my house where we had a very honest, long-overdue talk. I got the chance to tell her, from the bottom of my heart, how sorry I was for dragging her into my chaos. It was what she needed to hear, because that rekindled our relationship, a romance that was influential in me getting better from there on out.

Later that month, Nick and I flew to LA to meet our new bosses, Chris Long and Derek Chang, who are both head honchos at DirecTV, and they gave us the offical green light—generous salaries, a good budget, everything, just like that. The news was picked up by TMZ and all the entertainment blogs. I was just so happy to have my mother see that I was really back on my feet and out in the world. Her son wasn't going to end up another casualty. It was the best I could do, because I can't give her back all the hours she spent taking care of me instead of enjoying the golden years of her life. I'll never forgive myself for that, but I'll do everything I can to make her proud.

The first official *Nick and Artie Show* debuted at 10 p.m. on October 3, 2011, and we found ourselves a devoted audience very quickly—again, something I understand, but it still happily surprised the fuck out of me. It makes sense if you think about it, because sports fans like talk radio—the devoted like to listen to people talking about sports when there aren't any sports to watch—but until we came along, there weren't any late-night sports radio shows that were actually entertaining. There are almost no late-night sports shows to speak of, and all of the entertaining ones are on in the morning or during the afternoon rush hour drive time. Creating a late-night version of a talk show with sports had never been done. Put it this way, any guy that likes to catch *SportsCenter* at two a.m. is definitely going to be up for listening to the kind of sports radio on acid that Nick and I serve up every weeknight. The numbers proved it too: we did so well that after just a couple of months DirecTV put plans in motion to begin televising us. They rented a 6,500-square-foot space in TriBeCa and had the guys who do the show *Man Caves* build us our dream set. The thing has a full kitchen, a pool table that converts to a Ping Pong table, couches everywhere, air hockey, a functional batting cage, a basketball pop-a-shot, and a photo booth. They even let us put whatever we want on the wall and we took that to the limit. Nick had the producers commission an homage of the famous painting of dogs playing poker, this one featuring Michael Vick. For my part I asked for a photo of O. J. Simpson photoshopped next to a shot of Peyton Manning with the caption: "O. J. Simpson and a white Bronco." And God bless them, they let us have both. Our set is amazing, so great that basically if things get real bad at home, Nick and I can shack up there if we need to. That's not been necessary so far, but I'm not counting it out.

Since the start of the show everything in my life has been going great. I feel better than I have in a long, long time, and I've kept myself in line for the most part. My stand-up career is better than ever and I've gotten a new beginning in radio, which is an entertainment medium I really do enjoy. I'd say the only thing I need to do is lose about 100 pounds, and it really sucks that they don't make a pill for that. Listen, I know it's been decades since I've seen my fighting weight, but I do have an excuse right now. When you leave rehab they tell you to do anything you need to do to not get high. They say "eat whatever you want, have as much sex as you want with whomever you want, smoke as many cigarettes as you want, drink all the coffee you want—do whatever it takes to stay off drugs and booze." I had smoking down and I'm not a huge coffee guy, so that left food and sex, and since food was a lot more available to me than sex when I first got out, I went with that.

I ate whatever I wanted whenever I wanted, which turned out to be enough to feed medium-sized countries. I'm not happy about the weight I've gained, but if I had to do it to get where I am, then it's fine with me. I feel good and that's the only thing that matters. And I'm not saying I know better than AA, but if anyone out there reading this likes food as much as I do and is freshly sober, you might want to try something I wish I'd thought of when they told me to do whatever I wanted. See, if they'd suggested combining the things, I would be in a whole different place. If they'd said, "Eat as much as you like, have sex as much as you like, and if you really like food, have sex with food as much as you like," that would have changed things for me. I love food, so I would have tried it—I would have fucked a pancake. And fucking it would have kept me from eating it. Because I know my problems, and food fucking isn't one of them. That's not the kind of behavior I could live with, so if it happened, even once, I'd make some changes and never do it again. Let's face it, I've gotten pretty desperate, but even I wouldn't eat a pancake I'd fucked, would you?

———

As I've already mentioned, I'm the type of guy who's watched every single Super Bowl since I was ten years old. The first I saw was 1978, when the Cowboys beat the Broncos. I got started early gambling too, because I even bet on that first game: I took the Broncos over the Cowboys and I should have learned my lesson then because the

Cowboys killed them. My buddy Mike Ciccone, also ten years old at the time, took me for fifty cents on that game, which is something he enjoys reminding me of to this day. I can tell you who has won every single Super Bowl since then, and on a good day I'm pretty sure I'll be able to tell you who the MVPs were too. I have forgotten so much thanks to drugs and just getting older, but sports stats like these are literally a part of my brain and they'll never be forgotten. The Super Bowl is a big deal to me, which made the fact that I'd watched two in a row in institutions even more depressing. The first one I saw on a psych ward and the other one (well, half of it) from my bed in rehab, trying to ignore my roommate yelling, mad as hell, about the shampoo they'd taken from him when he'd been admitted because it had alcohol in it.

"They fucking think I'm gonna drink fucking SHAMPOO?" he kept saying. "What the fuck is that? They think I'm so desperate for booze that I'll drink my fucking shampoo? I respect myself, you motherfucking fucks! Who drinks shampoo?"

Apparently he didn't, but what I found out in rehab was that some people really do drink their shampoo, and from what I hear, Salon Selectives Level Six packs quite the buzz. Look, I've been pretty fucked up, but I've never been so fucked up that I've ever considered doing a shot of Prell. It just seemed so stupid and Nazi-like for them to take my shampoo, so I protested even when they explained why they needed to.

"But you can't take that. I need that, because I don't have manage-able hair. The alcohol is the only thing that manages it."

"Well, I'm afraid—" the orderly said, politely taking me seriously.

"I'm kidding, I'm kidding," I said. "I never wash my hair or any other part of my body. I don't believe in it. All of the products in my bag are just here for show. So when is the cavity search?"

After two years of what any sane person would call less than favorable Super Bowl viewing circumstances, in 2010, I came back with a bang. My DirecTV show was official and getting off the ground nicely, and if you don't know this already, DirecTV offers more NFL packages than any other network, which makes them a major player in all things football. I can't thank Chris Crane, Jim Crittendon, and the big honcho, the one and only Chris Long, enough for taking a shot on me—I wouldn't be here without those guys. Basically thanks to them, in 2012, I came back as a Super Bowl VIP employed by the best sports and NFL network around, which is how I ended up sitting third row on the fifty-yard line, watching the Patriots lose to the Giants. It couldn't have been any fucking sweeter. Plus they let me play in the Celebrity Beach Bowl, which is a touch football game the network televises featuring retired NFL guys, a few players, commentators, actors who like football, and lucky losers like me. It's a pretty fun event, and I'm not just saying that because they employ me; I'd watched it the three previous years they'd done it. Unlike the previous events in places like Miami, since Indiana is completely landlocked, my Beach Bowl debut was miles away from any actual beach. The beach had to be imported, so DirecTV put up a huge tent in the middle of downtown Indianapolis and filled it with a few tons of sand carted in by truck.

I salute them for the effort because it was insane and also proof that the guys in charge up there aren't the types to take no for an answer. Chris Long is literally the greatest executive I've ever worked with and in a sea of networks like Bravo and all of those making programming solely for women, working for him and his team is like working for a team of Goodfellas. When they set their mind to something they find a way to make it happen. For example, sand had no business being in downtown Indianapolis, but there it was. The sheer fact that it was there made the characters—homeless and otherwise—that populate the area stand out even more by the way. It was a car crash, this beautiful, perfect, celebrity-driven event in a Podunk urban center so rough that you had to step over a mother with a crystal meth problem clutching her shivering child to get to the artist entrance to the artificial beach. It was a strange backdrop to a four-hour, multimillion-dollar event, which unfortunately featured Pauly D from *Jersey Shore* as the DJ.

Listen, I was fresh out of my personal depression, so every cloud was gray for me, but all that aside, I stand by my impression that Indianapolis is pretty fucking depressed. It's not where you'd ever send a friend on vacation. On the drive in from the airport, every house I passed looked like the four-hundred-square-foot shack in Gary, Indiana, where the Jacksons grew up. That place looked small on TV, but in person, that same kind of Indiana McHouse was even smaller than I imagined. All I kept thinking to myself was *How the fuck did eleven Jackson kids plus two parents live there and have room to learn those routines?* The Jacksons had one bathroom and eleven kids and they sang and danced and mostly all of them were involved. If they just stood in line from tallest to shortest they'd probably take up the whole living room. How the hell did they practice those dance steps? I mean, at some point while they were all sitting around trying not to step on each other did someone just say, "Okay, we have to do ABC. Everybody lend a hand, get up off what you're sitting on, and help put all the furniture in the hall." Four hundred square feet is some asshole's scarf closet on *The Real Housewives of New Jersey*, and that's all the room they had.

It's all still a mystery to me, but that's Indiana for you. Here's something that didn't surprise me about Indiana when I found it out: in the southernmost part of the state they're real big on the KKK; basically Southern Indiana is the motherland of the modern Klan. I wanted someone to take me to a meeting during my time at the Super Bowl and even asked for a volunteer during our live broadcast. I don't want to be a member and I don't agree with the Klan's worldview, as interesting as it is, I just wanted to get a taste of what went down at a meeting. We're all human beings, but I find the ones that are that much different from me really interesting. Don't judge me. Here's what happened when I solicited audience members at the Super Bowl broadcast to take me to a KKK meeting. . . .

"So if anyone out there wants to take me, I just want to see a pure white bitch who is uncorrupted," I said. I pointed to a real white Midwestern guy in the audience. "Would you take me? They'd let you in no problem."

"I've only been to two," he said, dead serious, while everyone laughed.

"What? Why'd you stop?"

"It was just, whatever," he said. "It's not what you think."

"Well, that's good," I said, "because what I'm thinking is horrible! Were you disappointed? Did you expect lynching ropes hanging from the ceiling? Did you expect them to burn Bill Cosby alive? Were you upset with the food?"

The kid was on camera, and he started to look nervous, like he might lose his job if he kept talking, so I let it go. As much as I love busting balls, I've come to realize that putting your job in jeopardy to do so isn't as cool as I used to think it was.

Anyway, the Celebrity Beach Bowl was a great time. Joe Montana was the quarterback on my team, our coach was Cam Newton of the Carolina Panthers, and Maria Menounos was on my team along with a few others. Nick DiPaolo was on the other team along with Snoop Dogg and David Arquette and Deion Sanders and Kate Upton. Nick and I were the first ones in the locker room that day, so he got to witness the embarrassing moment when I realized they didn't have a shirt that could fit me. When they'd asked me for my size before the event I told them in all seriousness that I was "size Enormous" and if they had any question about what that meant they should measure the biggest jersey they had and double it because double XL wasn't going to cut it. They must have thought I was kidding and probably figured that since I was a celebrity I must be of normal human proportions. Clearly they weren't familiar with my body of work.

The shirt they gave me was tighter than any condom I have ever worn. I could barely breathe, let alone think about running. I could probably throw and if the ball were perfectly aimed, I could probably catch it, but I wouldn't have bet on it. I was not going to be the go-to man in the clutch with that thing on, that's for sure. I asked the intern handing out the shirts what size he'd given me and he told me that it was the biggest they had. I don't give a shit what anyone says, those jerseys were tiny. In the end I gave my extra one to David Arquette, who is normal-sized (and a really nice guy), because his was too tight. If Arquette's was tight, mine was a torture device. And I was screwed because contractually we had to wear these things, plus DirecTV had a deal with Reebok, so all of us had to wear the same bright yellow sneakers. Fueled by shame, I forced my way into my shirt, a shirt that was so tight I couldn't lean over far enough to tie my new shoes. After a few minutes of uselessly diving at my feet, desperate as a midget trying to order a drink in a crowded bar, much to Nick's amusement, I had to ask one of the LA publicist girls DirecTV had hired to run this thing for help.

The girl was such an LA cliché that it's amazing she even exists in real life. "Is there something wrong with your shoes?" she asked with all the warmth of a frozen tuna. "Are they too small?"

"No, that's not the problem," I said. "They fit."

"So what is it, then?"

"Well, I can't get them on because my shirt is too tight and I can't reach my feet, so what I need is someone to put my shoes on. Can you help me tie my shoes?"

She looked at me in abject horror, as if if I'd just gutted a kitten right in front of her. "Ohhh, okay," she said. It seemed like she was thinking of a solution. "Yeah," she said, staring at me through a wave of condescension. "That's not my problem." And then she turned and walked away. At that moment I wanted to strangle her.

By this time the rest of the participants in the Bowl had filed in, including Deion Sanders, who is just such a great guy all around, and Joe Montana, who confirmed my perception that he's a nerdy, ultrawhite dumb dummy. I got all the proof I needed watching him interacting with the black guys, and seeing how he and Deion talked.

It only took two minutes to confirm everything I already knew about Joe Montana: the guy had no idea what Deion was talking about (and he was a terrible faker). I even asked Deion about it later and he said that he never really "got" Joe Montana but somehow they knew how to relate as quarterback and receiver. There's a thing that players talk about that they call "football IQ," which means that a guy is dumb as a rock in real life but get him on a football field and he's a genius. Joe Montana is one of those. Think about it: the guy is a Hall-of-Famer, he's still alive and functioning, but why hasn't he been a commentator anywhere on any network, ever? Want to know why? I'll tell you—because he's dumb.

Everybody else in the locker room was excited to see Joe except for me. This had nothing to do with his regular IQ or his football IQ, it's much simpler than that. The guy was a graceful, incredible quarterback in his day, but I never saw it that way. He was the guy who regularly ruined my bets and made me lose. By my count, he's cost me around $24,000 over the course of his career, so basically I hate the motherfucker. It's not something I can hide, and just then I realized how much it sucked that he was going to be the guy ordering me to run patterns and telling me where to set up for the play. This made the fact that I still couldn't get my fucking shoes on just that much worse.

Great friend that he is, Nick might have called me every week when I was on the verge of ending it all, but the shoes were a bridge too far. Why, I have no idea—probably because he thought it was funny.

"I'm not putting your shoes on. That's gay," he said. "Just don't wear any. Save yourself the dishonor of having another man put your shoes on for you. It's disgraceful."

"Thanks, Nick."

I wasn't going to ask Deion Sanders, and fuck Montana, I'd rather play barefoot, but I kept thinking that there had to be someone in the locker room that would help me out and not make a scene out of it.

I kept looking around for the right person and the right moment. It felt like an hour went by before I saw what might be my only hope: Neil Patrick Harris. Not only is he gay, meaning he'd be sensitive to my predicament (unlike a callous asshole like Nick), but he's also a big *Stern* fan and he'd read my book.

Neil came over and gave me a big hug and told me he was glad I'd gotten myself together and was doing well. He was a class act; he continued to make small talk, and I did too, absentmindedly. That's because I was debating whether or not to ask Neil Patrick Harris to help me tie my shoes. This was a real problem. I mean it, this was an issue. I was also concerned that Neil might tie the laces in such a way, with too much of a knot, that they would look really gay. I decided in the end that I just couldn't risk it, so I didn't ask him. No fault of his—it was definitely me—I was just too worried about the final product.

That's when Snoop Dogg arrived and I realized that the coolest thing to do in this situation was ask Snoop Dogg to help me with my sneakers. I didn't think he'd actually do it, but it would look good if anyone else happened to see. And I already knew he was good with sneakers because on *Stern* he'd told us on the air how he liked to use them to beat his hoes in the head to keep them in line. The guy has millions but says he still keeps hoes—and beats them with sneakers. I think that's what they mean when they talk about "keeping it real."

In the end I zeroed in on David Arquette because Snoop spent every free minute promoting whatever his new project was—the guy is seriously the greatest businessman I've ever seen. Anyway, I'd given David my extra jersey, so technically he owed me one, but that wasn't the real reason. He's also just such a nice guy, but you know what, he should be after all the money I would guess he got from Courteney Cox. So in the end David Arquette got my shoes on and tied them for me and God bless him for it. We had Joe Manganiello from *True Blood* on our team, and I don't watch that show, so

I didn't know who he was but since he was six foot nine, really fit, good-looking, and wearing a Pittsburgh Steelers hat, I figured he was a pro player. We also had a black guy who I thought was a player, but it turned out that he was the night correspondent on ESPN or wherever. There were a couple of smoking-hot chicks on our team too: Erin Andrews, the ESPN correspondent who got videoed naked through the peephole of her hotel room door by some creep, and my good friend Maria Menounos.

Before we get to the game, I need to take a moment to tell you what happened when Neil Patrick Harris came into the locker room. He did that thing that gay guys sometimes do when they hang out with a bunch of straight guys: he tried to adjust for the occasion. It's just the worst when gay guys do that, and I'm not being biased—it's equally horrible when straight guys try to adjust to the gay thing. But that's what he did. There were people handing out bags with our jerseys and sneakers in them, but they weren't right there to meet us, so when Joe Manganiello walked in he asked, out loud to no one at all, where he had to go to get his gear. And here's what Neil Patrick Harris said: "There's a gaggle of people back there handing out stuff." A gaggle. A gaggle? That word means a noisy, disorderly crowd, and as much as it's an accurate way to describe a busy locker room, I'm pretty fucking sure that this was the first time the word "gaggle" was ever uttered in a football locker room by a player. I'd never heard a human being say the word in a sports setting until then, but who knows, maybe gaggle is trending right now in Super Bowl tweets.

Maybe Neil thought it was tough talk, or maybe he forgot where he was and thought this was an all-gay football-themed cocktail party. Maybe he was texting Beyoncé and got confused and spoke out loud. I don't know. I do know that it turned heads. Deion Sanders looked up from his phone when he heard that and just shook his head, confused, before looking down again. It made me think of Siegfried and Roy and their white tigers. I mean white tigers are tigers, one of the toughest motherfuckers out there, and those white ones are rare, so they've got to be even tougher, right? They're like the Jim Browns and Archie Bunkers of the jungle. What do you think it was like for them to go from being the king of the jungle, where they can fuck any female tiger they want, eat any antelope, or just kill the shit out of some animal for the fuck of it, to working in a circus? They're walking around like champs, the rulers of the jungle, one day, and the next they're captured and taken someplace where they don't get fed until they sit on blocks like poodles. Plus they have to live with two gay guys! It's no wonder someone got hurt. I just can't believe it didn't happen sooner.

Anyway, the field we played on looked like your average arena football field, about the size of a hockey rink, just enormous and filled with sand. The crowd was pretty much all people just like me—frustrated athletes, drunks, and others who wish they could play, most of them thinking that if they could play they'd do it better. Whoever they were there to see, enough of them started chanting my name as we walked out. There I was taking the field alongside Joe Montana, one of the winningest quarterbacks in the Hall of Fame, but all you could hear was a mob of drunken fools shouting, "ART-AY!" Montana looked over at me like he didn't even know I was Artie or that they were even saying Artie (this suspicion would be confirmed a little later). I could barely breathe, my shirt was so tight, so there was no way I could start or even play much. Chris Long and the DirecTV guys told me they'd be sure I got in on defense in a little while. Fine. I sat down on the bench next to the legendary running back Jim Brown, who was eighty-two and definitely there for show, though he could have given a few of us a run for our money. Jim was great; he was waving to everyone and the fans loved him. I was more impressed by Jim than I had been before meeting him, and I was already a fanboy, not just for his athletic career but for his acting. Not many people know how great his film work was for a sports star, which is usually passable at best. If you don't believe me, watch *The Dirty Dozen*, which is a classic and one of my favorite movies of all time.

The two of us were benched for most of the game. Jim's excuse was that he was in his eighties, and mine was being too obese for my jersey. There was an upside to being benched that I wouldn't trade for the world, and there is a generation of young men that I'm sure will agree. Since we were on the bench and since she didn't play much, Jim Brown and I enjoyed an eye-level view of Kate Upton's bouncing ass, mere feet in front of us, for nearly two hours. She was our teammate and was wearing bicycle pants so tight that they were literally painted on. Once I noticed that I didn't even know the game was happening. I certainly didn't give a fuck about the score, that's for sure. I kept looking over at Jim because I didn't want any warm-blooded heterosexual male within range to miss the show, but I didn't need to worry, he was right there with me. Anyone who thinks we're pigs can shut up because the girl was nineteen and perfect, just cheering her team on, jumping around, being free. Not appreciating that would have been a crime against humanity.

Jim and I were on the same page about this, but I couldn't think of a way to start a conversation with him, because there was a lot I wanted to ask. I couldn't think of a natural way to launch into asking him if Lee Marvin was as big of an asshole on set as his character was on camera in *The Dirty Dozen*. I was still debating my opening line when Jim waved me into a huddle and leaned in as if he intended to educate me on the finer points of the last play. When I got close enough, he acted as if we were talking then casually pointed at Kate Upton's ass and said, "I'd like some of that, huh?" Then he gave me a high five! It was amazing. That was the only interaction we had, and frankly I don't think it could have been any better.

By the second half of the game my team was down by seven points and that's when Chris Crane, Chris Long, and Jim Crittenden from DirecTV came over and told me that I had to play because the whole point of them paying to have me there was to promote the *Nick and Artie Show* as much as possible, so obviously they wanted both Nick and Artie to play in the game. I had to get over the jersey issue just as our coach, Cam Newton, had to get over the fact that he hadn't thought he had to play me. I can't say for sure, but I got the feeling he took me for disabled.

"All right, Artie, we'll get you in," Cam said. "You're going to go out there and you'll hike the ball to Joe Montana, okay?"

"I don't want to play center," I said. "I want to play quarterback. If I'm gonna play, I'm gonna play quarterback."

"Well, you can't do that," Cam said, "because Joe Montana is quarterback."

"I know that, but I want to play quarterback. And that's what I'm going to play."

We were at a crucial turning point in the game; we were driving and needed to score and time wasn't on our side. Cam didn't get what the fuck I was thinking, which was very simple: I wanted to see just how much arrogance I could get away with.

"Listen, I don't understand," Cam said, turning around, looking for help, from anyone.

"The DirecTV guys told you to put me in, right?" I asked.

"Yeah, we're all getting paid here."

"And they're paying you. And I'm not playing unless I can play quarterback, which means you have a problem."

At that point the publicist girl from the locker room came over to try to fix the situation. "Artie, we really want you to get in there— everyone does! Look at all these people rooting for you! And we know you want to play quarterback, but I don't know if that's possible, because Joe Montana—"

I can't tell you how much joy it gave me to be able to say the next words that came out of my mouth, because they were the same words that had pissed me off so badly earlier in the day: "Yeah, I know that. But you know what? That's kind of not my problem."

Payback time, bitch! Whatever. I'm sure that broad will become a show runner on *Modern Family* or some sitcom I'll have my sights set on in the future and she'll take even greater joy in turning me down than I did in getting her back.

The guys on my team all started laughing when they heard that. "You motherfucker," one of them said, laughing.

After the girl had a brief conference with Chris and Jim from DirecTV one of them walked over to Joe Montana and told him that Artie was going to come in as quarterback for a few plays.

"Who's Artie?" Joe asked. Then he looked at me. "This guy?" He was dumbfounded. "Can you even play? . . . Can you throw?"

I knew what he was thinking, because I looked like a Make-A-Wish guy in my too-tight jersey. "Yeah, man, I can play," I said.

So I replaced Joe Montana, and to make matters worse, since we had no one on the sidelines, Joe had to hike the ball to me. By then he had a real attitude about me and the look on his face said it all. He said he didn't remember me, which is good because I'd started tallying up all the times in ten years I'd called him either gay or an asshole on the *Stern Show*, and it wasn't pretty.

I started calling out the numbers: "Blue forty-two!"

And before I got any further, Joe Montana threw me the ball in disgust and jogged out to the sidelines. It didn't matter, because I was in the pocket and I might not have been mobile, but I could get my arm up high enough to throw. I sure as hell wasn't going to let Joe Montana be right about me—that guy had made a fool of me too many times for nearly twenty years. I had to put an end to that shit.

I looked to Terrell Owens because as the only open receiver with actual professional football instincts he was my only real choice. T.O. was being covered by the one and only Nick DiPaolo, so this was a shoo-in, but for the fact that Deion Sanders was helping Nick out. When T.O. cut to the middle I threw a spiral as hard as I could, which looked to be over his head. And this is where seeing a pro athlete, retired or otherwise, perform up close is just awesome, because T.O. took off past Deion like he had a rocket up his ass and caught up to the pass. The ball hit him between the numbers and he got a few more yards before Deion grabbed his flag, but it was a great play, so the whole place went nuts and started cheering my name. Joe Montana came out and gave me a high five, and I could not believe any of it was happening; I was having this great moment and finally, for once, Joe Montana wasn't—because of me! It was a victory I'd been waiting for for a long, long time.

Cam kept me in for the next play, with Joe Manganiello substituted for T.O. I didn't know this, but Joe had played ball all his life and if he hadn't taken up acting he would have gone on to the NFL. He's built like a player, so I thought we could just repeat the same play and get on the board. I told him to run the same pattern and we got set up and hiked the ball. Maria Menounos was in and she put heavy pressure on me but I was able to get a pass off. The only problem was that Joe Manganiello must have forgotten all of his ball knowledge when he started memorizing lines for a living because he cut the wrong way. He's come on the *Nick and Artie Show* since then and we talked it over and he insists that he knows a post pattern from a down-and-out, but I'm not so sure. Whatever happened, I ended up throwing the ball right into the arms of a player on the other team—Snoop Dogg. I looked over to the sidelines and saw Montana shaking his head. And I couldn't have been picked off by a worse person because Snoop is such a natural entertainer that he showboated the hell out of it. The network had told us to keep things PG, and considering Snoop's body of work I guess this was PG for him, but he looked into the camera, drew an imaginary spliff in the air, and took a hit. Then he set the ball down the way you would before a kickoff, slowly got to his knees, and began doggy fucking it until the producers ran on the field and made him stop.

We lost the game, and I was so bitter. I blamed Joe Manganiello, which was bullshit—it wasn't his fault at all. I'll say that officially: Joe did the right thing and I didn't. I did my best to stay away from Snoop in the press room and at the after-party but he kept following me, saying shit like, "Hey, man, you throw good, you put that football right at my head!" He said that between quips about his new sneaker line, which he joked features steel in the heels so that pimps can properly keep their hoes in line.

I asked him why pimps didn't just slap their women around with their hands the way other men do.

"A pimp got to keep his hands clean, Artie," he said. "He don't want to ruin his nails educating a ho."

As I mentioned earlier, thanks to my amazing employers, the great Chris Long and his team at DirecTV, I got to enjoy the game from the third row on the fifty-yard line, with a bird's-eye view of the Giants beating the Patriots. And since my cohost, Nick DiPaolo, is from Boston, this afforded me endless opportunities for ball breaking, which is the greatest gift you can give a guy like me. The whole thing even inspired me to write a song about how much Boston sucks, called "Boston State of Mind," to the tune of Jay-Z's "New York State of Mind." It was my first attempt at a rap song, and I'm proud of it because it features lines like these:

> *Boston, the birthplace of Facebook, and the comedy of*
> *Dane Cook.*
> *Boston, where Bucky Dent made the Red Sox look like the*
> *cast of* Rent.
> *Boston, this town is a big joke, where Len Bias bought bad*
> *coke.*

And my personal favorite:

> *You know New Yorkers are always stuck in traffic on the*
> *packed Upper Bruckner, the only thing getting through*
> *is a ground ball to Buckner.*

After viewing two Super Bowls from box seats in hell, there I was, with my own radio show, watching my team defeat the evil Patriots from the best seats in the house. The Marriott where we were staying was covered in broads wanting to hang out with anyone connected to the broadcast, so I was in heaven.

The only downside was that I had to go home and be back on the radio the next day and they'd routed me through Atlanta, which made what should have been an hour and a half flight into a five-hour ordeal. Nick and I had to leave early in the morning and do the show that night, and his flight was even worse because for some reason he had to deal with a transfer through Charlotte. He was bitching about it nonstop, and it only got worse after his team lost—the guy was incapable of speaking a positive word. Anyway, he and I agreed to leave together at seven a.m. and share a ride to the airport.

That was before I ran into this kid Ross, whom I used to work with at Sirius, who was flying back on his friend's private jet. "Art, you should come with us," he said. "The guy is a huge fan of yours; if you come hang and bring him a signed copy of your book I'm sure it'll be cool. We have room for you." He checked with the guy and it was in fact cool, so Ross told me he'd pick me up in the limo at my hotel around seven a.m. and we'd head right to the jet. I couldn't believe my luck—this was going to cut seven hours of travel out of my day. This was also yet another chance to fuck with Nick, even more so once I learned that aside from Ross and his buddy and me, all the other passengers on this ten-seater plane were girls who had just posed for *Maxim*, all of them twenty-one or twenty-two years old. I was so excited to bum Nick out in the morning that I could barely sleep that night.

I was out in front of the hotel bright and early knowing that Nick would probably be early, which he was, as usual. I was there already, all smiles. "Hey, man, how you doing today?" I asked him.

"Whatever, fuck you," Nick said, almost spitting at me. "Yeah, I know, I get it. Giants win."

"I mean, yeah, but I'm just happy to see you, man," I said.

"Whatever. Let's get going, There's a cab over there."

Just then the limo pulled up and three girls leaned out the window. "Hi, Artie!" they said.

Ross leaned out the other side: "Hey, Art, let's go. We don't want to miss the plane, man."

Nick looked like Walter Matthau standing in a cold New York City rain. "What the fuck is this?"

"Oh, shit, I forgot to tell you," I said. "My buddy Ross got me a private jet home, so I'm going to head out with him and the girls. Enjoy that ride to the airport with Sandip from Pakistan. Sounds like that cab has a bum muffler. Tell the guy he should really get that checked out."

"I hope your plane crashes, you asshole," Nick said. "You're a fucking bastard, you know that?"

"Artie! Come on, let's go!" The girls had opened the door and were sipping champagne, all of them in tight shirts and short skirts.

"This has got to be a joke," Nick said.

"Afraid not, man," I said. "I'd have you along, but the plane is full. So have a great flight and I'll see you in the studio. It's gonna be a great show tonight."

Nick finally realized that this was happening. "Have a great flight, asshole," he said, "and fuck you."

"I will, Nick," I said, getting in, as a girl sidled up on each side of me. "Oh, and Nick? Fuck the Patriots and fuck you."

By ten forty-five that morning I was in my apartment watching *SportsCenter* as Nick landed in Charlotte, completing the first of his three flights. I decided to check in with him and was shocked that he didn't pick up. I left him this message:

"Hi, Nick, it's Artie. I'm home safe. I'm all right, just wanted to let you know because I know that you're worried. So don't worry, I'm very comfortable. I have a sandwich, I have *SportsCenter* on, and a few of the *Maxim* girls are here keeping me company until I head into the city to work later. Now, I know you're married, so I probably shouldn't tell you this, but one of the girls thought you were really cute. I'm taking one of them out Thursday and her friend wanted to tag along if you were going to be there. But don't worry, I told her that you're married and put an end to that. If you get back in time and want to come here to my place instead of driving back to Westchester, give me a call. I'll be here with the girls. I'm comfortable, just unbelievably comfortable, so don't worry about me at all."

Around two o'clock in the afternoon he sent me a text. It was simple, but the rage still came through. All it said was, "Delayed in Charlotte. Sitting on my suitcase." It's too bad that I didn't read it until much later, but I couldn't help it. I was busy napping.

CHAPTER 10

THERE'S NOTHING LIKE PARIS IN THE SPRING

You've gotten this far, and I salute you for that because it hasn't been a joyride. It has been the truth, though, and the truth is all I have to stand by, easy read or not. It wasn't an easy "life," either, believe me. I say this now because I'm about to tell a story involving someone who means the world to me, but up until now in this book I haven't said so at all. Her name is Adrienne and Stern fans know all about her, but to understand what I'm going to tell you now, I need to say a few things about myself first. Keep in mind I've only recently learned these things and can only now actually say them out loud, so bear with me.

I've got a gruff exterior and what an analyst of human behavior might call a "cynical-sarcastic comic attitude." I'd never argue with that; it sums up my public persona perfectly. But that's not me in my personal life at all; I'm very emotional and I fall hard for people I care about, especially women. Yeah, yeah, I can hear you fans who think that means I "act like a pussy," because that's what I've had friends tell me through the years. But I don't, I just fall hard and when things don't work with my girlfriends I experience a spectrum of emotions that are very extreme: anger, sadness, depression . . . but I can't lie, mostly anger. That's what swells up inside me when things don't go my way.

If you're a drug addict like I am, anger is the most dangerous emotion of all because anger is at the root of all impulsive, destructive behavior. In the AA program, which I've done my best to stay with (though my batting average is fair to middling so far) the biggest drive in those moments when I've lost my way has always been anger. I mean, let's face it, I nearly killed my former assistant Teddy over some pretty trivial bullshit. Anger is the devil on my shoulder; it's the slippery slope to relapse and I'm no delusional fool—I know that relapse isn't ever far behind me. Anger has a twin brother, and his name is Resentment, and they are best friends who are bound at the hip. Every time I've fallen off the wagon, whether it's been a day or a week, I can pin the blame on one or both of them. I have to be honest, I've been doing my best, but sometimes they get the best of me. I'm an addict. I know this. I am wired to consume and self-destruct. My struggle every day is to not do that.

When you love somebody you're vulnerable, and when you're vulnerable your emotions get the better of you. When you're in love you have no control, which is a tricky thing because at that point your emotions take control of your actions. When you're in love everything is amplified, both inside and outside of you. It's such an intense state of mind and it affects different people differently, but no matter how it does, the results are always elevated. Being in love can make you controlling and obsessive simply because you want to be with the person you love every single minute of every single day. Whether we're talking about the Stones, Springsteen, Jimi Hendrix, Dylan, or The Who, all of their best songs are about women who did them wrong or confused them enough that they had to create something to try to figure out the "why" of it all. They had to find a way to use their yearning and dissatisfaction. If they didn't it would eat them alive. I take those same feelings and put them into my comedy because I have to send them somewhere. I may bust balls all day professionally, but that doesn't mean I don't have feelings. If you ask me, I have too fucking many and most of them are too much for me to live with. Without comedy I don't know what I'd do . . . actually I do, I just don't want to think about that.

What I'm trying to say is that this chapter is about feelings and this chapter is about Adrienne, but what I want to be clear about is that she wasn't the first girl I've ever loved. There have been several whom I considered my true loves at the time. What I've found out to be true is that Adrienne is someone that I've loved more than anyone else I've ever known outside of my family. I've never had the depth of passion I have for her for anyone else in the whole world. I fell deeply in love with her when we were together and though the dynamics changed between us, my feelings always remained the same.

———

On May 14, 2009, I got temporarily clean after Joe the Cop and Helicopter Mike saw me through the Subutex withdrawals down at my beach house. That was when I got healthy, when I lost forty pounds, when I hit the gym daily, and started to look like something resembling good. And that's when I saw Adrienne for the first time. She literally was the most beautiful girl I'd ever seen in my life. She had, and still has, these eyes I could see from twenty feet away. Years later I described them in a letter I wrote to her like this: "If heaven had green lights, they would be your eyes." If anyone reading this wants to punch me in the face for writing something so corny and sending it through the US mail to a woman, don't worry, I couldn't agree more. In fact I'm going to do that right now.

There. Done. I feel better. I hope you do too. Now we can move on.

When I went into the tanning salon, I was relieved to find out that she was just filling in for a friend. Because I downplayed this fact before, let me be honest about it now: I think tanning salons are a sign of the apocalypse. I think they are ruining Western civilization from within. They are making everyone orange and dumb. They should all be destroyed.

As I've already told you, I managed to sweet-talk her for a while, making plans to get a shave a few days later, then I kept at the small talk until it evaporated. I asked her where she was from—Cherry Hill, about an hour and a half away—and I was thankful that she was a Yankees fan, not a Phillies fan. And after that I took her to the *SNL* party at Rockefeller Center and soon after that we started dating seriously. That's when we started spending as much time as we could together.

I fell deeply in love with her, though she is very different from me in every possible way. That was new for me, because all of my girlfriends, aside from Dana, were pretty much all like me. My past girlfriends had been Jersey Italian types, pretty much across the board. Even if they hadn't been Italian they might as well have been. I had never in my whole life dated a WASP before, and Adrienne is the Jersey version of that.

My last girlfriend Dana was nothing like me, not only because she was adorable and sexy and I'm not, but because she didn't like the same things I do. But the funny thing was when we fought Dana would yell, and when she did, she sounded like Andrew Dice Clay. Which, in a weird way I care not to explore ever for the rest of my life, really turned me on.

As I was saying, Adrienne is none of those things. She isn't Italian, and she didn't grow up in an Italian neighborhood. She comes from a really great family, all very classy people. That's not to say my family isn't classy, we're just louder and more obnoxious. Adrienne's family is a refined one, and she's a brilliantly smart girl. She did a semester at Oxford and went to Australia to study, she's traveled abroad and met all kinds of interesting people, and all of that fascinated me. She is everything I'm not, from the way she was raised to the way she looks. If you see a photo of us side by side, your first thought will probably be that we'd never work. I'd say the same if

I were you because I get it, I'm much better looking. But joking aside, the truth is that Adrienne and I do work. We genuinely have true love for each other.

When we were first together, during that time when I was sober, my love for her became very, very deep. She gave our relationship her all, trying to help me through my problems. I warned her that she was walking into the eye of a hurricane, but she assured me that she could handle it. I gave her a copy of *Too Fat to Fish* at that point just to be sure, telling her that it was required reading if she planned to be with me for a week, for a month, or for the rest of either of our lives. I wanted her to know where I was coming from and that even though I was in a good place, she should understand what I would be trying to fend off each and every day. I told her that if I relapsed she needed to be strong enough to walk out, no questions asked. "You will need to save yourself. You will need to get the fuck away from me, right away," I told her. She agreed that she would and could do that. And so we went on.

I guess that pact was our prenup, because once we'd had that talk, we set off on a great romance. Like I said, she and I should not have worked, just by looking at us, just on the basis of how different we are, but we did. I made her a part of my life in every way, right away. When I did *Letterman* I made jokes about dating a younger girl, because at the time she was twenty-five and I was forty-one. My joke was innocent enough: I told Dave how women always want to "do something," and how that was a full-time job. They don't always know what they want to do, but they want to do "something." When we came back from commercial, they had a camera on Adrienne, in the greenroom, and she looked stunning. She looked like Christie Brinkley's younger, better-looking sister. It was unbelievable; she's gorgeous in person, but on camera her beauty just popped. She was tan and those eyes were incredible and she was wearing this cross necklace by Lazaro that I had bought for her.

"Is that your girlfriend?" Letterman asked.

"Yeah."

"Artie, if I were you, I'd start doing something," Dave said.

That got huge laughs, of course. And he was right.

None of that was planned, which made all of it cooler. Adrienne was very shy in front of the camera too, which made me even more attracted to her.

By the time I began to relapse, she and I were so connected and so serious that she didn't run away. I slid all the way down, back to heroin, back to pills and any other drugs I could find. She saw it all and she fought for me. She fought for us, really, because by then there was an "us." I'm well over two hundred pounds and she's just over one hundred, but there were many nights when she tried to wrestle the drugs away from me, unafraid. She fought for me and fought to save what we had. She was the light of my life for those few months. Every time she smiled I saw everything good in the world. I'm a very dark person, so that's not what I look for or ever see if left to my own devices, but when she smiled I did. In those moments I saw everything I'd been missing in life.

My career had taken me all around the world, but I'd still never been to Paris. It's hard to believe that the Funny Bone comedy empire hasn't staked its claim in Paris, otherwise I may have been booked there. Adrienne is well-traveled in every way, so during her time at Oxford she met people who were in a different zone wealth-wise and had subsequently been to Paris a few times. She loved Paris and she always told me all about it. She told me how romantic it is and how beautiful it is to walk those streets. We both love the movie *Casablanca*, and like so many other couples we always quoted the line "We'll always have Paris," even though we'd never been there.

Adrienne always promised that if we ever went to Paris she'd show me everything, and I couldn't imagine anything more romantic than that. I was forty-one and she was twenty-five when we met, and I can't describe how great it is to find true love at forty-one because it rejuvenates you. It was like I was born again. Just as I'd come to believe that I knew what this world is all about, she came along and reminded me that all the good exists here right alongside the bad. It made me happy to be alive. Adrienne was my little angel.

She wrote me the most beautiful card I've ever gotten from anybody about what we were going to do when we went to Paris, all the activities she had planned for us, and it became a dream and a plan we talked about. We were going to Paris and we were going to experience it together. This was before I completely crashed and burned the first time. After we said good-bye on December 9, 2009, I never thought I'd see her again. I didn't have the capacity to think about how she felt; I was too caught up in my own spiral into hell to be capable of that. Or to care. I didn't realize, because I couldn't even understand what it meant, that she was stuck on me just the way I was on her. In the moments I thought about her, I figured she would walk away and have a happy life because she wasn't like me—she could do that. But that wasn't the case because what I didn't realize is that real relationships aren't like that. True love runs both ways.

Adrienne's birthday is January 1, which makes New Year's Eve a big night in her life. When we were at our best she told me that, so I concocted extravagant plans for that first birthday of hers we'd spend together. The first of many, I'd say, but it never happened, though I tried. I left rehab early, pretty much to be with her, just to try to fulfill at least one promise because I'd fucked up so many others. I came home with every intention of celebrating her and proving that I was changed. All I did was retreat into my broken lair and get high, drunk, and as fucked up as I could, just everything I'd done before, once again. She was living with her parents at the time and I didn't even call her, I didn't make any kind of effort at all, because I was in full addict isolation mode.

New Year's Eve 2009 was awful. It was the cherry on the crap cake. I wanted to be with Adrienne and I wondered where she was. I didn't know because I hadn't reached out. I hoped she was somewhere free of the kind of bullshit I'd made her deal with. I hoped she was smiling, having a good time, and enjoying her birthday. I hated every single second of those two days because all I wanted was to be with her. I didn't have the courage to even call, text, anything. In that hole I went and dug for myself there in my living room, I didn't even know how to communicate with someone who had become closer to me than anyone. So I did drugs, I drank, I numbed myself to the point of oblivion so I'd not think about how fucked up that was and how alone I felt. And I kept going and, as I've described as honestly as I can in these pages, on the morning of January 2 I stabbed myself.

That was my rock bottom. I'm fine with declaring that moment officially as my rock bottom. I mean, shouldn't it be? If it wasn't I'd like someone to step up and tell me what is, because I can't think of a deeper pit of hell. If it exists, I'll take your word for it and hope I never go there. When you hit rock bottom as a heroin addict you realize something that is very simple and very clear. It's something that people tell you all along your path to that dark existential shit hole of a place. It mystifies me how this easy-to-remember fact gets lost in the shuffle for all the months or years that addicts like me insist on stumbling along.

Here it is—and please listen up. Heroin addiction is a story with only two endings: death or quitting. You will die or you will quit, and that's it. When an addict finds their rock bottom, that might be their end, because they might not live through it. If they do, unless they're completely deluded, that last straw will turn their ship around and make them want to get better. I hate to spoil things, but given that those are the only two options and that you're reading a book by me, it's safe to conclude that I chose the second option.

If you're math-oriented you already have calculated that it took me a full two years to get straight. From psych wards to rehab to my mother's house, I marched through my own personal hell and brought too many loved ones with me. When I came out of it and got back on the radio, Adrienne came back into my life, and as a sober man, that relationship and all the love I feel for her was more powerful than ever. I really couldn't believe that I was getting a second chance. The love of my life, who I finally realized loved me too, was back. And I had a new job!

Adrienne had tried to come see me when I was in rehab, but my family wouldn't let her. They kept anyone from my life who wasn't actual blood to me (a very Italian move) at a huge distance. I can't blame them. I was a completely vulnerable person, but they didn't realize that she would have helped. My family wouldn't let Adrienne visit when I needed her most and I'm still disappointed by how much they misjudged her. I couldn't explain to them how much seeing her face would have cheered me up during those dark days. They were trying to save my life—and they did—and I understand why they didn't want me to see her. I love everyone I'm talking about so much, for very different reasons. All of them had the right intentions, so I hold no grudges, and neither should they.

I called Adrienne once during those bleak times, during a period when my life coach/sober coach was living with me at my mom's place. I'd flown him in from LA to be with me twenty-four-seven. He was sleeping on the couch at my mom's, doing all he could to get me to leave the dark bedroom down the hall. He was there when I called Adrienne, and she was still taking classes and studying at the time. I had come a long way by then and under the sober coach's supervision, I was allowed to have my BlackBerry back again. Maybe a day or two later, as fate would have it, I got a text from Adrienne telling me how she was at Radio City Music Hall seeing a band that she said reminded her of Springsteen.

When Adrienne and I were together, she made me feel young, she tuned me into what it is to feel young and happy again and in return I turned her on to Springsteen. She and I were like "Thunder Road," and she texted me that night to tell me she was crying because of the memories of us there. I texted her back from the heart. I said, "I hope you're okay." It was the start of a conversation, because the next day we got on the phone.

We talked for a long time and I thought that seeing her would be really good for me, but that's when she told me that she'd started seeing someone a few weeks earlier. That is why she'd been so emotional at the concert the night before—she was there with him. I couldn't blame her for dating someone else, but at the same time, I realized just how much I still loved her, because hearing that she was with another guy broke my heart. I was happy that she'd moved on, but it tore me to pieces.

What surprised me was just how much she'd fallen for me and how she hadn't forgotten what we had. She'd been so moved by the memories of us that she wasn't able to contain that emotion at the concert. I was surprised but so fucking happy to hear how much she still loved me. I'd been too fucked up to realize it when we were first together, so it was a complete shock in the best possible way.

"Artie, please just let me see you," she said.

I was speechless.

"You want to go for ice cream?" she asked.

I didn't want to do that. I couldn't. I love going for ice cream, but I just couldn't. She'd call and ask and I'd just say no and hang up. I didn't want to see her if I couldn't have her. I expected I'd never hear from her or talk to her again. She was going to be just another good thing that left me because of me, because of drugs.

But against all odds, and against how I saw things, our romance started up again once I began to crawl out of the dark. We had a few months of bliss where we'd go to dinner in downtown New York and we'd walk around Greenwich Village. She'd come see me do sets at the Comedy Cellar. It was almost like we were dating again, but also for the first time somehow, because I was clean and everything was brand-new to me. It was like we were dating the way we should have when we first met.

When we came back together, Adrienne was trying to get into medical school and was studying and working like crazy to do it. She had her schedule and I had mine, which was pretty open compared to what I was used to before I crashed and burned. But the better I got, the busier I got, and that schedule filled up. When I started going on the road again, things changed between us. I don't think either of us could have predicted it, but feelings of resentment and anger came over the two of us. She had never been able to express them and I'd never acknowledged that she should have them. I was also seeing my life clearly for the first time and had a bundle of uncomfortable feelings to deal with. I loved what I saw of our past and I wanted another shot, but I knew that she was worried about dealing with me and how hard it was still going to be, to say the least. All of these things bubbled up between us and we went through a few really bad months.

No matter how hard it got, we never stopped talking about going to Paris together—it was like this promise we wouldn't let go of. And that, to me, seemed like the best way to get us back on track. I wanted what she had talked about in her card—all those plans and dreams—to come true so she'd see that it could work. I told her that I had a vacation from the radio show and that I wanted to go to Paris. When it came time to book that trip, we had been fighting nonstop, and what I should have done was say that the best thing for us to do was stay home and work out our problems during my time off, but I didn't do that. Instead I went for the grand gesture and booked a trip to Paris during a moment when she and I weren't even talking. What a fuck-you that was! I didn't get her a ticket or anything, I just told her about it, I guess to rub it in, but I guess also because I wanted her to come. Somehow we made up before I left, so I ended up using a bunch of air miles to get her on my flight at, literally, the very last minute. It was a recipe for disaster before we even left, because we hadn't resolved anything we'd been fighting about.

There was another reason I wanted to go to Paris in July 2012 rather than any other time: Bruce Springsteen was playing two shows there over the July Fourth weekend. There is nothing more patriotic than seeing Bruce—and seeing him in Paris was a double win—so

I planned to fly out on the fourth after doing the *Nick and Artie Show* to catch Bruce on the fifth. Thanks to my friendship with the E Street Band's brilliant and kind guitarist Nils Lofgren, whom I am lucky enough to call a friend, I was able to arrange tickets and passes for me and my friends. I can't say enough how much Nils Lofgren has been a source of inspiration and a positive force in my life in every single way you can imagine. We first met in 2004, when he and his wife, Amy, came to see me do comedy in Arizona, and after my set Dan Mer, the owner of the venue (which was the Tempe Improv), introduced us. Dan came back to my dressing room to let me know that Nils wanted to come meet me, and honest to God I've never said, "Please bring them back," quicker in my entire life. We have been friends ever since and I've grown to love him and his wife very much. I almost feel bad saying this because I'm just not worthy, but I'm so privileged to say that Nils has even begun to give me guitar lessons. It was his idea: as a guy who has been sober for decades, he told me I'd need to find a hobby, a passion, something to put my energy into aside from what I already did, and that guitar was perfect. He's right; it's a great meditation for me and I don't care that I'll never be Hendrix, Clapton, or Nils, I just like the practice. It's a habit I won't have to quit. And guitar lessons from Nils Lofgren? It's great to be alive, as far as I'm concerned. I also hoped that I'd see Bruce for at least a minute or two because I really wanted to tell him just how much that phone call from him when I was at my lowest had kept me going. He really helped save my life—I mean that very literally.

All in all, even though Adrienne and I had been fighting, I had high hopes for this Paris trip. I booked a really nice hotel and I invited a small group, which included some good friends, like my cowriter, Anthony Bozza; my radio show producer, Dan Falato; my AA sponsor, Don; and my travel guru, John Valestri. And I might as well come clean now: I planned to ask Adrienne to marry me on that trip. I'd set up a place for us to go ring shopping, and I was going to propose under the Eiffel Tower. Once I was there I changed my plan;

I decided an evening cruise would be more romantic. It would be more of a cliché, but I didn't care, I wanted to be as romantic, cheesy, whatever you want to call it, as possible. Because that's how she makes me feel.

Unfortunately my anger and overall addict behavior took over the moment we landed in Paris. I started a massive fight with Adrienne at the airport that just kept going all the way to the hotel and resulted in her not coming to the Springsteen concert that night. This is something I'll regret forever. She and I had talked about how much we wanted to hear "Thunder Road" together in Paris. I heard it, and she didn't, because my knack for being an asshole ruined the evening. What's even worse is that Nils, in addition to getting my friends and me passes for the E Street Lounge and whatever else we wanted, invited me to have a bite to eat with him and his wife before the show, where I got to meet Roy Bittan, the genius piano player in the band. After that my friends and I went backstage and we hung out with Steve Van Zandt, which was incredibly cool. I've gotten to know Steve over the years, so it wasn't strange when he came up and said: "What? Were you just in the fuckin' neighborhood?"

Steve has seen it all, and I'd been honest with him about my struggles with heroin, so for that reason I was excited to tell him that I'd beaten it and was finally clean. Steve grabbed my cheek and, in the way Silvio did when he scolded Christopher on *The Sopranos*, said the most simple, truthful thing anyone could ever say about heroin—take note of this.

"Why would you ever mess with that shit?" he said. "It ends one of two ways, and one is death." He had one more observation that's equally important: "Why would you mess with something that gets in the way of your fucking?"

The show, as any Springsteen fan who keeps up with the band can tell you, was amazing. There was no air-conditioning in the sold-out arena full of seventeen thousand for two nights. I'm overweight, so that kind of heat affects me, but I don't care what anybody says: it felt like it was about two hundred degrees in that place. The air was so hot it was almost visible. But let me tell you something: the first time I saw Bruce in concert was August 31, 1985, at Giants Stadium in New Jersey. He played for about four hours and I was sitting in the very last row of the upper deck with my friends Danny McGrath, Charlene Cole, and Sue Solofski. We were all seventeen. That is still the best show I've ever seen in my life. I've been to fifty-plus Springsteen shows since then and I can say with no doubt about it, that the Paris show on July 5, 2012, was easily the second-best Springsteen show I've ever seen. It's a natural follow-up to my first show way back in the sumer of '85.

Bruce opened that Paris set with "The Ties That Bind" off of *The River*. That is one of his greatest songs, if you ask me. It's a track about being young and rebellious, and it's something hard-core fans know and love. It's the kind of song that would make sense for him to open with in Jersey, though it would still be a welcome surprise because it's a very rare thing for him to do. But in Paris? I couldn't believe what I was hearing! During the show he played about seven tunes off of *Born in the U.S.A.* and Nils outdid himself during the solo in "Because the Night."

The most surreal thing of all was hearing seventeen thousand people sing "Born to Run" in thick French accents! And as he did throughout the tour, Bruce took the house down with a heart-wrenching video tribute to Clarence Clemons in the middle of "Tenth Avenue Freeze-Out" that came right after he sang the classic lyric, "When the change was made uptown / And the big man joined the band." The show ran just under four hours with no intermission and no air-conditioning, and it was nothing short of amazing. I had to piss four times during the show, because it was that long. The man is sixty-three years old! I have no idea how he does that, I'm just glad he keeps doing it.

I figured I'd missed my chance to chat with Bruce, but after the show, Amy Lofgren, who was sitting near me, invited me to the band's after-party at the Four Seasons. She said the whole band would be there and Bruce would be too, since he had his mother and his in-laws in town for the show. I was missing Adrienne bad, but I had to go. I chose to ignore what was going on between us because I'd probably never get a chance like this again. I left my friends behind and went off on my own. It took me an hour to hail a cab to take me over there because it was chaos outside of the arena, but I did it and I'm glad I did. I was escorted into the bar, where the band was hanging out and Nils greeted me. As I was walking in, Ryan Seacrest was walking out. Fuck him.

The whole band was there, including Bruce, who was sitting quietly chatting and laughing with his mother. It was such a great hang, just talking about music and life with Nils and Amy. I also talked to "Mighty" Max Weinberg at length, as well as his wife and daughter. For a Springsteen fan like me it was seventh heaven. Nothing else in my life mattered just then. An unexpected bonus was meeting NBC anchor Brian Williams, who is really cool, really funny, and was a great guy to talk to.

The evening couldn't have been better for me, just sitting there by the bar drinking water (at that point), chatting with all of these people that meant so much to me and made music that has been my life's sound track since my teens. I didn't think for a second I'd get a moment with Bruce, and it didn't matter to me: I was having the time of my life. I couldn't believe it when, over Amy Lofgren's shoulder, I saw Bruce get up from his table and walk toward us. Surely he was just getting a drink? No, I was this lucky—he was coming to talk to me. He tapped Amy on the shoulder, pointed at yours truly, and said, "Excuse me, Amy, I wanna talk to this guy." He shook my hand, asked how I was doing, and I got that chance to let him know just how much his call, his concern, and his words meant to me.

"Bruce, I just want you to know that your phone call saved my life. It really did. I'm out of hell now. Thank you, man."

He didn't say a word; he just gave me a hug.

"That's great news, Artie. I'm glad you're here."

We talked for a while and had a few laughs and I asked him something I've always wondered about, because in my small way I can relate, though he's on such another level. I asked him how he came down from performing.

"Yeah, that can be the hard part," he said, grinning a little. "After all that it's tough to relax."

After a while Bruce said his good-byes, and the last thing he said to me was this: "Much good fortune." What a cool way to say farewell. Bruce escorted his mother to the elevators, and watching that guy, arguably the greatest American rock star we have, do something so humble and natural warmed my heart. Of all the roads a rock star can take, of all the horrible self-indulgent places they can end up, of all the pitfalls that can take them too early, from Hendrix to Cobain, seeing Bruce Springsteen, age sixty-three, chivalrously walk his mother, who is in her eighties, to her room in the Four Seasons in Paris did my heart good. It made me want to stick around long enough to do the same with my ma one day.

Riding back to the hotel I was on cloud nine. And I can hear some of you fans of mine snickering as you read this. Yeah, I get it, I'm being corny. I'm a forty-four-year-old sappy sentimental loser. I know comedians are supposed to be cynical and sarcastic above all, and I agree with you. But also, I have this to say: Fuck you. Really, go fuck yourselves. No human with a heart and conscience can be that way all the time. Everyone must allow themselves to be romantic, at least about a few things in life. You get to choose what they are, and for me the music of Bruce Springsteen is one of them. It's helped save my life and hopefully my soul. I'll probably not be able to let you guys know if that happened, but if I can I will.

When I was eleven, I was hanging out at my cousin Jeff's house because to me at that time in my life, Jeff was the coolest person in the world. I wanted to be exactly like him. I was waiting in his room while he took a shower or something when his mom, my aunt Jo (who is simply one of the greatest human beings of all time), came in to clean up. She was dusting off a photo of a thin guy with long hair, sunglasses, and a guitar. That guy, whoever he was, looked to me like the only guy I'd ever seen who was probably cooler than Jeff.

"Aunt Jo? Who is that?"

"Artie, who's that?" she said incredulously. "That's the Boss!"

———

By the time I got back to my room, it was close to seven a.m. I found Adrienne, the only other thing I'm romantic about in this life, lying there, awake and upset. Actually she was half-asleep, half-crying, and completely mad at me. I've come to realize that it's possible to be too in love with someone. That state of mind probably means different things to different people, but completely sober, in a foreign country, I discovered exactly what it means to me. I became controlling, I became obsessed, and I found out how destructive those emotions can be. We didn't make up completely, but we tried our best and things remained tense for the next few days as we went sightseeing with our friends.

One night Adrienne wasn't with me. Our group was supposed to go out together, but I didn't follow that plan. I decided to go to the hotel and take a nap, so she had dinner with my cowriter, Anthony, and the plan was for me to meet them afterward when I woke up. But I didn't take a nap; in a crazy, angry, resentful state I got some booze and started drinking in the room, hard, the way I used to when I had nothing to lose and didn't care about shit. I must have downed a bottle of vodka in half an hour and was in a blackout state before I knew it. And then I got nutty enough to accuse her of cheating on me with Anthony, which could not be further from the truth. I was irrational.

I took a cab to where we were all going to meet, which was a burlesque show in the heart of Paris. When I got there I stood outside listening to music, screaming the lyrics at confused French passersby on the street. I wanted to see Adrienne immediately and I started screaming that. I started screaming that I hated my friend Anthony and I wouldn't talk to him when he came over to me to try and calm me down. Nothing I was saying made sense. I ran around the street, I ran at oncoming traffic, I ducked into an underground parking garage, and I would not listen to reason no matter who was talking. My friend Dan came down and he and Anthony both tried everything they could to get me out of harm's way, but it was no use. I don't know what I expected to happen at that point. All I wanted was for Adrienne to talk to me, but I was acting so insane that she was too terrified to come out of the theater.

She had every right to be scared; I was in a blind rage, standing in the street, harassing people, hoping a car would hit me, and yelling at two of my best friends as they tried to save me. I tore off my shirt at one point, threw it at someone, and began to walk directly at oncoming cars. The street was wide, with traffic going both ways, but there weren't streetlights, so it's a miracle that I wasn't hit. At one point I lay down in the middle of the road, with my arms and legs spread, as cars passed on both sides of me, hoping one would run me over. My friends Dan and Anthony risked their lives, standing on either side of me, directing traffic away from me on a dark, busy Paris street. I found all of this out later, of course, because I don't remember it. At the time I hated them both and I told them so in every possible way I could think of. I told them to leave me. I told them I wanted to be hit and that I hated them. At one point I even kicked Dan in the chest, nearly sending him into an oncoming car. He bumped the side of it but thankfully he didn't get hurt. Those two were just trying to keep me from getting killed or arrested, and they did a pretty good job from what I understand, but there was no end to my spiral by that point. It was just a matter of time before the authorities got involved because I had become a spectacle.

The French police arrived, the gendarmes, which aren't your average beat cops. They carry submachine guns like a paramilitary unit, so when they show up, things change pretty quickly. By that time I'd stopped responding to my friends altogether apart from accusing them of things that made no sense and insisting that someone bring me Adrienne. I was shirtless, lying on my back in the center of a busy street, and it had begun to rain, so this was just a mess. Adrienne was inside the theater still, scared out of her mind, hiding in there with the managers.

I kept yelling that I didn't want Dan or Anthony anywhere near me because I hated them, even as they talked to the gendarmes, begging them not to take me to jail. It took two gendarmes plus my two friends lifting me up by my arms and legs to drag me out of the street and harm's way, into the gutter on the side of the road. As they put me down, I took a wild roundhouse swing at one of the officers. Let me tell you something, as different as Europe and the rest of the world is from America, certain rules remain the same. I've now taken a swing at a cop in LA, New York, New Jersey, Miami, and Paris, France, so I'm somewhat of an expert on this: it is NEVER a good idea. Trust me, if you swing at a cop it's not going to work out well for you. It should be at the top of everyone's list of worst ideas to ever do, wherever you're from and wherever you are. Swinging at a cop eliminates every other alternative they have to taking you in. So that's what happened. There was no longer anything my friends could do, once the gendarmes slapped the cuffs on me. They pulled me up out of the gutter, sat me down on the curb, and kept me subdued until the paddy wagon showed up. It was my first international arrest, which, in a sick way, is somewhat of an achievement that I have no right to be proud of.

Once I was carted off, Adrienne emerged from the theater and my friends escorted her back to the hotel. Despite all the names I called them and how much I told them I hated them, Dan and Anthony did everything they could to help me out. They went to bat for me with the gendarmes, which is probably why the cops decided that if I was only drunk and not on drugs, that they'd let me sleep it off and release me without charge. The only problem was that apparently I kept insisting that I was on drugs. Every time my friends would say, in their best French, that I'd had a fight with my girlfriend and was just very drunk, I'd yell in English that I fucking hated them and that they were wrong because I was drunk and on all kinds of pills. That wasn't true at all, I was just very, very drunk.

The gendarmes got to the bottom of it by making me pee in a cup at the jail and once they learned that I was clean of all narcotics they kept their promise and let me sleep it off. I have to say that the Parisian authorities were fantastic, just very calm, very professional, and for very no-nonsense law enforcement officers, they were very compassionate. Their American counterparts should take note. I had a cell mate who looked like Casey Stengel when he was ninety-two, who was lying with his head on the toilet, talking nonstop all night. He sounded like a maniac speaking in tongues, but in French. The only thing I could understand, because he said it over and over, was "*la plume*" which is some kind of bias of mine. When some- one speaks French at me, to me, or near me, I only hear "*la plume*," which I've come to discover means "pen." So whatever this scary old guy was yelling about, to me it was only pens. When I couldn't take it anymore, I called a guard over and told him that the guy belonged in a psych ward.

"Monsieur, come here, read this," the guard said.

"I can't read French," I said. "You have to tell me what it means."

"This means that you *are* in the psych ward."

That was a wake-up call, and another first—a foreign psych ward. So the old guy belonged there, but thank God he was old and lack- ing in stamina: he fell asleep in an hour or so, after which I managed to doze off for a while too. I woke up around seven a.m. And what scared me more than the guy's crazy voice the night before was the fact that he was still comfortably asleep, with his head pretty much inside the toilet bowl. Put it this way, I had to move him in order to take a piss. Even then the guy didn't wake up; he just let me move him over a bit. I know I sprayed urine on him, but I can't imagine he cared. I just hope that weirdo is doing okay, wherever he is.

At that point the guard came over and decided I was sober enough to get the hell out of there, so they gave me back my possessions and signed me out. I wasn't charged with anything and that was that. Once again, the French police are wonderful people. As I mentioned, I threw my shirt at a car or a person sometime the night before, so I had no choice but to wear what anyone would call a sure sign of trouble: the blue plastic hospital-style smock they'd given me the night before. It was the kind that ties in the back, pretty much leaving you hanging out in the wind, especially if you're my size. Basically I looked like an escaped mental patient (something I also know quite a bit about) which didn't help me any when it came time to hail a cab.

The sun was coming up by then and I started walking as bits and pieces of the night before came back to me, none of them good. The jail was just off the Champs-Elysées, near the Arc de Triomphe, smack in the center of a beautiful, busy tourist destination in Paris. There was no getting lost in the crowd or going about my business unnoticed on a Wednesday morning at seven a.m., being an obese American in a blue smock who spoke no French. I wandered, trying to get any cab I saw to stop for me. After about an hour I found a cabbie willing to take me, who coincidentally looked exactly like Susan Boyle from *Britain's Got Talent*. I mispronounced my hotel's name, but she was patient and cool, and got me where I needed to go, God bless her.

I texted Anthony to tell him that I'd just gotten out of jail as I pulled up to the hotel. He and Dan had taken Adrienne to get her things out of our room because she wanted to move to another hotel, and I can't blame her for that. But I got out earlier than anyone expected and showed up while they were still there waiting for her to finish packing. I got up to the room and found the two of them standing there, but what I didn't realize was that Adrienne was in the room too, hiding behind the door. I barged in like a maniac and went straight to the bathroom and when I did, she ran out and went to Dan's room. I literally just missed her because I came out a minute later and told Anthony and Dan to get the fuck out of my room, out of my life, and to go to hell, because I hadn't sobered up enough to be rational. I told them they were "traitors," "liars," I told them they were fired, crazy shit like that. All I cared about was being alone and taking a shower. That's the first thing you do when you get out of jail, by the way, you take a nice hot shower. It's the only way to get the stink off.

I was confused, I was angry, and that anger hadn't gone away during my evening in jail. I wanted to see Adrienne just as badly as I'd wanted to see her when I was drunk, playing chicken with Peugeots, the night before. But I'd scared her so bad that she'd checked into another hotel, and since I'd been acting like a homicidal maniac, neither she nor my friends thought it was a good idea for me to know where she was on the off chance that I'd show up and storm the walls to get to her room if she wouldn't see me. I found out later that Anthony and Dan even refused to let Adrienne tell them the name of her new hotel because they didn't want to know. They'd had enough of our drama, for one thing, but more importantly, they wanted to be sure the two of us would stay apart until I calmed down. They also didn't want to have to lie to me; it was just better for everyone if they didn't know. Adrienne knew how to find them if she needed to and when she was ready to talk to me she would—that's how they left it. This may come as a shock, but in my mental state, drunk or not (and I did continue to drink immediately after my shower), I didn't believe my two friends at all. I was convinced that they knew where she was and I got more belligerent about it at every opportunity. I was pissed as hell and believed that the entire world, starting with them, was against me. I just had to see Adrienne so badly that I was going to scream her name from the balcony of the room until someone brought her to me.

There's one thing I need to say about Adrienne: I love her to death, but I don't think any woman overpacks more than she does. Listen, all women pack a lot of shit, but this girl is ridiculous. Left to her own devices she will pack three suitcases for a two-day trip to the beach where she'll only end up wearing one bikini. I'm all for being prepared, but she takes it to another level. She's got this one bag she takes everywhere with her (because it could, literally, fit everything the average family of four might take with them on vacation), and that's what she had in our room in Paris. This might sound crazy but looking back I'm not surprised at all that the couple hours I spent in the drunk tank weren't enough time for her to get her shit packed back into her bag and out of the room. A midget could live in her bag; it's like a studio apartment.

Anyway, when I came in and Adrienne ran out to Dan's room, there was no way she could have snuck out and taken her bag, so she left it behind. And there was no way I was going to let Dan take it down to his room, because that bag was the only leverage I had to get to see her. I was so angry that as I sat there all alone, I began to stare at her bag and just get more and more pissed off. I called Dan's room and started asking him, calmly at first, where Adrienne was. When he couldn't tell me because he said, for probably the tenth time, that he really didn't know what hotel she'd moved to, I just started yelling. Eventually I told him to fuck off and hung up. I called Anthony, insisting he knew where she was and started yelling at him to tell me, but it was no use because he didn't know either. I called him a bunch of names and threatened his life, and then hung up on him too.

I was so full of rage and had no outlet for it. I stomped around the room, like a caged animal. I kicked over the furniture, I broke a glass coffee table, and then I went to the minibar and began to empty it, bottle by bottle. It was the first time I'd felt calm since our plane took off from Newark. I've emptied minibars on my own many times in my life, so I consider myself an expert on what I've come to refer to as a Noah's Ark drunk. A minibar, you see, is the Noah's Ark of little liquor bottles, because, like the ark, it's a structure that contains two little bottles of every liquor known to man. If you consume the entire minibottle ark, the insane variety of liquor creates a very specific type of buzz, and it's not pretty. It's a Noah's Ark drunk. If you're doing that in the first place, it's safe to assume that you're not doing it for pleasure, which means you're probably going at it the way it should be done: downing the wine like it's water and putting away the Pringles and M&M's while you turn the inventory into a pile of little plastic empties. All I can say is that the mixed booze and all the trimmings make for one Biblically out-of-control drunk once the sugar, salt, and alcohol collide. Just hope you don't puke, because it is no fun coming up—I can tell you from experience.

So like hanging out with the worst kind of old friend, that's how I dealt with realizing I'd fucked up the night before, which was a terrible idea. I'm not sure of the timeline, but at some point soon after I started sailing on Noah's Ark, I know that Anthony and Dan came by to make sure I was okay, both of them hoping I'd gone to sleep. Nope! The found me in full rage mode, stalking around the room. After I told them to fuck off for the tenth time and threw bottles at them, they left, leaving me to destroy everything in sight, from the one remaining coffee table to the bathroom door. When there was nothing left, I got to work on the mother lode: Adrienne's suitcase.

I knocked it on its side, opened it up, took armfuls of her clothes to the balcony, and threw them onto the street below. We were staying in this particular hotel because Bill Murray, who is one of Dan's close friends, had recommended it. He'd told Dan that if anything went wrong with me, if I fell off the wagon or otherwise misbehaved, the staff there would take care of everything and no one would be the wiser. I can't even begin to tell you how right he was. When I threw Adrienne's clothes off the balcony, the bellboys looked up and without a word began to catch what they could and fold it. They waved up to me a few times as if what I was doing was one of the amenities in the brochure: Throw your girlfriend's clothes down to one of our doormen and they will fold them and bring them back upstairs to you!

That's the least of how cool they were if you think about it. I'd just come in like a maniac wearing a hospital robe, smelling of prison, and within an hour I was drunk again, throwing my girl-friend's clothes out of our window as I screamed every obscenity known to man at the top of my lungs. If that's not cause to call the cops, I don't know what is. But they didn't. Instead the doormen and bellboys picked up her stuff as it landed, some of it in traffic, some of it on the median in the middle of the road, all of them smiling as if it was just another day on the job. During a brief moment of clar-ity I realized I'd probably be arrested again and if I were it might cost me my job, and at that point I stopped. When my phone rang I figured it was the hotel and that I was fucked, but I couldn't have been more wrong. It was the front desk, but instead of threatening me, they'd just called to ask when I'd like to have Adrienne's belong-ings brought back up. I'm telling you, this place is a dream hotel for fuckups. By the time I was done, there was smashed glass all over the floor. I'd destroyed two end tables and the coffee table, ripped the bathroom door clean off its hinges. At some point I passed out on the floor, between the two mattresses that made up the king-size bed. When I woke up, it was like magical elves had been there: the coffee table was cleaned up and replaced, the door was fixed, and all of Adrienne's clothes were in the drawers.

I'm ashamed to say that it took a couple more days full of manic fits of drunkenness and anger before I got control of myself and so-bered up completely. As I mentioned before, my AA sponsor Don was on the trip, but he was staying in a different hotel, so, like a true addict, I made sure I got wildly drunk—and irrational and crazy—whenever he wasn't around. Then I'd spend time during the days with him without any of the others around and I'd act like nothing was wrong. After my emotions ran their course I began to get control again and truly calm down. I knew we'd flown out there with problems, but I'd had such high hopes for Adrienne and me on this trip that when it didn't happen I literally lost my mind. After my friends told her that I was doing okay and that I seemed somewhat back to normal, Adrienne agreed to talk to me, so long as the guys chaperoned our meeting by waiting outside of the room. If things got heated, they'd hear it, and if it got out of control they'd step in.

The two of us went into the bathroom and she sat in the tub, looking as beautiful as ever, wearing a little flannel shirt like you'd expect to see at a Nirvana concert in 1991, just so gorgeous. And there I was in Paris with her, the love of my life, the woman I'd planned to ask to marry me, as I realized that anger, resentment, jealousy, and everything else had probably ruined us for good. Those drives within me always ruin everything I care about.

I got into that bathtub next to her and the two of us cried.

"Maybe you've got to move on," I said.

"Maybe I do."

She went back to her hotel, and she still wouldn't tell me where it was. She wouldn't live with me there or anywhere else anymore. She even changed her flight because she didn't want to be on a plane with me. I'd been so crazy that she didn't feel safe around me and she worried that if we got into a fight on the plane I'd be arrested in the States, which would have ended my career with my employers at DirecTV. So I left Paris without my baby; she came home a couple of days later. That wasn't the end of the drama between us. A few more crazy events happened and after those we decided that there was no way she and I could possibly work. Adrienne was still so very mad at me and that wasn't going away. She told me, to my face, that she couldn't see me anymore, that she couldn't have me in her life in any way at all. Her parents and her family agreed—actually they insisted, and I couldn't argue with their point of view at all because they were right.

And so we had another awful, gut-wrenching good-bye. For me

this one was the worst of them out of what I must say have to be some of the world's most horrible good-byes. We got that Paris trip in, but instead of it being the romantic adventure we'd dreamed of, it was a train wreck. We had a couple of moments—and those I'll never forget—but it could have been so much more. We had one insanely romantic night during the trip, and that gave me great comfort. It still does—no matter how things ended, at least Adrienne and I had one night in Paris. We had one night where things were great, one night where we were the way we used to be back when we first fell in love, back before everything else got in the way. Paris is where we always dreamed we'd go, but that's where we ended too, and it's sad. Due to my self-destructiveness, my anger, my resentment, and my self-hatred, I lost the light of my life. I lost that smile. I lost those beautiful eyes, the eyes that were going to show me the path to happiness. I lost all of that because of me.

—— —— —— ——

We didn't speak at all for a couple of months, but that wasn't the start of a slide back into drinking for me. Instead it was a wake-up call that my feelings could throw me off. Paris was a misstep fueled by—you guessed it!—anger, resentment, and the rest of it. I was strong enough to see it for what it was and not let it take me over. A couple of months passed and then Adrienne and I got back in touch. She texted me: "I want you to know that I don't hate you." Just more proof of how big her heart is. "I hate the things you've done," she wrote. "I'll never understand them, but I want you to know that I don't hate you. I miss you, but I can't have you back in my life."

It wasn't what I wanted to hear, but who could blame her? Not me. As of now, as of the writing of this book, I've respected her wishes. I've stayed out of her life although I don't want to. I want to be in her life, and it seems that I stand a chance of getting there. I hope so. I hope this isn't the last paragraph of the last chapter in the story of my life with Adrienne. I hope I'll write that last paragraph forty years from now, just before I prepare to enter the next life, where I'll wait for her to join me. That's what I'd like, but I don't know if I'll get that. Whether I deserve it or not is another story, and it's not one I'm discussing here. Let's just leave it alone and let me hope for the best, okay? For now I'm respecting her wishes, I'm staying out of her life, and I'm happy knowing that she's all right. It was so sweet of my baby doll to text me to let me know that she doesn't hate me and that she misses me. That meant more to me than she may ever know.

———

So that was Paris. A classic Artie Lange self-destruction tour, international edition. Jesus, the minute I think I'm out of that cycle, it draws me back in! There's never a dull moment in my life and I guess I'm trying to come to terms with the fact that the good is always mixed in with the bad in equal doses. I've realized that my job is to keep the bad from taking over—which is a hell of a lot harder than saying it out loud or writing it down here or anywhere. Admitting it is important, but that's just the first step.

I know a lot of you reading this admire me, so let me tell you something: your admiration and appreciation is what keeps me going. Please hear that and know that I mean it in every possible way, but also know that I'm more flawed than even you think, and if you've followed my life story this far you know we're talking pretty flawed. Seriously, though, I'm more fractured, more twisted, confused, and dark than these pages and the book before this could ever do justice. I don't want any of you to see me as a role model, I don't want any of you to think that my story is something to aspire to. My way of living is no way to live. It is what it is, and I couldn't help it because I can't help who I am. But if you can? You should. Please, for my sake and for the sake of those in your life, do.

As much as all of you fans love me and as much as I love you, I think if you got to know me personally the way those closest to me like Adrienne have, you'd see someone else. I think you'd see that I'm not the guy you think I am. You'd discover, unfortunately, that like most people I'm just a jerk-off. And some of you would really hate to learn that, I'm a jerk-off with a very sentimental side that, dare I say, borders on the romantic. Call me a sissy, call me a pussy, call me whatever you like, I don't care. This sentimental jerk-off has something to say: I love you all. And more than that, I've got to say something I should have said a long time ago. Fuck it . . . Okay, here I go. . . . I'm sorry, Adrienne, and I love you.

What you just read was written many months before this book went to press, and as usual, a lot happened in my life. I'll tell you why this book didn't get out there to you in a more timely fashion at a later date: right now we're talking about Adrienne. After Paris, when I wrote the words you just read (which was several months later), I believed with all my heart that she and I were done forever. When she and I were together, I saw the possibility of being another Artie, and I'd like to think being with me allowed her to be who she really wants to be. Whatever it was, when we were together and things were good, I felt deep down in my soul that I'd finally found my girl, the one I wanted to be with forever. When she was on my arm I felt like I was doing something right.

There's a theme to this memoir that the learned scholars among us have probably picked up on by now. For the stoners in the back of the class who don't even know their names, let me fill you in on a concept we've touched on repeatedly in these pages: hitting rock bottom. Did you guys get that at all from this book so far? It's cool if you didn't, I'm known for my subtlety. What I'm getting at here is that Paris was rock bottom for my relationship with Adrienne. Luckily, I learned from it. I didn't walk away from that drama and deny it, I didn't ignore it and I didn't blame what had happened on her and pretend it didn't matter. I saw the writing on the wall, and it made me realize that I'd lost her and getting her back was a cause worth fighting for.

So that's what I did. It took a long time because I'd done a lot of damage and our bond had been put through the ringer. But I kept at it, and slowly, over time, I showed her that I'd learned my lesson. We didn't talk for a while, but slowly we started talking again, and step by step, she saw, through my actions, that I was worthy of her trust. She understood that, going forward, I wasn't going to lie and tell her that everything was fine when it wasn't—the way I had in the past— and she was okay with that. I told her that every day was a struggle for me but that I wanted to struggle if that meant I could have her in my life. We started spending more and more time together and she saw that I meant what I was saying; I really was trying. Eventually we got back to where we were, and it hasn't been perfect every day because nothing is. Having her back is a blessing I never thought I'd have, so when the time was right, I did what any sensible man who values the woman in his life should do: I asked her to marry me. And lucky for me, she said yes. As of this writing we're engaged and I'm the happiest, luckiest motherfucker in the world. So there it is.

CONCLUSION

IT'S TIME TO SAY GOOD NIGHT

This book is mostly about the darkest time of my life. That's saying a lot because my life has seen a lot of darkness. I'd like to make it clear that those dark times were caused 100 percent by my own fuckups, because I wasn't born into hell. My life hasn't been the male version of Fantine's from *Les Misérables*. I created my own misery and I know it. And this misery was pretty much completely brought about through drug abuse. Booze was in there too, but dope is the thing that really fucked me up—opiates, heroin.

I realize that to some of the people reading this what I'm about to say is a utopian goal, but please, do yourself and the world a favor and try to avoid drugs. There's nothing romantic or cool on any level about drug addiction. It's pathetic, plain and simple. Drug addiction isn't feeling euphoric and being insanely creative. It's crying like a baby when you need more drugs. It's needing people to take care of you as if you're an infant. It's your skin turning green or yellow from abuse or withdrawal. It's just flat-out embarrassing, and there's nowhere to hide.

When you are truly down and out the way I've been, you really find out who has got your back . . . and whose friendships have been nothing but a steaming pile of bullshit. I'm happy to say that ninety-nine percent of my friends were amazing, all truly great people who helped me in ways I can't describe and can only hope to pay back. But there was also one percent who were the opposite. I won't name them here because I plan to let them know sometime in the future, in a more surprising and more hurtful way. These people treated me so badly that their behavior could have only come from a place of insane hate and jealousy. Now, I know when you look at me it has to be hard to believe that someone could be jealous of me for any reason. Don't ask me how, but these jerk-offs found a way. They treated me as if my career, and my life in general, were completely over. I might as well have been dead and buried. On the one hand, look, who can blame them? They were just playing the odds, and I was in bad shape, so if you hate me for some reason, why not pile on?

In the end they lost, because with the help of the ninety-nine percent who were good to me, I made it. I'm back, I'm not going anywhere, and my hatred for that one percent runs deep—very, very deep. As a matter of fact, if it were legal I'd have them killed. Don't worry, I'm not going back to the joint for one of those dirtbags, but if I were sure I could get away with it? Yeah, I'd make a phone call or two and rid the world of those scum-fucks forever. However, that is not the case. I know for sure there's no way to get away with it, so this is the last I'll speak of it because I'm not going to do anything to get in trouble—I've had my fill of it.

I'm guessing a few of you are reading this and thinking, or saying aloud if you've chosen this book as your children's bedtime story, "Christ! Artie, what the fuck did these people do to you?" If I were you I'd be asking me the same question and I'd be disappointed when I didn't get a straight answer. This is all I will say here: what they did was serious and devious. The kind of things that trigger the level of anger that gives you the chills—and they did them to me at my very lowest point. They know who they are. They range from being very wealthy and successful, to flat-out broke drifters, and at least two of them have names that you, the general public, would recognize. It sounds so childish, but one of my biggest incentives for staying clean and in showbiz now is to prove them wrong and stick it in their smug, giggling asses. To that one percent who screwed me over, when you get a chance, do the world and me a favor and go fuck yourselves.

Glad I got that off my chest.

Let's not end a dark tale on a dark note, shall we? Let's try to stay positive, so please allow me to take this opportunity to thank a few of the good people in the ninety-nine percent who helped me and who can't be thanked enough. My mom, my sister, the great Colin Quinn, and obviously the rest of my family; Adrienne, who has proven to be an angel; Norm MacDonald; DirecTV's Chris Long, who is truly a stand-up guy, and the great Howard Stern . . . thanks, guys.

———

If there is anything I've learned from my life and if there's anything I hope to impart to anyone else who cares to listen to my story, it's that addicts are not like other people. I'm not saying we are better or worse, worthy of praise or ridicule, I'm just saying we are different. A normal person could have a bad day and come home and have a drink because of it and not have another drink for two months. A normal person could also have a drink every day and not have it affect their life. An addict like me needs chaos. I need the action, I need the juice; it's like gambling to me, except that I'm gambling with my life and the lives of those I love. But I love the risk, no matter what the odds. And that's an urge that is never going to leave me.

I've realized something lately and this might come as a surprise, but I think gambling is my worst vice. It's the one that led me down the path. Because if you think about it, when you gamble, especially the way I do, you really get the adrenaline going—and isn't that what addiction and abuse are all about? I saw a friend of mine recently whom I've known since we were teenagers and he told me a story about myself that revealed a lot to me.

We were out one night about twenty years ago watching a Monday Night Football game and my buddy wanted to go home pretty early into the game.

"You're leaving?" I asked.

"Yeah," he said.

"Why? What's wrong with you?"

"It's a pretty boring game, Art."

He was right. It was the Browns versus the Rams, and both teams sucked. "I'm gonna go home and get some sleep. I have to work tomorrow."

"Hold on," I said, as a true addict and degenerate gambler would. "I know a way to make this game *not* boring."

My friend laughed at me. "Oh yeah, how's that?"

"How much money do you have in your bank account right now?"

He looked at me funny. "Um, probably six hundred bucks."

"Okay, bet $1,600 on the Browns. I've got a bookie we can call right now."

"What are you talking about? Why would I do that?"

"C'mon, it'll be fun. We'll see what happens."

He really looked at me funny then. "Art, why would I do that? I don't know anything about the Browns."

"Well, that's perfect, that makes it even better! If you knew about them, if it was an educated guess, it wouldn't be any fun! C'mon, man, let's do it!"

Going in blind: that's the action, that's the juice. Not knowing what's going to happen, not considering the consequences, that's the high. The consequences are so insane when you're betting more than you're worth.

I got so worked up trying to talk him into it that he saw my true inner self and he never forgot it. Just the thought of placing that bet— not even with my own money—got me so excited I could barely sit on my bar stool. I have a gene in me that's not found in most people.

"Artie, calm down, man. I'm not doing it. I'm going home."

He did go home and we're still friends, but I was definitely disappointed in the guy.

I now know that I've got a fire inside. I've learned not to romanticize it, but I've also learned the hard way that I can never say I've beaten it into submission and eliminated it because that would be a lie. You can't destroy what's a part of you, you can only learn to live with it. I'm going to do my best to live with that demon each and every day. Sure it's going to come out, and I know there will be times when that part of me wins. Hopefully it's during football season and I'll get lucky, because let's face it, there's nothing like winning a long-shot bet. I can't imagine a greater high than winning a ridiculously large wager because of a fluke like a Hail Mary. Which is pretty much what I am, as a person, if you think about it.

What can I say? Rooting for an underdog is not a winning strategy, but I can't tell you not to do it because somehow it's worked for me. It hasn't been easy, in fact it's mostly been hell, but it's never been boring. And since my life is far from done and is changing every day, this won't be my final answer, but after all I've been through I'd like to say this about my life right now, from the bottom of my heart: just being here is all right by me.

There's something I figured out in therapy and through the writing of this book, so before I sign off, I'm coming clean, because I want to be honest with you guys. Basically this is it: I was completely suicidal on January 2, 2010. My intention was to kill myself. I did not want to wake up alive. Life as a heroin addict had become unbearable and I could think of no other way out. I am deeply ashamed and embarrassed by this and that is why I concocted the story of wanting to pass out and go to sleep, a story that I believed myself for a long time because it was easier to do than facing the truth. It's taken me years to admit this to myself, but now that I can I'm admitting it to you. If I weren't honest about it here, I'd be doing you, my readers, a gross injustice.

I need to be honest about something else, too. I'm writing this book for the money, but I sincerely hope it helps people who are addicts and the family members of addicts in some small way. I hope it helps everyone who reads it understand what addiction is and that there's no quick fix, no magic pill, no miracle cure. I hope that admitting that heroin got me to a place in my life—which by the way, by anyone's standards was a great life—that I willingly took a knife and plunged it into my gut nine times, hoping to die, will be a deterrent to anyone considering using drugs at any level. I make no moral judgments; people should do whatever they feel needs to be done to achieve happiness. John Lennon said it best: "Whatever gets you through the night, it's alright, it's alright."

Just think of me and others like me before acting on certain things, because my mom, my sister, Adrienne, and other great people in my life are still here and that's for now. I'm still kicking, I'm still performing, I'm still writing, I've got my radio show and I'm on TV and in the occasional movie. It feels good; it feels really good. I want to thank you all for sticking with me. All of my fans, you're truly wonderful to me and I wish all of you happiness. If any of you are lost, hopefully this book will help you find your way somewhat. That's the most you can ask of anything.

Until the next time,
Artie

ACKNOWLEDGMENTS

To Richard Abate, my loyal agent, for never giving up and helping with business and creative issues equally great. Thanks again brother! Two books! Stacy Creamer! What can I say? You are my newest angel! THANKS! Here's to the future as well. Much love to Dave Becky. As good as a friend and a manager gets! Jared Levine—brilliant lawyer. It's always good news when Jared's on the phone. Love you Jared! Tony Burton and Don Buchwald, you guys stuck with me! Thanks. Nick DiPaolo—the funniest guy I know, who doesn't even know how to say something other than how it is! Respect! Julie Grau, your brilliant mind is all over this book. I will never forget the success we had together. I wish you nothing but happiness. Much Love! Chris Long, you are quite simply the coolest and most creative executive I've ever known! Thanks for taking a risk and believing in a slob like me. Much love and respect. Danny Falato, the coolest Cubs fan I know—seriously brother, I'm proud to call you a friend! Ted Knuetter—miss you. Melissa in Richard's office, your help is unreal! John Valdastri, my travel God! Love ya, JV. Tim Sullivan: a friend and a coworker who takes care of me like a brother. He has become a brother! Chris C. and James C. at DirecTV! Everyone at Sunrise Detox in Jersey and Ambrosia Drug Rehab Center in West Palm Beach, Florida, for saving my life. To Frank Sebastiano for being insanely smart and funny—and for being my friend. And, of course, Anthony Bozza—The Wolf! You're a genius! We are two for two partner—love ya! Lastly, all my family and closest friends! For always taking time to ask, "how is Artie doin'?" AND YOU FANS! 'Til the next one, guys.

—Artie

ABOUT THE AUTHORS

Artie Lange is a comedian and actor who has performed in sketch comedies, movies, TV, and radio. In 2001, Lange joined the cast of *The Howard Stern Show*, where he quickly became one of the most popular characters on the show. He is the author of the #1 *New York Times* bestseller *Too Fat to Fish*, a collection of narrative episodes from his life. Currently, Artie is very happy hosting *The Artie Lange Show* on the Audience Network for DirecTV. Find out more at artiequitter.com.

Anthony Bozza is a former *Rolling Stone* staff writer and coauthor of the *New York Times* bestsellers *Whatever You Say I Am: The Life and Times of Eminem*, *Tommyland* with Tommy Lee, *Slash* with Slash, and of course, *Too Fat to Fish* with Artie Lange. He lives in New York City. Visit him at anthonybozza.net.